KALEIDOSCOPE

BRENDA L. THOMAS

KALEIDOSCOPE

Copyright 2023 by Brenda L. Thomas
ISBN 978-0-9797622-9-1 / 09797622-9-4
Phillywriter, LLC www.brendalthomas.com
First Edition September 2024

All rights reserved. No part of this book may be reproduced in any form or by any means including electronic, mechanical, or photocopying or stored in a retrieval system without permission in writing from the publisher except by a reviewer who may quote brief passage to be included in a review.

Manufactured and printed in the United States of America.

If you purchased this book without a cover, you should be aware that this book is stolen property. It is reported as "unsold and destroyed" to the publisher, and neither the author nor the publisher has received any payment for this "stripped" book.

Also by Brenda L. Thomas

FICTION

Heartless, when love isn't enough.

Woman On Top

Every Woman's Got a Secret

The Velvet Rope

Fourplay, The Dance of Sensuality

Threesome, Where Seduction, Power and Basketball Collide

NON-FICTION

Sayin' A Taste

Laying Down My Burdens

SHORT STORIES

Bewitched

Secret Service

Every New Year

ANTHOLOGIES

Four Degrees of Heat

Maxed Out

Kiss The Year Goodbye

Every New Year

Bedroom Chronicles

The Experiment

Indulge

The Watcher

Contents

Prologue	1
1. Peninsula Papagayo	15
2. Casa La Paz	31
3. Lean on Me	49
4. Every Little Bit Hurts	67
5. Pura Vida	83
6. Dreams and Nightmares	99
7. The Lodge at Sugar Hill	109
8. Sugar Hill Gang	133
9. Float	157
10. Barren Hill	165
11. Mother's Day	179
12. Operation Unicorn	197
13. Ditch Plains	209
14. Heartless	221
15. Mercy, Mercy, Me	233
16. Beast of Burden	241
17. Homecoming	249
18. Unrequited Love	267
Epilogue	275
Also by Brenda L. Thomas	281

"It always seems impossible until it's done."

NELSON MANDELA

Prologue

Happy Valentine's Day
Alpine, New Jersey

Sasha Borianni

I refuse to apologize. My husband is dead, and not even his daughter could have made me deny his instructions to be cremated. Trent and I made a pact three years ago not to be laid out stiff and cold in a church, waiting for mourners to say, "*Oh, she put him away nicely.*" Briana though, was insistent, and it grew contentious with her lashing out resentments I'd never known she'd had against me. I told myself it was her grief talking; still, I wanted to push her off my condo balcony. Thankfully, her brother TJ intervened, making me realize Trent's children, unlike me, had to identify his body; they needed to see their father one last time.

Bottling up those emotions, I poured them into the funeral arrangements, answering awkward questions and consoling well-intentioned friends and family who repeatedly expressed how sorry they were. In the last two months, I've come to hate the word *sorry* and whatever meaning it has in a time like this. Yet pieces of my heart crumbled with every kiss on the cheek, money-filled sympathy card, and nauseating smell of food that never stopped coming.

A private service would have been easier, but I had to stand before left and right-wing politicians, allies, and enemies from his term as a New Jersey senator and those he led as President of IBEW. Did any of them care how I felt, or had they come to share how they felt? I'm sure that the reality of my husband's death will come crashing down upon me, fracturing every piece of my heart and soul that I've been holding together with Ambien and alcohol.

We arrived in Alpine, New Jersey, a few days before Christmas to celebrate the holidays, followed by Briana's nuptials. After leaving her three children behind to live in Los Angeles in search of an acting career, she finally settled down with a woman who was smitten with her. Her father paid for the elaborate wedding attended by 200 guests, not even close family or friends. Trent hoped this would cut the financial cord. TJ was a lot less needy, more of a ladies' man who never imposed his financial burdens on his father and made his money as a self-appointed restaurant broker.

An aviation mechanic discovered my husband in hangar number 8 at Teterboro airport. The coroner said he suffered a massive heart attack. I didn't know how that was possible when he'd recently had a stress test before we'd left home. Isn't that always the case, *'healthy 63-year-old drops dead of a heart attack?'* What I couldn't understand was why he'd been at Teterboro. We were planning to leave Jersey the next day for our vacation, and he'd insisted on making a trip to Target to replace my damaged suitcase.

Following a beautiful wedding, I found myself unexpectedly planning my husband's funeral and dealing with the distribution of his estate. Despite Briana receiving property and substantial insurance money, she's determined to take more than what is rightfully hers. My urgency to reach JFK airport also stems from my struggle with a heavy Target Tote containing a wooden box filled with my husband's cremains.

Esterillos Puternarus, Costa Rica
Isabella Washington-Moore

Valentine's Day has been special to me ever since I was a little girl when my Daddy would bring home candy-filled hearts for my mother and me. I know it's a commercial holiday, but I like that it's one day dedicated to love worldwide. For that reason, I always ensured that any man I was dating knew I had expectations on February 14. It didn't have to be an expensive gift, but it had to be a romantic gesture. This evening's Valentine's sendoff might not include a gift from a lover, instead I will celebrate in the love of my Esterillos community

The closer I get to my home, the more I realize nobody can live in paradise forever. I dread returning not only to the cold temperatures of Philadelphia but also to an employer I desire yet despise. For that reason, I've gone to the dark side, compiling her financial information into what I've named Operation Unicorn; it's a slow process, one that will put her in a jail cell. Until then, there's a party to get ready for; the Twins have probably already arrived to put the final touches on the decorations and finish preparing the evening's bountiful feast.

I've owned my home on this tranquil side of the island for 10 years; these past six months have been my longest stay to date. Blessed with dual citizenship, I can travel from the United States to Costa Rica without restrictions. When my business in the U.S. is complete, I plan to make this my permanent home and set up a boutique accounting firm, offering my intuitive skills to the locals.

Except for family, I entertain few visitors. My most recent guests departed the island this morning. White Magic, Tampa Bay's franchise quarterback, missed his third chance at a Super Bowl ring due to a hit from Eagles defensive tackle Fletcher Cox breaking his clavicle. The other not-so-ideal visitor, Lady Zoë.

With my belly full of my morning Casado from Guava Café and my legs weak from my visitors, I build up a sweat steering my bike up the road, greeting "Pura Vida" to everyone who passes me by. I will miss this community of friends who now call themselves my family. That's why I'll hand out the gifts for this Valentine's Day.

Turning into the bottom of the driveway, I pull my bike to a stop to check the mailbox painted to replicate my house. As usual, it's empty, and then I take time to smell the flowers that outline its perimeter. Picking an equal number of colorful Guairá morada, speckled plantillas, and red ginger flowers. Placing them into the bicycle's basket, their fragrance carries me the rest of the way. That is until I'm damn near thrown off my bike when a Mercedes Town Car whizzes past me. Seeing luxury cars in Esterillos is odd; maybe someone has decided to surprise me.

Esterillos, Costa Rica
Malcolm Moore
Formerly known as Elijah Moore

Cruising along the Pacific coastline, I realize, as I have many times before, that choosing to live my life as someone else was the worst choice I ever made. The Federal Marshalls tucked me away in Witness Protection; after all the back and forth to court and those I'd testified against were behind bars, outside of their monthly check-in calls, they didn't give a damn what happened to me. My handlers think I should be grateful to have a new life with a $60K salary while employed as a Home Depot data analyst. Then again, they have ideas about this new life that I can't agree with because I don't believe my old life is over.

Except for the funds I stashed before becoming a nobody, the only thing I do outside the view of the Feds is run a tax preparation business, which allows me to build a cash reserve with no taxes to report. There is satisfaction from cheating the government, especially when I see the joy on my clients' faces when I get them a return they certainly wouldn't have gotten from H&R Block.

The weight of losing everything and everyone I loved is immeasurable, far outweighing my meager income. My wife, Isabella, chose not to join me in the program, and my closest friend, Sémile, wrongly believed I had betrayed him. The loss of my mother, who passed away shortly after our relocation to Colorado Springs, was devastating. I was unable to notify family members of her funeral until I reached out to Sémile, and together, we arranged for her cremation with the hope of someday returning her ashes to Philly. Sémile's presence in Colorado enabled me to clarify my decision to cooperate with the authorities as a witness against Russian arms dealers. Unfortunately, it left my wife to face the repercussions alone.

My transformation from Elijah Moore to Malcolm Moore came with much growth and acceptance. To keep from losing my mind, I started walking every morning, which led to full-on hiking through the mountains with fellow hikers. When I started seeing results, I got serious, joined one of the outdoor gyms, and hired a personal trainer, causing me to shed over 70 pounds. That, I'm sure, will be surprising to my wife, who's the only woman I ever really thought about after leaving Philadelphia. There were other women, even one who seemed to be a good match. However, the jealousy over things she didn't understand was too much. I'm sure part of the fault lies with me, so I won't commit to her until I confront Isabella and know it's over.

For many reasons, showing up to my wife's Costa Rican hideaway is risky, but what do I have to lose? Is anyone still looking for me? The only person who knows I've come to win back my wife is Sémile, who also thinks he's discovered the person behind my fall from grace.

I leave my bag in the car, along with her Valentine's Day gift, to avoid being presumptuous. After announcing myself using the knocker on her wide front door and peeking inside the glass panels, I receive no response, and to my surprise, the door is unlocked. Stepping inside, I am greeted by the delightful aroma of spices, igniting a desire for her cooking. The vibrant interior offers a new perspective on Izzy, from the Spanish floor tiles in the foyer to the enormous sofa adorned with giant pillows. I notice about 50 red gift bags filled with white tissue paper lined against the wall to my right. Could she be planning a party?

As I walk across the room, the first thing that gives me hope is a framed picture from our wedding day on a crowded bookshelf. Through the patio doors, tall potted plants stand, their leaves swaying on the veranda, centered around an in-ground swimming pool. This reflection of Izzy's life reaffirms that coming here to reclaim my wife was unquestionably the right choice.

Esterillos, Costa Rica
Bryce A. Goodman

I'm not a man with a list of regrets. If I had one, it would be having allowed Isabella to slip from my grasp, which is why I find myself in a country that's so fucken hot I should've known to change my clothes on the jet. The detective I'd paid for guaranteed she'd be here, hosting a party, then leaving to return to Philadelphia in the morning, so my timing is perfect.

On the drive to her house, rather than looking at the landscape, I immerse myself in work, responding to emails and text messages and returning client calls. This shit never ends. As the driver climbs the hill to her driveway, I see why this place was a respite for her. Where I expected her to be living in a bungalow, she's living in a house that, depending on the lot size behind it, must be worth close to a million, even in these parts. Once again, my expectations of Isabella have been exceeded.

Where I failed was when Isabella needed me to be emotionally available; I came up short. My focus had been to satisfy her like I'd satisfied all the women in my life. Isabella needed me to be vulnerable, and I couldn't give that. In retrospect, I should've been gentler and patient and made love to her. However, that's exactly what I didn't want to do, make love, fall in love, or be tied down, yet here I am.

I reasoned I'd be her savior once her ex-husband was gone. I was wrong. Rather than answer my calls, she left the city. I tracked her down, first to Houston to visit her mother and then to Costa Rica. If what she's running from is to get out of this business, I'm the only one who can make that happen. The problem will be getting her to trust me.

I'm man enough now to admit my insane desire to hit my financial goals outweighed any chance I had at love, yet this last year without her, I plan to try it. Hence, I'm here on Valentine's Day with a gift that will undoubtedly show my commitment and bring her home, even if it reveals my dark side.

JFK Airport
Sasha

This airport has always been a nightmare. Today, it's even worse as I navigate my way around college kids burdened with oversized backpacks on cross-country adventures, foreigners headed home with cheap trinkets from their vacation in the

States, and professional travelers rushing to reach their next meeting.

Luckily, I have TSA Precheck, so I won't be humiliated by removing my shoes and being randomly patted down by a stranger. Reaching the security checkpoint, as instructed, I lay my purse on the conveyor belt yet am hesitant to set down the Target Tote.

A suited-up businessman behind me groans, "Lady, you're holding up the line; I got a flight to catch."

His impatience alerts the agent, who turns away from the monitor and says, "C'mon, ma'am."

Reluctantly, I place the Target Tote on the conveyor belt and then make hurried strides to pass through the body scanner in time to see the belt stop. The agent calls over another to take a closer look at what I can only assume are my husband's ashes.

"Is there a problem?"

"Ma'am, we'll need you to step aside to search your bags."

"Why?"

"Ma'am, please step aside."

With everyone watching, I do as I'm told. Three agents are at the belt; my purse and Target Tote are carried to a table.

After a female agent pats me down, another agent pokes his rubber-gloved hands inside my purse. The young man holds the Target Tote, asking, "Ma'am, what's in this bag? Are you carrying an illegal substance?"

Try as I might, it's hard to keep my composure; I whisper, "Please don't touch that; it's my husband's cremains."

"Remains of what?"

"His ashes, I'm taking him home."

"Naw, you can't do that." His eyes cut to a trash bin filled with items travelers had to leave behind. "You gotta dump 'em."

"Are you out of your mind? That's my husband, and you want me to dump him in the goddamn trash!"

"I don't know what to tell you. Maybe you should've packed

him in your suitcase; then he wouldn't have to go in the trash," he smirks.

I get in his face. "Listen to me, you fucken 12-year-old punk I'm not putting my husband in a suitcase for you to lose; now give me that damn bag!" I yell, reaching out to take the Target Tote from his hands.

He pulls back, and I yank the other way, fearing our tug-of-war will cause Trent to be spread all over JFK; I grab hold of his wrist, digging my nails in for him to let go.

Hurriedly, a uniformed woman approaches us, hopefully with the authority to end this fight.

"Excuse me, ma'am. Please calm down and tell me the problem."

"The problem is my husband's cremains are in that bag, and I'm taking them with me; if you don't like it, lock me the hell up!"

"Ma'am, there's no need for all that, but did you say cremains?" She gently unpeels the agent's hands from the Target Tote.

"Cremains remains. What's the fucken difference? It's my husband!"

She hands the bag over to me. "I'm sorry; of course, you can take your husband. Can we get you some water, or would you like to sit briefly?"

I snatch the bag and stare at the agent, asking her, "Do I look thirsty?"

Before I'm out of listening distance, I hear one of them remark, "That bitch is crazy."

I find two seats in the Admirals Club lounge, one for me and one for my bags. I draw a deep breath and glance around the room, littered with men who look like the last place they want to go is wherever they are headed. I feel the same way.

Squeezing my eyes tight, I try convincing myself that going home will help me figure out the next steps in learning to live without my husband. First, I'll hire someone to pack up Trent's things and donate them to Goodwill, and then I'll move out of the villa and into one of the suites.

When I open my eyes, the man across from me is staring in my face, and when he speaks, I ignore him by pretending to answer my phone, not realizing I've pressed Trent's number. His smiling face fills my screen. Covering my mouth to keep from screaming, I snatch up my purse, pick up the Target Tote, and rush to the bathroom, where I use a wet paper towel to cool off my face and wipe away the tears that have my mascara running. Deep breaths are the only thing that relaxes my heaving chest. When I'm finally somewhat calm, I question the person who looks back at me in the mirror. I don't like her.

What's puzzling, though, that I haven't shared with anyone is I can't understand why I'm so horny. The moment the police showed up, informing me that my husband had died, I began to crave him with an intensity that hasn't let up. I know death affects people in different ways, all the same, I never expected it to build up so bad that when the casket closed, my entire body orgasmed.

I've also been wearing black since the funeral, and now here I stand in this overpriced black dress, black suede ankle boots with black back seam stockings, and this Hermès scarf around my neck. No wonder they think I'm a crazy woman. I exit the bathroom and the lounge and walk into New Jersey Sports & More, where I change into an I Love New York hoodie, sweatpants, and a pair of Nike sneakers.

Desperate to ignore the rise of my libido, I stuff the dress, boots, scarf, and stockings in the recycle bin. All that remains are the Japanese Akoya pearls I haven't removed since Trent placed them around my neck the morning of Briana's wedding.

My phone alerts me to a text.

> Bree: Expect me at Sugar Hill next week to discuss my father's property.

The property she's referring to belongs to me. Trent had been a New Jersey Senator who lost his re-election bid when his rival dredged up the fact that Trent had sold drugs in college and sometime after. A few months later, when Trent's Uncle Thomas died from a stroke, passing the ownership of his deteriorating ski lodge onto my husband, we moved to Utah. Rather than accept one of the numerous offers to sell the over 2,000-acre property, we refinanced The Lodge at Sugar Hill, turning it into a 5-star ski resort. Who knows, maybe it's not too late to get the hell away from Briana and everyone else.

Scrolling through my phone I text *My Travel Agent*, requesting she change my flight. I may be alone, but I'm taking my vacation.

Bryce

Now that I'm standing in front of her house, if my sources were right, then that fucken quarterback and Lady Zoë should be gone; if not, that will be a problem.

Upon opening her unlocked front door, the central air cools me until I'm faced with someone who should've been dealt with months ago, Elijah Moore.

"Bryce Goodman, what are you doing here?"

"No, the question is, why are you here?"

"I don't know what happened when I left, either way, she's still my wife."

Before we can debate where Isabella is and who has the right to be here the glass patio doors shatter.

"ELIJAH WATCH OUT!"

He turns. It's too late.

POP!

"E-L-IIII-JAH!"

He crumbles to the floor.

The shooter stands over him.

POP! POP!

Unprotected and with no weapon, I lunge toward the gunman, and he fires again.

Isabella

Leaning my bike against the carport wall, I peek inside the green Hyundai with Enterprise tags beside my car. A weathered black duffle bag with flight tags sits on the floor of the front seat. This looks more like a visitor than someone dropping off items for the party. I gather up my flowers from the basket and head into the house.

I attempt to enter through the French doors of the breakfast room, but when I turn the knob, surprisingly, it's locked, and I don't have my keys. That's when I sense the eerie quiet on the property. Most of the time, when the Twins are cleaning and cooking, they have the music blasting, singing along to Celia Cruz or their favorite Marc Anthony.

Needing to know why the food in my stomach has turned to acid, I walk around to the front of the house. Finding the front door ajar, I call out, "Trisha, Tiana?"

No response.

Pushing the door further open, I'm barely inside when the rubber of my flip-flops sticks to something on the tiles. When I glance down to see what has spilled, my bouquet drifts to the floor, and the piercing sound of someone screaming penetrates my ears.

Dropping onto my knees next to his body, I cry, "Elijah, Elijah, please, my God, Elijah!"

His lips move. There's no sound. His eyes roll left and then right.

Holding onto Elijah, I turn to Bryce, lying only a few inches away. His strained voice murmurs, "Is-a-bell- call."

"IZZY, MS. IZZY! WHAT HAPPENED?"

When I look up, the Twins are running in from the kitchen; their screaming drowns out Bryce's weak voice. Tiana comes with towels for Bryce and Elijah's wounds while a frantic Trisha screams Spanish into her cell phone.

It's too late.

Elijah

I'm dying. I know it. If it were not for the pain, it would be peaceful. Isabella is here, pleading with me to hold on, but the suffering is unbearable.

I long to reach out, but my heavy arms weigh me down. Even as I fade, I am certain, once again, Isabella will not be coming with me.

Peninsula Papagayo

Liberia Guanacaste Airport

Sasha

"Ms. Borianni, we've landed," the flight attendant whispers, attempting to wake me from my Ambien-induced sleep, where Trent's voice asks, *"Why don't we go to Costa Rica for Valentine's Day?"*

"We're here, Trent," I whisper.

"Ma'am?"

I glance at my watch; it's quarter past six in the evening; reaching between my legs, I grab the handle of the Target Tote. After deplaning, I follow the crowd toward customs, handing my purse to the agent for inspection.

Nodding toward the Target Tote, the officer tells me, "Ma'am, *necesito inspeccionar tu bolso.*"

"Please, be careful," I lower my voice, "It's my husband."

"*No entiendo?*"

"It's my husband."

Another agent walks up, and my first thought is here the fuck we go again.

"Yeah, well, we gotta check his bag, too. Where is he?" she asks, glancing behind me.

"He's inside, it's his ashes."

"Sorry, ma'am you can't be spreadin' the foreign debris in our country."

"Debris? I told you it's my husband's cremains. I'm begging you not to do this."

"You should've put him in your luggage," she says, holding her hand out. "We have to check it."

I briefly consider turning around and heading back home, but then they might think I'm smuggling something.

With trepidation, I hand over the bag, and instead of peeking inside to confirm what I've told her, she pulls out the box, opens it, removes the plastic bag tied with his ashes, and unties it for a closer inspection.

"What are you doing?" I plead in a panic after noticing the oversized whirring metal fans above my head and imagining the horror of Trent's cremains blowing across the customs area of Liberia Airport.

"Need to check you not hiding nothin' down in there; your people do it all the time."

Not to make a scene, I say, through gritted teeth, "You TOUCH those ashes, and I will break your scrawny neck!"

Backing away, she replies, "You know what, lady, I don't care; take your damn Target bag, your husband, and go!"

Without any luggage to claim and my heart filled with angst, I rush through the nearest sliding doors toward a kiosk marked Four Seasons Resort. A young man greets me, "Pura Vida, Ms. Sasha, I will be your driver to the resort!"

Stepping outside the airport, the island's warmth immediately embraces me, leaving me momentarily breathless. The driver kindly offers to take my Target Tote, but I hold onto it, feeling its weight against my chest as I follow him to a waiting black SUV. The interior is a welcome contrast, cool and comfortable. I gratefully gulp down the water in the back seat and use the cool towels to soothe my sweaty face and neck. The struggle to remove my heavy sweatshirt is a physical exertion, but I'm relieved to find a camisole underneath, which will serve as my shirt for now.

During the drive, I'm awed by the unrivaled views of the bay and the lush greenery of the hillsides filled with a variety of flowers I've never seen, along with brightly colored homes nestled in between. I crack the window and take in the fresh air. "Is that a monkey in the tree?" I ask my driver when I notice two of them playfully following each other from limb to limb on what appears to be coconut trees.

"Yes, ma'am, lots of wildlife; we can schedule a tour if you'd like."

"Thank you, I won't have time for that," I say, realizing this trip will be short, not the 10 days we intended.

In less than an hour, we are approaching the gates of Papagayo. Once inside, it takes another 20 minutes to round the resort's circular driveway, where two valets await my arrival.

"Pura Vida, Ms. Sasha, welcome to The Four Seasons Peninsula Papagayo!" the young man says when he opens my door.

"My God, it's beautiful here."

"Ah, yes! Ma'am, I'm Manfred, your concierge. May I relieve you of your bag?"

"No, I have it. Thank you, Manfred," I tell him, gripping the Target Tote.

When I step through the busy open-air lobby, the resort's beauty continues to impress with its simple yet luxurious island décor.

"While with us, I'll be available to fulfill all your requests," Manfred tells me while using his iPad to check me in, a process that only takes five minutes. Meanwhile, a smiling woman offers me a tray with a refreshing glass of fruit-garnished coconut water. Another extends a tray of warm, wet towels for me to wipe my hands.

It feels as if the entire resort has been awaiting my arrival. Is this normal? Do they know that I'm grieving? If they do, I'm thankful no one has said, "Sorry for your loss."

"Ms. Sasha, if you follow me, I'll escort you to your villa."

Seated beside Manfred in a golf cart, I notice his young, stress-free features, which haven't dealt with the complex realities of life. Yet, a tingle dances up my spine when his tanned leg brushes against mine.

I shift my focus and listen as his accented voice gives me an overview of the property.

"All the villas are within a 5-minute walk from the main lobby, except for some larger residences."

"People live here?"

"Oh yes, they come year-round, especially to relieve themselves of the cold. I believe you had a tour scheduled for one of the residences."

"That won't be necessary," I say, realizing Trent and *My Travel Agent* had planned this trip. Did he really think we'd purchase a property?

"Understood, Ms. Sasha. Our amenities include a luxurious pool, five restaurants of various cuisines, and a world-class spa. Should you need anything, the 22 Knots boutique will open anytime for our guests' convenience."

I'm sure that's a reference to my lack of luggage.

"Nice."

"Your villa is located further from the main area, perched high above the sea, and surrounded by the tropical rainforest. This also means a golf cart will be at your disposal. Now, as for the beach, we have some that we claim are the world's most pristine beaches, where, in some areas, you'll find volcanic black sand. I should mention that the property is hosting a wedding tomorrow; it could get a little hectic."

"Manfred, how long have you been working here? You're so knowledgeable about the resort."

"About nine months; my last post was at the Four Seasons in Jackson Hole, where I was for about two years. Before that, I was in Johannesburg, South Africa. Now, that is a place I'd suggest every guest visits. It is Pura Vida, and it is my home!"

"May I ask what 'Pura Vida' is?"

"It's our way of life, the simple pure life. You'll know when you feel it."

I want to tell this young, magnetic man that Pura Vida is far from becoming part of my life.

Upon reaching my villa, I thank him yet decline his offer to show me around. Manfred refuses my offer of a tip, bows, and then makes his exit. Once he's gone, I flip the Do Not Disturb sign to the outside doorknob. Housekeeping will be optional during my stay.

Inside the villa, I set my purse in a chair and lift the Target Tote onto the dresser, asking Trent, "Is this where you want to be?"

My answer is to uncork the bottle of Chateau Margaux that sits in a temperature-controlled cooler with a handwritten notecard that reads, "May your memories guide your future," signed *My Travel Agent*.

On the bed, folded neatly, are two brightly colored sundresses, an adult romper, a pair of sandals, a two-piece black bathing suit, and a bag of assorted lingerie and toiletries. I'm sure that with the assistance of The Four Seasons, this was also a gift from *My Travel Agent*. I appreciate her thoughtfulness since Trent's and my suitcases have already landed at Salt Lake City Airport. Packing Trent's bag was a force of habit, whenever we were traveling, that became my responsibility.

"Sasha, did you pack my razor? Sasha, don't forget to pack my gym clothes!"

"You could always pack it yourself."

"I like knowing your hands touched every piece with love, so get on with it, woman," he would say before smacking me on the ass.

Who will smack me on the ass now, and who will reach for me in a one-arm embrace when I'm attempting to get out of bed?

Nobody.

There will also be nobody to touch me, to make love to me, and tell me, "Get ready," as Trent often whispered to me during the day, letting me know he had plans for the night.

I consider turning on my phone to let someone know I've altered my trip; however, the last thing I want to hear is someone's opinion of my decision to travel here. After giving myself a generous pour of wine and taking the bottle, I step onto the terrace.

Outside the doors is a low-lit plunge pool with a spectacular view of the sun lowering itself behind the rainforest. I strip my clothes, kick off my sneakers, and slide directly into the perfectly tempered pool. To fight the shudder threatening to tear through my body, I wrap my arms tightly around myself, posing the question, "God, what am I supposed to do without my husband?" Again, I'm gutted by the lack of a reply.

Our door attendant, Rahim, called, "Ms. Sasha, you have guests."

"I do? Who is it?"

"It's the state police. You want me to bring them up?"

By the time the New Jersey State Troopers reached my floor, I was standing in the doorway, my body tight with anxiety. What made it even odder was that Rahim stood wide-eyed behind them.

"Are you here alone?" the white trooper asked, glancing behind me into the condo.

"What happened?"

He tells me his name and that of his partner, which I still can't recall, then states, "There's been an accident. Your husband had a heart attack."

"My husband, are you sure?" I ask, feeling some relief that my health-conscious husband couldn't possibly have had a heart attack."

"Ma'am, may we please come inside?"

Through tightened lips, I ask, "Where is he? Where is Trent?"

"I'm sorry, ma'am. He didn't survive."

It is late morning when I wake up sweaty and sticky under the covers. Despite the air conditioning being on, the open sliding doors give off the humidity of the East Coast. I carry my aching body into the bathroom; staring back at me in the full-length mirror is the reflection of a woman ten years older than my actual age of 62. Trent's death has aged me faster than menopause ever did. If I'm lucky, maybe I'll die soon too.

Upon further inspection, my puffy eyelids are swollen from weeks of crying, and seemingly stitched together by crow's feet that have permanently etched themselves into my skin. Pulling at the short, tight curls of my dry and matted gray hair, having outgrown my typically edgy close cut, I cry again, asking, "Who are you?"

Desperate to escape the answer and the ugliness of my appearance, I wash down an Ambien with the remaining wine and bury myself under the cocoon of my comforter and sweat-drenched bed sheets.

The voices in my Ambien haze tell me that when I wake up, Trent's ashes will have formed back into the person he was, holding me, and loving me. It's surreal visions of him that move from my head and course through my body, landing in the worst spot, between my thighs. I slide deeper under the covers and force myself to think about the reality that there is no coming back for him. My husband is dead.

"He's in a better place," claimed Pastor Lamb. I didn't understand what that meant. What place is better than being here with me? I hated everyone who came to the funeral, attempting to console me. They had no idea what it was like seeing your husband, who one moment was making you laugh across the kitchen table, and days later, he is stiff in a casket. I wanted to run out of the church as soon as the choir started singing their rendition of Smokie Norful's, *I Need You Now*, followed by Pastor Lamb's eulogy of what God had promised.

Hours later, my head feels filled with bricks instead of feeling refreshed from my sleep. Since I'm in no shape to be seen by anyone, I slip into one of the hotel robes and make coffee from the pot in my room. Out of habit, I swallow my Metoprolol for high blood pressure, Lipitor for cholesterol, and Prempro for my often-debilitating menopause symptoms, followed by two Excedrin.

I return to the terrace, turn on my phone, and scroll through the never-ending text messages and voicemails, deleting those that start with, "I'm sorry to hear… "If you need anything," and especially deleting the three voicemails from Briana.

The first message I listen to is from my son Owen.

"Mom, I hope you're getting some rest. I know it's not a good time, but I need to talk to you. I need some advice."

My son is seeking advice on how to fix his failing marriage. I have no answers for that.

Next is Marquise Andrew Price, who grew up at Sugar Hill. His parents worked there, and he started cleaning skis as a young boy until he learned every aspect of operations, and now he excels in his role as general manager. Two years ago, he married Jacque, a maître d' at a Venice restaurant who'd visited and never left. Recently, they completed the adoption process of a six-month-old little girl from Cameroon, solidifying them as parents.

Knowing he was awaiting my return yesterday, he's my first call.

"Ms. Sasha, I'm so glad you called. Cosay said you were a no-show at the Salt Lake airport. Are you okay?"

"I didn't mean to alarm you. I needed some time alone before coming home; I'm okay."

Okay. Another lie.

"Understandable. I wanted to make you aware Trent's daughter has phoned and is demanding that we email her a copy of the deed for Sugar Hill."

"Briana has no authority to access anything without my consent."

"Good, because certain documents must be transferred to your name."

"I'll be home by the end of the week, probably Friday."

"Excellent! And thank you, Ms. Sasha, for returning my call, and please take care of yourself."

I refresh my coffee and add a splash of rum from the bar before calling my best friend, Arshell. Her guidance in knowing what needed to be done kept our family sane during the arrangements for Trent's services. She must've been the one who put Trent's death notice in the newspapers, as I have no recollection of calling anyone except Briana. It was also Arshell with whom I had a laugh after Trent's funeral when some of his family requested ashes be put in rings and necklaces. We both thought it was ridiculous. Now, I fear if I toss his remaining ashes into the ocean what will be left of him for me to hold onto?

"Sasha Borianni, where are you right now?" Arshell demands to know when she answers the phone.

"Costa Rica."

"Your vacation? Oh, sweetie, you went by yourself. Do you need me to come there?"

"No, I'm only staying a few days to spread his ashes. Then I'm going home."

Her voice softens with sympathy. "How are you managing?"

I glance up at the Target Tote.

"I'm okay. I wasn't sure his ashes were going to make it."

Not okay.

"What do you mean?"

Not ready for a lengthy conversation, I tell her, "Long story. Can you do me a favor and call Owen? Tell him I'll call him in another day or so?"

"Of course. Sasha, you will thrive again, I promise."

She can't make that promise. No one can.

Once we hang up, I don't try to hold back the tears. I'm free now to cry, to scream, and let out the pain and anger that's been trapped inside me without anyone comforting me. These are my tears and my pain; I own them.

Later in the evening, I order room service, and when the chicken quesadilla and second bottle of Chateau Margaux arrive, I prop myself up on the bed. Retrieving my iPad from its case, I google "releasing ashes in Costa Rica." The first response is that it's illegal. These ashes have become problematic at every turn. What's the point? I'll take them home with me.

Thinking it might make me feel better, I open my phone to listen to Trent's old messages. When his voice fills the room, my body yearns with so much desire for him that all I can do is squeeze my thighs tight, praying it will subside. I shut off the phone, pop an Ambien, and for the second night, I cry myself to sleep. Maybe the morning will be different.

The morning is no different.

When I climb out of bed to use the toilet, I'm hit with an unpleasant odor, reminding me that I haven't showered since leaving New Jersey. This is not the way I want to grieve. After a much-needed shower and feeling slightly refreshed, I check the sizes of the dresses that have fallen to the floor and pull on the Mandarin bareback midi dress. Surprisingly, it fits my wanted and unwanted curves. For shoes, I opt for the sparkly Stuart Weitzman flat sandals.

Determined to scatter my husband's ashes, I pull my sunglasses down over my puffy eyes, and with my Target Tote in hand, I make my way outside. As I'm getting situated onto my golf cart, Joe Thurmond, the branch manager at Chase Bank, rings my phone.

My watch shows an hour difference in Park City, but there's still no reason for him to be calling. I answer.

"Ms. Sasha, I'm sorry to disturb you. Please accept my condolences."

"Thank you. Mr. Thurmond, how can I help you?"

"I was instructed to let you know your husband set aside a special savings account to be transferred to you upon his death."

"A savings account? Are you sure? We already have an account, several accounts at your bank."

"He said it was an emergency fund, and also, Ms. Sasha, there's an additional safe deposit box."

I know about the box where we kept my jewelry and legal documents for the lodge and the various properties we owned in

Jersey, Philly, and a one-bedroom condo in Park City; nevertheless, why did he feel like we needed another one?

"When did he do all of this?"

"The savings account was set up three years ago. The box he opened it before you left for your daughter's wedding."

"Why?" I ask, feeling like I'm in a movie scene, about to discover things about my husband I never knew. I pray he doesn't have another wife and family somewhere.

"All he said was he wanted you to be protected. Shall I expect you at the bank?"

"What's the balance on the account?"

"He only made one deposit when he opened it."

"And the balance?"

I hear Thurmond swallow before saying, "One hundred and seventy-two thousand dollars."

This doesn't make any sense. "Are you sure? Where'd he get that money?" I ask, knowing he doesn't have an answer.

"Ma'am?"

Praying my husband wasn't doing anything illegal, I tell him, "You'll see me in a few days. Thank you."

After bringing the golf cart to a jerking stop outside the Bahia restaurant, I scan through my phone and call our attorney and friend, Adam Selzer, only to be told he's on vacation until Monday.

At the restaurant's entrance, the smiling hostess greets me, and following her inside, I see it's filled with tall plants and colorful flowers, overlooking the bluest ocean I've ever seen. The place is busy, with servers jostling and diners seated on couches and at tables, everyone enjoying this beautiful island except me. When I hear a group of giddy young women enter behind me, I recall the wedding Manfred mentioned, and I want to be far from it. Aware that I'm alone, she properly seats me outside in what feels like a treehouse.

Before I can look at the menu, a young waiter delivers coffee, toast, and a fruit salad medley filled with the brightest colors of thinly sliced papayas, mangos, watermelon, two soft-boiled eggs, and fresh squeezed orange juice. Realizing again that my husband planned every detail of this trip, except to tell me about his unexpected windfall and whatever he's hidden in a safety deposit box, makes me smile. I want to be mad at him, except I want to believe he'd planned to tell me during our vacation.

"Pura Vida, Ms. Sasha," greets Manfred with what should be infectious enthusiasm.

"Morning, Manfred, I need to ask you something personal."

"Please, whatever your needs."

I wish he'd stop staying that.

"My husband died recently."

"*La condolencias.*"

"Thank you," I say, grateful he didn't say, *sorry*. "I've come to your island to spread his ashes. Do you think there'd be somewhere discreet where I could do that without a permit? You see, we were supposed to spend our vacation here," I get choked up, "but he…"

"No need to explain, Ms. Sasha. I have the perfect spot for you," he smiles toward my Target Tote, "and for your husband."

I lay my hand over his, which is unbelievably soft, sending a teasing tingle in places it shouldn't. I pull away and say, "Thank you," only to realize I'm also sick of repeating those two words.

"Allow me a moment."

After I've finished drinking the best coffee I've ever tasted, Manfred returns with instructions. "Here's what to do: When you leave the restaurant, stay on the path toward the quiet beach, about a half mile to the left of the resort. There, you'll find the perfect spot. And take these with you," he says, handing me a small cellophane bag filled with multicolored stemless flower buds.

My tear-filled eyes ask the question I'm too choked up to say.

"To carry your loved one out to sea."

Unable to stomach the soft-boiled eggs, I get up from the table, and on foot, I head to the quiet beach. Along the way, I see the staff setting up white chairs and an altar for the wedding. Delicate white and sky-blue flowers are strewn along a white aisle runner, and a string quartet is tuning up while a DJ places his equipment further off to the right, where a hardwood floor has been laid.

Try as I might to resist, I recall the memories of my nuptials at Lake Trasimeno in Italy. It was a simple ceremony with about 60 guests who raved about every aspect we'd planned. There was no need for décor, as Agriturismo was a breathtaking estate between Tuscany and Umbria, providing all the scenery needed.

Now I wonder how I will spend our wedding anniversary, our birthdays, Christmas, New Year's, and all those holidays people say are so hard to endure once you've lost someone. I'm assured the pain will be unbearable.

Walking on the warm, gritty sand, I kick off my sandals and pick up my pace, increasing my anxiety. A few more feet down the trail, I come upon a remote area that must be the place Manfred suggested. If not, what place could be better?

Realizing that the ocean will be Trent's final resting place, I lower myself into the sand to calm my pacing heart. I should've Googled a special prayer. Instead, I draw deep breaths of the sea air and tell myself it's time to let him go.

With the bottom of my dress dragging behind me, I walk out into the ocean. Stooping down in the water, I'm hesitant to open the box since after the cremation, before offering up containers to Briana and TJ, it was Arshell who knew to sift through the ashes, removing bone fragments that would've certainly been a disaster for us to see.

I pull the bag from its box, remove the twisted tie, and stare at what remains of my husband. How could a man I loved so much and who gave even more have been burned down to ashes? Isn't this how we were created?

Using the gold scooper, I begin sprinkling my husband into the ocean. I scatter ashes from side to side, followed by stemless flower buds. Wading further out into the warm water, I feel my feet sinking in what's left of the sand beneath me, and when I'm up to my waist, I find myself encircled by flower buds and ashes. Maybe he doesn't want to go. Lifting my sunglasses from over my eyes, I swish the clear water with my hands, and the stemless flowers begin trailing behind Trent, carrying him further out into the warm ocean waters. If only I could go with him.

Instead of feeling lighter, I feel heavy. No burden has been lifted. I step backward until I can lie flat in the wet sand, where I whisper my final goodbye.

Dear God, thank you for my husband. I didn't want him to go, it was your will to bring him home. I'm hurting; my family is broken, and I don't know what to do. I pray for peace and acceptance of your will and that it be your will for us to be together again. God, please make this ache in my heart and body go away.

Struggling to sit up, bleary-eyed from the blistering sun and unstoppable tears, I am completely stunned to see a naked man walking out of the ocean. I blink my eyes. Maybe it's Trent, reincarnated from the ashes. It must be!

Sitting erect, I remove my sunglasses and cannot stop staring at this strange man formed from my husband's ashes. Squinting, I can see the sun glisten off his sculpted, tanned brown skin, from which water droplets cling. Before he can get close enough for me to see his face, he notices me and attempts to cover himself with his hands. It's too much to cover.

Stumbling to get up, I start walking backward. My haste causes me to trip up in the sand. When he stretches out his hand to assist me, his act puts me at eye level with what must be a gift from God

Casa La Paz

Isabella

"NOOO, NOOOO! MY GOD NO! DON'T LEAVE ME!"

Rocking back and forth, cradling Elijah in my arms, where crimson blood bubbles from a hole in the middle of his forehead, police encircle me, coaxing me away. I fight them off until I'm not given a choice as they lift me up, away from him, carrying me into the kitchen.

"We got two male victims. Send another unit and call for the coroner. This one took two in the chest and one in the head. No pulse."

In disbelief, I watch as EMTs cut the clothes from Elijah and Bryce's bodies in search of their wounds.

Someone behind me exclaims, *"Fuck qué sucedió, Fuck qué sucedió!"*

"Está vacío," an officer yells while descending from my second floor. What were they doing up there? Where did they come from?

"Call it."

"11:48 a.m."

An officer at the kitchen counter casually thumbs through Elijah's wallet and then announces, *"Muerto Malcolm Moore muerto."*

"No, he's Elijah, my husband," I scream.

"This one's been hit in the groin and the shoulder; we gotta get him outta here!"

"He's losing lots of blood. *Rápida! Rápida!*"

Within minutes, they lift Bryce onto a stretcher, pierce an IV into his arm, and place an oxygen mask over his face, rushing him out to a waiting ambulance, calling out codes on the radio alerting the hospital as to his status.

A wide-body officer has been positioned to block what has now become a crime scene. When I see them cover Elijah's body with a sheet my legs give way, and I pass out.

Upon regaining consciousness, I find myself seated in a kitchen chair with Trisha and Tiana standing on either side of me, each with a hand on my shoulder. When did they arrive? Did they call the cops? Were they here before me? Did they see what happened?

I see now the wide-body officer is a woman with brightly colored hair partially covered with a black baseball cap that reads POLICIA printed in yellow across the front of it and on her bulletproof vest. In the living room, more police have arrived, including those dressed in white hazmat suits, draping crime scene tape across my furniture and to my walls. What's worse, two people with CORONER written on the back of their shirts are kneeling beside Elijah's body.

"They busted through here," an officer barks into the kitchen.

"Collect, package, everything!"

"Recuperas un arma?"

"No weapons and no shells yet."

I'm lost in a chaotic symphony of sounds and movement from the police, who walk around Elijah's sheet-covered body and the blood that has started to seep through, to the ones roaming throughout my house. All of them are wearing a collage of vests, hats, and shirts with varying logos, and all take glances at me, seeking answers I don't have.

That's when a man wearing a police-logoed polo shirt and baseball cap approaches, giving me a nod of familiarity. He kneels in front of me close enough that I can see the melting peppermint bobbing on his tongue. Do I know him? His sympathetic voice says, "Ms. Isabella, I'm Detective Mora. I'm sorry this has happened."

"Eddie, she knows who you are."

He cuts his eye at Tiana and mouths, "Be quiet."

Now, I remember. He's Tiana's boyfriend. I've done his taxes, and I know he hates being called Eddie while working.

"Ms. Isabella, is there a gun in the house?"

"No, Eddie, there's no guns here; we would know," replies Tiana.

"I'm serious, Tiana, I'll have you escorted outta here."

"No iré a ningún lado hasta que apague esta comida," she tells him, making her way to the other side of the island, where she lifts the lid from a simmering pot causing me to hold onto my griping stomach.

"Ms. Isabella, can you tell me what you saw when you came home?"

Why is he being so formal? He always calls me Izzy. "I found them," I answer.

He repeats the question.

I repeat my answer, louder this time, "I found them. They were on the floor."

Wide body who's squinting at me from across the kitchen island says, "Awe shit, she's bleeding. Get somebody in here."

Glancing down, I see blood on my knees and a piece of glass jutting out from the right side of my left foot.

"I'll take care of it," says a woman with EMT printed on her baseball cap. She snaps on blue gloves and then kneels in front of me. From her bag, she pulls out tweezers that she uses to remove the thin shard of glass.

Trisha notices me turning my hands over and using a wet dishcloth; she wipes the blood from my hands and knees; still, I pick at the caked blood under my nails.

"Ms. Isabella, I know this is difficult. The first officers on the scene heard you calling the deceased Elijah."

"I'm his wife."

"Ma'am, his identification says he's Malcolm Moore. Are you his wife?" he asks me, looking toward the Twins to see if they know the answer. Nobody knows.

"Malcolm Moore. Ma'am, do you know him?"

"Malcolm, who is Malcolm?" I ask; they still ignore me.

Trisha answers, "Can't you see she's in shock? She's not talking."

I am talking.

Nodding toward the even more crowded living room where I can no longer see Elijah's body, Tiana asks, "Would you, after witnessing that?"

"Mora, I found a picture of 'em. He looks a lot different. He must've lost a ton of weight or had the squeeze," offers a young officer.

Eddie eyes our silver-framed wedding picture and then back at me he asks, "Ms. Isabella, were you expecting these men?"

"No. I don't know why they came here."

From her shaking hands to mine, Tiana passes me a glass of water that spills after a sip. I give it back to her.

"What about her party? All the guests?" Trisha wonders aloud.

An irritated Detective Mora tells her, "The party is over; this is a crime scene. And I need you two to provide a witness statement about what you saw when you arrived."

"Really Eddie?"

"This is my last warning and cut it with the Eddie shit."

Tiana throws him a kiss and mouths, "I'm sorry."

The Twins—I'm not sure which one—whisper in my ear not to talk until I get a lawyer.

In a tone she rarely uses, Trisha asks, *"Detective Mora, can my lady get out of these bloody clothes?"*

I glance down and see blood covering the front of my halter-top and shorts.

"I'll get an officer to go upstairs with her, now you two are outside!"

A young woman who can't be more than 18 enters the kitchen and says, "Hey, Sarge, there ain't no footprints in the dirt behind the house; besides that, not one shell casing was left behind. It looks like a professional hit."

"Yeah, I get it; I need you to take Ms. Isabella upstairs so she can change."

She rolls her eyes in defiance, yet does what she is told and follows me up the back staircase to my bedroom.

Finally, alone, when I step out of my shorts and untie my halter top, the familiar scent of Elijah's Bond No. 9 cologne overtakes me. Before I realize it, I've slid onto the floor of the shower, biting into my washcloth, crying, and screaming for God to make it all go away.

The door slides back; the young officer peeks inside and asks, "Hey, are you okay?"

Go away.

"Are you okay? Do you need help?"

When I realize she can't hear me, I shake my head from side to side. She closes the door.

Now I panic. What's happened to my voice? Has the shock taken it away? Will I ever be heard again? I need to get out of this house. I'm not safe here.

Wiping the steam from the mirror, I notice that the natural white streaks in my freshly braided hair are covered with blood particles. Bending my head in the sink, I stick them under the running water. It doesn't help; my hair is too thick, and I need scissors. I scramble through the drawers in the bathroom vanity and then in my toiletry bag. As soon as I get them in my hands, the officer opens the door again, and with surprise at what she thinks I'm attempting, she takes them from me and says, "Whoa, you don't need to be handling those. You should get dressed."

On the back of the bathroom door hangs the white cotton eyelet dress I'd ordered from Anthropology to wear to the party. Forgoing undergarments, I slip the dress over my head and step into a pair of rainbow Teva's pushed halfway under a chair. That's when my cell phone rings.

"You wanna get that?" the officer asks.

Ignoring her, I shove the phone into my dress pocket, pull my braids back in a rubber band, and head downstairs. As if there were more room in my house for police, a burly man enters the kitchen and circles around the island. Along with him is a woman who isn't dressed to be here.

Directing her question to Eddie, I hear the woman ask, "What the fuck happened?"

"Besides the obvious, I can't say yet."

The impatient burly man states, "Goddamnit, I don't like open murder cases in Esterillos, especially ex-pats bringing trouble to our island. Somebody better get me some fucken answers."

"We're working on it, Cap'n."

With her bare back to me, the unidentified woman asks Eddie, "You're saying she hasn't spoken yet?"

"Not a word. Here she is now. Ms. Isabella."

"Where?"

When the woman faces me, I'm awestruck by her resemblance to Salma Hayek. Her straight black hair is parted down the middle and pulled back into a low ponytail with swoops circling her ears. Changing her tone slightly, she's still irritated about being here, and it's obvious why. This woman is standing on four-inch Louboutin sandals, wearing a form-fitting red bareback dress, and donning a pair of Tom Ford private collection sunglasses. Who is she, and why is she here?

"Ms. Isabella?"

Keeping my eyes on her, I weave through the officers towards an empty chair where I notice the Twins through the open patio doors, seated at one of the poolside tables, each writing what I assume is a statement for the police. This is when I become aware of the colorful party decorations with paper lanterns strung from the trees, inflatable slices of oranges and lemons floating in the pool, and a bar stacked with boxes of liquor still to be put away.

The burly man who spends too much time lifting and even more on his gelled-down hair introduces himself. "Ma'am, I'm Captain Carlisle Castro."

I ignore him and instead focus my eyes on the living room where Elijah's body lay stiff alongside an unzipped black bag. Eddie motions for the wide-body officer to block my view; even so, it's obvious she's not wide enough.

"Ms. Isabella?"

I turn to give my attention to this Salma Hayek lookalike.

"Ma'am, I'm Special Agent Luciana Solano of the FBI. I'm so sorry for your loss and what's happened here."

I nod, and she sees that I understand, but will she be able to hear me when it's time to speak?

Captain Castro adds, "Ma'am, can you explain your relationship to these men, Malcolm Moore and Bryce Goodman?"

"Stop calling me ma'am. I'm not old," I tell them, my voice unheard.

"Ms. Isabella, do you know who might've done this?"

Is she serious? How would I know?

"Ms. Isabella is there anyone you wanna call?" asks Eddie.

Trisha, who's now re-entered the kitchen, speaks for me: "Who would she call? She can't talk."

There is someone I want to call, *"Sémile, I want to call Sémile,"* I plead.

"Eddie, send your girlfriend and her sister home," Captain Castro orders him.

Tiana easily corrects the captain. "Nobody sends me and my sister anywhere. Maybe if you get her away from here, she can breathe. We don't have to be cops to know that."

Mora and Castro look at each other dumbfounded, with Mora adding, "Ms. Isabella, I'm going to have an officer take you over to the station, okay? We'll be right behind you after we wrap some things up here."

By wrapping, do they mean Elijah's body?

My cell phone rings. All eyes land on me. Without removing it from my dress pocket, I silence it and follow the young officer out the door. Behind me I overhear Solano telling Eddie and Castro, "She better hope by the time we get there she can answer some questions about this fucken love triangle."

Yellow crime scene tape outlines my otherwise colorful landscape outside the pool area. Its flowers are trampled, while the driveway leading to my house is filled with police cars and vans. Glaring among them is a dark blue van marked MEDICAL EXAMINER.

As the police car approaches the end of the driveway, I lower my head and close my eyes from the clamoring neighbors and reporters hungering for information and photo opportunities. This show demonstrates that my home and I have become a spectacle for the town of Esterillos and probably beyond, which tells me I can never live here again. Someone has taken away my paradise.

I text Elijah's best friend.

> Me: Elijah is gone

> Sémile: Don't understand gone

> Me: He's dead. Bryce is shot

> Sémile: fck

Of all the places I've been on the island, I've never had a reason to visit its community police station, and it's a lot different from those in the U.S. It doesn't even look like a police station; it's more like an army barracks, tucked safely behind tall wooden fencing. Then I remember Eddie telling me that some officers, primarily women, live on the premises.

Inside, the largest of the buildings and although it may not be as gritty as those back in Philadelphia, it still makes me feel like a criminal. Walking behind the officer, I might as well be in handcuffs, the way everyone is staring at me in disdain as if I've messed up a perfect day, which I have. I'm sure all the chaos of ringing phones and an overabundance of chatter inside is from the case I've presented them with. It's not as if Costa Rica is without crime, but I brought this here, and as much as it's personally painful, it's also embarrassing.

Instead of an interview room, I'm seated in the break room; the television on the counter is turned to Channel 9 with the caption reading *Murder at Casa La Paz*. I don't need perfect Spanish to understand what they're saying, especially with the footage of my home, my face, and Elijah's. So far, the only mention of Bryce is as *"The other man, possibly her lover, embroiled in a domestic dispute that turned fatal."*

I need to call my mother. I can't allow her to hear this from anyone except me, as it will undoubtedly make national news.

On the stove over a high burning flame, a pot of Olla de Carne bubbles, filling the room with its aromatic blend of cumin, cilantro, and oregano, forcing me to swallow the nasty taste of vomit. When another familiar face, Officer Martina, whose first home mortgage paperwork I processed, wanders in and stirs the pot, she whispers, reassuring me that everything will be alright, then sets a bottle of water in front of me.

I finish off the water, hoping to push back the nausea and keep my composure so I can call my mother. Before I can make the call, Special Agent Solano, Captain Castro, and Detective Mora enter the building and walk my way. I pray my voice has returned. If not, they can give me the paper to write my answers to their questions and sign their statement. My only question to them is if Bryce survived.

Salma Hayek begins, "Before we start the questioning, I need you to understand the relevance of my being here. These folks," she nods toward the police outside the room, "they ran Malcolm Moore in the system, and it sent a red flag to the Department of Justice and FBI. It so happens I'm here on vacation and it was kicked to me. This man known to you as Elijah Moore was a government informant under WITSEC, but you already know cause you were his wife."

"I'm still his wife."

The reality that Elijah is dead brings with it a swell of unexpected tears. Observing from her desk, Martina rushes in, handing me a roll of brown paper towels and another bottle of cold water. She then stands beside me, her hand on my shoulder as a comfort until I can stop the flow.

"You okay?" Eddie asks.

Captain Castro could care less when he says, "Maybe you take your time and start telling us about your day, from this morning when you woke up until the time you returned home from the café."

How did they know I was at the café? Of course, they know. This is Esterillos; everyone knows everything in this community. It also means they know White Magic and Lady Zoë left this morning.

My phone vibrates in my pocket, announcing a text. I glance down.

> Sémile: how

"Is there anyone you'd like to call? A lawyer perhaps," Castro adds.

"Why would I call a lawyer?"

"I know she hears us because her eyes are moving," Solano states.

"I'm not dead."

Frustrated, Solano removes her oversized Tom Ford sunglasses from her oblong face and tosses her Salma Hayek ponytail hair over her left shoulder.

"You understand the most likely suspect is the Russian oligarch your husband testified against? I'm certain he ordered the hit from prison, and your other guy, the one in the hospital, your boyfriend; it's my guess he was in the wrong place. Do you understand that?"

I can only hope my facial expression reveals my disdain for this woman.

When she asks, "Did you invite them to your little party?"

Luckily, she can't hear me when I say, *"You bitch, why would I do that?"*

Not realizing how hard I'm gripping my cell phone when it rings, it slips out of my sweaty hands and drops to the floor.

Solano picks it up and slams it on the table before me, "Just answer the thing."

I'm perplexed as to why this woman doesn't like me. My guess is I'm the reason her vacation has been delayed.

The call is from Sémile. I can't answer in front of them, and he might not be able to hear me either.

"Guys, the woman witnessed a tragic scene; go a little easier," Eddie suggests.

Solano tells him, "It's my job to find out who killed a government witness."

"He's nobody's witness anymore."

"Malcolm Moore belongs to the federal government."

"In this jurisdiction, he belongs to us," states Captain Castro.

While Solano and Castro argue over who my husband belongs to, I reply to Sémile's call with a text.

> Me: CR

When they see me texting, they watch me waiting.

He doesn't respond.

Then it strikes me that the one person I need to talk to who won't want to hear from me, especially this news, is "His mother," I mumble, this time hearing the words.

"Excuse me?" Solano asks.

"His mother, call his mother," I say a little louder after clearing my throat.

"His mother's dead," she spits out, then catches the disapproving eyes of Eddie and Castro.

Attempting to ease her harsh remarks, Eddie says, "I'm sorry, she's right. The DOJ sent over his file, and his mother is listed as deceased."

This can't be happening. Life can't be this cruel.

"How? When did she---?"

Solano is the only one who can answer that question. "About seven months after they entered the program."

Although Ms. Moore was cautious of me when Elijah and I first started dating, she eventually warmed up, and we built a good relationship until her son got into trouble. She believed it was my fault. Unbeknownst to her, Elijah had been involved with the Russians before we met.

"When can I go home?"

"That's not happening until they finish processing the scene. It could be a few days," Castro states.

"Home to Philadelphia?"

Salma pulls her hair from whatever holds back her sleek ponytail and shakes it loose, telling me, "You're stuck here until your story checks out."

I feel my voice rising and the tears gathering. I refuse to cry again, especially in front of this woman. "My story? There is no story. It's what I came home to."

Castro adds, "Now that you're talking, I need to get a statement. Mora, get someone in here."

A young woman sits next to the refrigerator and is poised to write down the answers to their questions. Eddie stands near the stove, taking his own set of notes.

"What is it you wanna know?"

"What happened when you came home?"

"I came home, and they were there on the floor."

"What time was it?"

"I don't know."

"You didn't look at your phone?"

"No."

"Did you see anyone fleeing the scene?"

"A car, a Mercedes town car, was coming out the driveway."

"That was the driver for Mr. Goodman."

Solano chimes in, "When was the last time you had contact with either man? Did you know your husband had relocated to Colorado Springs? Had you visited him there?"

"No! I never knew where he'd been taken to, and if I did, I wouldn't have gone."

By now, it doesn't matter who's asking the questions since my eyes are focused on the ticking clock over the door behind them, whose arms aren't moving, giving me no idea what time it is.

"Do you think they planned to come here together to confront you, make you decide?"

"I don't know why they came."

"Yet you had a visitor, the football player, and another woman; they left on a private jet."

"They're clients."

Solano's smirk turns into a laugh that she attempts to cover with her hand.

Castro takes a turn. "Was anything missing from your home? Were you holding anything for your husband, money, guns, drugs?"

"No."

"They're searching your house. Anything they find, love letters or gifts he may have sent, will go into evidence," warns Solano.

I shrug my shoulders, not caring what they find.

"It's hard to believe you didn't know they'd be together at your house. Did you invite them, lure them?"

This unrelenting bitch must think I'm stupid.

"I answered that question. Now, where'd you take him? Where's Elijah?"

"He'll be at the morgue until we decide how to process his remains."

"What do you mean process?"

"As I stated, the man you knew as Elijah Moore is no longer. Our *Malcolm Moore* remains the government's property."

"Then how was it you allowed your *property* to get killed?"

"That's what we're trying to find out—exactly what made him leave the program when he knew the rules and the risks. Every time, though, these informants go back for love," Solano says, twisting her lips into a condescending smile.

I hate her.

"So, there's no funeral?"

"A funeral would draw unwanted attention. And who would come anyway?"

Eddie saves me when he says, "That's it. We're done for now. Ms. Isabella, please sign the statement, we'll have an officer take you wherever you wanna go."

"Bryce, where's he at?"

"Hospital, in surgery. You need to pray he makes it."

Eddie waves in a uniformed officer, informing me he will be my bodyguard for the next few days.

Once I'm in the back seat of the police car, I text Sémile.

> Me: I NEED YOU

No response.

With my battery at 10%, I call Ms. Ana, who owns Black Sands Bungalows. Having been her bookkeeper for the past six months, together, we were able to tighten up her books and find profits she'd ignored and almost lost. We even discovered that her land covered more acres than the county had allotted her.

30 minutes later, we arrive to find Ms. Ana walking with a basket of vegetables from her garden. The officer lets me out of the car and walks over to relieve Ms. Ana of her basket.

After releasing me from a much-needed motherly embrace, she says, "Izzy, *bienvenido de nuevo*. I have what ya need."

"Thank you, Ms. Ana. I'm so sorry to bring this here."

"*Nada, nada, ven adentro conmigo.*"

Stepping inside the bungalow that serves as her home, the television above her desk is reporting the news, featuring me. "You don't need to see this right now," she says, turning it off.

"It's okay."

Along with the key to Bungalow 8 and a fresh set of bath linens, she hands me a container of fried platano maduro and redfish, which I'm sure was caught this morning from the nearby fishing village.

"*Aqua en la habitación* and Twins, they drop your things. Here's your backpack. You *necesitas comer*, weakness, grief, and pain are easier to handle when the body is strong. And take this," she says, slipping me two perfectly rolled puros.

The last thing I want to do is get high, but they might be helpful later, especially if I stay on the island. Plus, she is not a woman you want to argue with.

The quaint one-bedroom Bungalow is painted an early morning blue, with various hues of white furniture. The main room holds a queen-size bed, dresser, and a small writing desk and chair. The narrow kitchen is complete with a stove, refrigerator, overhead cabinets, and microwave, all squeezed in between a new countertop and cement sink.

If this place were listed on travel sites, tourists would invade it, allowing Ms. Ana to charge hundreds of dollars a night to stay there. Her interest and intent, though, are in keeping it comfortable and nostalgic for those who can appreciate it. People only find their way to her place through personal referrals.

The selling point of Black Sands' sold-out Bungalows is that the back porch dips into the ocean right where it meets the sand, and from there, you can sit on two blue Adirondack chairs or a few steps away; you can stretch out in a hammock swaying between two palm trees. I shut the door to the view.

Inside my backpack are my wallet, scratched-up Warby Parker prescription glasses, a charger, and two changes of clothes. I plug in my phone, refusing to scroll through the screen full of text messages or listen to the 32 voicemails. Horrified at the events of the day, I head to the bathroom, my hands shaking and my neck sweating from the lingering scent of death, blood, and Bond No. 9 that has seeped into my skin.

Seated on the floor, my back against the tub, I call my mother. When her cell phone goes to voicemail and her home phone goes unanswered, it reminds me that she's on a cruise with Mr. Rich, so I text her.

> Me: Elijah has died. Please call me when you land. I'm okay. I love you.

Next, I make the dreaded call to my employer, Lady Zoë, a woman I befriended, only to be lured into the underbelly of a sexually charged lifestyle that I've yet to shake loose. To make it worse, when Elijah testified against her lover of sorts, I was blackmailed into picking up the pieces of the business he left behind. Making our relationship the worst case of mixing business with undeniable pleasure.

"Isabella, *My Love*, I did not expect to hear from you so soon."

"Elijah's dead."

"Your husband, the informant? I hope you don't think I orchestrated this. I figured he was in some remote country, you lured him to you."

"I did no such thing, and how'd you know he was here?"

"When it comes to you, *My Love*, there isn't much I don't know."

"Mr. Goodman's been shot. He's in surgery."

"Now, that is a shock. You must admit, there is power between those tight thighs of yours. Even I can't stay between them."

I hate this woman.

"Are you even listening to what I'm saying?"

"Ah, yes, *My Love*. Check on your Mr. Goodman. If you need a lawyer, call Lemuel, and we'll see that it's taken care of. Bury the informant, and I'll see you back in the States. Business as usual."

Lean on Me

Sasha

"*Permettez moi?*"

I am indeed dreaming until, with one arm, this freckled nose stranger lifts me up a little too close to him, while with the other arm, he holds onto a towel that barely covers what was so vivid a moment ago.

"Your things?"

"I—I'm fine. Thank you."

"Are you sure? I can stay if you need me?"

How does he know what I need? Is my grief evident?

Still holding my hand, he offers, "Perhaps a beverage would be good, water?" he smiles. "Something stronger?"

Before I can answer, the stranger glances at my sparkling wedding rings.

"I didn't realize you were married. Please, I would never disrespect a man's wife. What if you and your husband join my party for dinner tonight?"

"My husband won't be able to join me, ever!" These words

leave me with the stark reality that I no longer have a dinner partner.

Touching the sand-covered Target Tote with my big toe, I murmur, "That was my husband; I'm a widow, a widow, do you understand, so no, I—" and before I can finish, my grief rises, leaving me gasping for air.

"Mademoiselle, please allow me to comfort you."

Too emotional to deny him, the stranger tucks in his towel and then gathers me in his arms, and with my head buried in his naked, wet, and slightly hairy chest, I cry. Big, ugly sobs escape me, and I don't try to hold them back. Instead, I attempt to talk through them, sharing my pain.

His one hand massages my head while he whispers words of comfort in another language—French, maybe, or am I too confused to hear straight? Why does this stranger feel more comforting than family or friends I've known most of my life? Then it happens. My hormones defy me and become fully alive from his touch, and when I feel him rising against me through the towel, it's obvious he feels the same.

"Je suis désolé," he whispers.

"No, no, it's my fault, I'm so sorry," I blurt out, running away, with the heaviness of my wet dress weighing me down.

Back in my room, I'm emotionally exhausted yet relieved to finally cry the tears held so deep in my gut. I also can't deny that had he followed me, I may have given in to my throbbing libido.

Stripping out of the wet and sandy dress, I find the bottle of Ambien and swallow one, chasing it with a glass of wine.

Realizing it's the first time I've identified myself as a widow, I crawl under the covers with my iPad and google precisely what that means, *"A woman who has lost her spouse by death and is not remarried."*

I know that much, but how do you define it? I google, "How to be a widow?"

Responses flood my screen with website links, podcasts,

articles, essays, and books from professionals, and widows, complete with instructions on how to grieve.

"I'm in a dark tunnel."

"How I processed my grief."

"10 steps of grief..."

"Widow brain."

"A Widow's Journey."

"Widows Wear Stilettos."

"From Widow to Bride in 90 days."

"Losing your husband and finding yourself."

A knock on the door interrupts my research. I slip into a robe, check the peephole, and open the door.

"Manfred, is everything okay?"

"Yes, Ms. Sasha. I have a package for you."

"From who?"

With a suspicious smile on his fresh face, he hands me a large shopping bag with the 44 Knots Boutique logo. "It came with a note."

Assuming it's another package from *My Travel Agent*, I thank him, taking the bag.

Already feeling the Ambien, I climb back under the down comforter where I read the handwritten note card.

> *Mademoiselle Sasha,*
> *Please consider joining me this evening at 6:30 p.m. and bring the contents of this box.*
> *Azmar*

Neatly folded inside the shopping bag are my Target Tote and the plastic Ziploc that still contains a sprinkle of Trent's ashes. How awful of me to have left it behind. Indeed, I am the worst widow.

That's not the only thing in the bag. There's a box containing a red bib apron with the slogan *Sayin' a Taste* and a book of the same name. Underneath sits a clear box containing a shell cutter, two seafood forks, and a claw cracker. How odd a gift for a grieving widow.

Checking the time on my phone, it's 1:30 pm. Back in bed, I drift in and out of sleep, wondering why this man came into my life when Trent was washing away in the ocean. I certainly don't believe in reincarnation; this man is nothing like my husband. Don't we reincarnate differently though?

The only person I can share my crazy experience of spreading Trent's ashes and how a strangely handsome man came to my rescue is Arshell. Turning my phone back on, as soon as she answers and we get past the *am I alright* a few times, I dive into my story, starting with how horny I'd been from the moment I'd learned about Trent's death. As I'm sharing with her about the naked stranger, I notice that she has not once interjected. Is she mad at me for something I have no control over? She's certainly not one to judge me. I've never cheated on Trent in all the years we were married. There were some missteps before we tied the knot, but I was faithful to him once we did.

I pause long enough to hear what she has to say, and that's when my friend launches into the most ridiculous story. Apparently, her husband's niece lives on the Caribbean side of the island in a place called Esterillos and has gotten herself wrapped up in a murder investigation. Arshell is asking me to check on her.

"Have you lost your mind? I'm sorry," there I go, using that meaningless word. "Arshell, you know I'd do anything for you, but not this, not right now. I'm releasing Trent's ashes, and you're asking me to handle some PR nightmare your husband's niece has gotten into, you're asking too much. I mean, did you forget I'm mourning?"

"I know you loved Trent deeply, so I expect you to be

grieving deeply. Sasha, I'm not asking you to be her publicist. I only want you to check on her. She's there by herself."

"And I'm here by myself. I can't check on anyone. I can only tell you that whatever situation she's gotten herself into, she needs to get a lawyer and get off this island."

"That's the thing. Her husband was in Witness Protection, so the Department of Justice is involved with the FBI and the State Department, making it complicated. They know she didn't shoot either of them, nonetheless, they won't allow her to leave the island."

I recall a few years ago, Arshell phoning me with the news of her niece's husband, insisting I follow the story on CNN where he was arrested for gun trafficking for a Russian oligarch. She can't be surprised he's dead. More importantly, why the hell would she want me to get involved? My days as a publicist are in the past.

"Wait, how many people were shot, and how old is Isabella now?"

"Her husband is dead, and the other man, I guess, was someone she was seeing. Her age? She's probably mid 40's maybe. All she'd need you to do is navigate any press until she can come home."

"I can't, Arshell. My own grief is too heavy and will probably be for quite a while."

"You can't allow yourself to marinate in grief forever."

My friend needs to be corrected. I'm drowning in it.

"Listen, I understand if you don't want to help. Maybe I can fly over there and bring her back."

"I thought you said she lived here?"

"Only part-time. She has dual citizenship."

"It sounds messy and beyond my scope of experience, especially in a foreign country. Plus, I have too much going on in my own life to help anyone else."

"My friend, checking on Isabella might be better than lusting after some stranger. Don't become a cliché. You're not Stella, and you don't need your groove back. You've made that mistake before."

"That hurts Arshell."

"I'm sorry, you're vulnerable right now, and I'd hate to see you taken advantage of by some slick island character looking for a free ride. I mean, what do they call it now, pig-butchering?"

"What the hell are you talking about?"

I think that man, Azmar, doesn't need a free ride. If anything, I'd like to ride him. I can't say that to Arshell; I shouldn't even be saying it to myself.

"I love you too much to let anything happen to you. I'm sorry for asking."

I don't realize I'm screaming when I say, "Damn it, Arshell, I'm begging you, stop saying you're sorry. Everyone is sorry; we can't keep saying that word like it's a placeholder for not understanding that the idea of being without Trent is terrifying."

"You're right, calm down. I haven't known what to say since the day you called me, but I know you, and I thought you might want to shift your focus."

She's right. Arshell has shared every moment of my life, and even though she may not have agreed with some of my reckless choices, she held my hand literally and figuratively through it all.

"From my husband dying? I don't think that's even possible. You don't understand how hard this is. I'm not sure I should've even come here. This was supposed to be our vacation, and now I've become a widow and don't even know how to check that box."

I'd always hated checking the boxes on anything that referenced your marital status. What difference is it if I'm married, single, separated, divorced, or widowed? Am I getting approved for whatever I've applied for or not?

"Oh sweetie, I'm…listen, when you get home, you should see someone, like a grief counselor, to help you process all this."

I need to get off this phone and out of this room before this heaviness crushes my chest and chokes my throat. Maybe I'm having a heart attack. Is this what Trent felt?

"I don't wanna go home, the chalet, the lodge; I can't do it."

"You don't have to. I'll meet you there. We can mourn together," she tells me with tears in her own voice.

"Listen, I gotta go," I lie, and she probably knows. "I promised the concierge I'd attend the Chef's Tasting tonight."

"Allow me to say this. Please don't be foolish and think sex with some island hottie is going to alleviate your pain. It won't."

"I'm too old for that. It's merely a strange coincidence; you're taking it too far."

"Am I?"

To prevent myself from feeling guilty about lying to my friend, I drag myself out of bed and into the shower. While shampooing my hair, I realize how badly it needs to be cut and how much gray has taken over, making me look like some version of Florida Evans from *Good Times*. Trent loved massaging my close-cut hair; when I'd complain that I needed a new look, he'd tell me that what I had was all the crown I needed. Before changing my mind, I massage oil throughout, then pat it down, hoping to flatten my now small afro.

My excitement is squashed when I look at myself too closely in the mirror while brushing my teeth. It scares me to see my face so old and drawn. I should consider Botox. My friend Parker would be thrilled to assist with that and possibly a lift to these sagging breasts. Who besides Trent could be turned on by what was once an inviting body to most men? Still, I push my body and its fluctuating waistline into the red halter maxi dress embroidered at the hem with small white flowers that resemble a muumuu.

When I step outside into what I now realize is always perfect weather, using the resort map, since I left my cart at the beach, I make my way on foot to the location indicated on my invitation. I'm not alone for long when Azmar slows down, driving his golf cart from an adjoining path.

"Azmar, hi. Thank you for returning my things and for the invitation."

"For a lady going through such a tough time, you," he looks me over, "*Eres hermosa!*"

"Your compliment is appreciated. I know exactly how I look—old and tired. Thank you."

"*Betise*! Does this mean," he glances down at the small box in my arms and says, "You've decided to join me. If so, climb aboard."

The only thing I want to climb is him. I push those thoughts back and take the seat next to him. Grateful for the armrest between us, I remind myself to do another search, more specifically about the libidos of widows. I'm sure he can feel the heat emanating from my body at this rate, and it's not a hot flash. Taking care not to fall out of the cart by holding onto the handle above, I scoot away from him to the edge of my seat.

"You might be a little overdressed. It could get messy."

"I do feel bad crashing someone else's dinner. I'm sure one of these beautiful women I've seen around the resort will be disappointed if you show up with me."

"I have no interest in these young women. But you, I'm sure you could use a delicious meal."

After my stupid comment, I breathe in the subtle hint of his cologne and ask, "Are you French?"

"Egyptian. Primarily raised in Paris, so I'm fluid in French and Arabic. My father was a diplomat and a businessperson. I had no time for romance. Education was prioritized."

"Married? Children?"

"No to both. Maybe one day."

Why does his wanting to have children disappoint me?

"Tell me, how long will you stay in paradise?"

"I don't know. My chief of staff has gotten married, and the festivities end tonight. What about you? How long will you stay?"

"To hear my best friend tell it, I'll be grieving forever, so perhaps never."

"If I'd loved someone for 15 years, Trent? I don't think I'd ever recover."

"How much did I tell you this morning?"

"It was mostly muffled, my chest and heart absorbed it all," he says, placing his hand over his heart.

I appreciate that Azmar doesn't try to diminish my grief, yet his words spark a flame under my dress. I secretly wonder if I'm being filmed for a *Lifetime* movie.

"You were listening?"

"Your heart has been wounded. Every day, it will heal, even if it's a little, but the wound will never totally close. It just fills up with memories."

How can he be sure?

When we pull to a stop, before I step down from the golf cart, Azmar quickens his step to my side, offering me his warm hand. When we brush against each other, I notice his scent is a blend of saffron and citrus. I allow my shaky hand to remain in his as we walk together along the beach, bringing me a bit of calmness under the evening sky dotted with early stars and a setting sun that barely touches the ocean.

As we approach the far end of the beach, the crashing waves blend with the sound of maracas and steel guitars of calypso music, which have me moving my hips ever so slightly. Once we're close enough to be noticed, I can see about 50 jovial guests, most under 40. Everyone calls out to Azmar, and he acknowledges everyone by name, introducing me as his friend, whom they eagerly welcome.

Without warning, Azmar slips the red Sayin' A Taste apron

over my head and ties it around my waist; I steel myself from his touch. When we take our seats at one of the five 6-foot-long tables covered in white paper tablecloths, at each place setting are the same utensils I've carried with me and large ceramic containers posted at every other chair, which I assume will be for crab shells.

After we're seated, a bell chime rings out, followed by a parade of waiters arriving with trays of steaming lobsters, shrimp, mussels, oysters, clams, and crab clusters. There's also bread and colorful tossed salads with peek specks of yellow and white corn, coconut rice, and beans. There are so many other dishes I'm not familiar with, yet the mere sight of them makes my stomach growl. I waste no time digging into the delicious meal. Somehow, in between eating, and talking, we manage to have a conversation, toasting our first drink of the night, a Guava cocktail.

"Where do you consider home now?" I inquire as he skillfully cracks open a lobster tail. Rich, buttery juices cascade down his arm as he offers me a generous piece of succulent meat, which I savor with delight.

"I follow the biggest waves. Costa Rica today, maybe Oluwatu next. And you?"

Before answering, he spoons what he tells me is arroz arreyado and chayote onto my plate, then refills my cocktail to wash it down.

"So, you surf and swim naked! Where is Olu..." I laugh, unable to pronounce the name.

"Bali! A beautiful country, and yes, I apologize that you had to see that. Have you ever tried it?"

"Which one?"

"Either or both."

"You seem pretty good at it."

"Ah, Sasha, since you haven't seen me surf, I will assume it was my embarrassing nakedness."

I smile at his correct assumption.

"Tell me, where do you call home?"

"Utah. Park City."

His face lights up, and his nose freckles bounce around when he states, "I've been there! Black Ski Summit a few years ago."

"You ski too?"

"No, I was dating a woman who was a club member, so I tagged along. We stayed at an African American-owned lodge, a jewel of a place."

"The Lodge at Sugar Hill, that's our place!" I proudly respond before realizing that Sugar Hill is now my place.

"Wait, yes, I met your husband at the cigar night! A good man, now I see why you loved him. That's a lot to go missing from your life. Is that where you're originally from? You don't seem like a cold-weather woman the way this sun is taking to your skin."

"Philadelphia is my real home. Still cold, but not like Park City."

"The City of Brotherly Love," he says before glancing at his vibrating phone on the table and then excusing himself to answer the call.

Turning slightly to watch him walk away, I take note of his contoured back and an incredible ass that fits nicely inside a pair of natural drawstring linen pants that matches his short sleeve button shirt vented on the sides. With his bare feet digging into the sand, he takes a moment to glance back at me. Briefly, I close my eyes and recall his naked body, the way his manhood hung on him, and the way it felt against my body when it hardened. Swallowing a sip of the sweet cocktail, I find myself swaying to the calypso music though I'm not prepared to handle the mini orgasm that dampens my thighs. Arshell is right I'm being ridiculous.

When Azmar's call ends, I jump from my seat, rattling off,

"I'm leaving in the morning for a day trip to the other side of the island."

Standing close, his warm hand lightly touches my back, yet his fading smile shows disappointment. "I apologize if I was disrespectful in taking my call."

"No, it's not you. It's me. I shouldn't be here."

"The meal isn't finished, and I ordered something special for you."

"Why would you do that? Why are you being so nice to me?"

"This is a time when you shouldn't be alone, and I wanted to be a friend. If you must leave, I'll escort you."

"That's not necessary; please stay with your friends."

"Why would I stay without you?"

His question tells me that he knows his effect on me, and I assume this is his effect on all women. Now I feel foolish, as this man has gone out of his way for me.

"You know what? I am still a little hungry," I say, retaking my seat.

"*Bien*! Share with me, Sasha, where are you going tomorrow? Is it an excursion?"

Ugh, does he have to say my name like that? Like it's sweet in his mouth.

Until now, I had no plans to check on Isabella. "It's a day trip to Esterillos Puternarus. I'm checking on a friend. I plan to ask Manfred if he can reserve a driver."

"I was there a few days ago on business. It's a four-hour drive; it might be easier if you take a commuter flight. I can arrange that for you."

I don't want to be indebted to him; however, I'll lose my mind in a car for four hours.

"Ah! Here's your dinner."

By the time I've finished eating the tableside fileted snapper and had too many Guava cocktails and several champagne toasts, I know it's best to depart from this dream of a night.

The gentleman he is, Azmar, offers to escort me back to my room.

"No, you've been so kind already. I need to walk all this food off."

"I'll give you my number if you need me or get stuck somewhere. I also need to text you the details of your flight."

"Sure," I respond, knowing that taking his number could lead me in the wrong direction.

He hands me his phone; I punch in my number.

"Goodnight," he kisses my cheek, "Sasha."

When I arrive back at my villa, I text *My Travel Agent*, who is always responsive, and have her arrange my flight to Utah the day after tomorrow. I then slip naked into the plunge pool, and this time, with my iPad on the side, I attempt to google Azmar until realizing I don't know his last name or the name of his business. Arshell was right; I need something else to focus on. I google Isabella Washington + Costa Rica.

The first of many headlines reads, *"FIESTA CANCELADO."*

"Deadly domestic dispute."

The local *Costa Rica News* boldly states, *"TROIS GONE MAUVAIS."*

"...her husband and lover surprised each other at her home, and the husband wound up dead and the lover, shot and in critical condition by an unknown assailant."

I can't read Spanish, but on the cover of their tabloid, *Diario Extra* is a triangle of Isabella's face and the two men. She looks younger than 40, with bright eyes and fresh braids framing her narrow face. A few of them hold natural gray streaks. The other photo is of her getting into a police car.

The following article, written by Tara Torres, states, *"Either there was a fourth party, or Malik and Elijah Moore are the same person who was killed while under witness protection. Sources tell me that this could have been a murder for hire. It is rumored that a man may have left the island earlier that morning on a private jet. OIJ and*

DOJ will hold a joint press conference in the morning. Until then, they tell us there is no threat to the island. The question our community is asking is, 'How well do we know Isabella Washington?'"

Members of the community who've been interviewed express how much they love Isabella and that she's part of their family. Most of them were expecting to attend her CÉLÉBRATION DE PARTIR. Thankfully, Isabella is smart enough not to defend herself publicly. There is no mention of her having retained legal representation, which is what she needs to do.

The U.S. newspapers don't have a big splash, yet *The Philadelphia Inquirer* does mention, *"...local man murdered in Costa Rica and another in critical condition but is expected to survive. The story is developing and will be updated."*

Thankfully, after checking Facebook, Instagram, X, and even TikTok, it doesn't appear that Isabella has a social media presence. On LinkedIn, she lists employment as a forensic accountant. Wait, why am I researching this? I'm not interested. This isn't my problem. Unfortunately, I've dived in too deep and feel committed to going, if only, as Arshell said, to check on her niece.

> Me: Will check on Isabella tomorrow; send me adz

> Arshell: I love u & I owe u.

While I've been buried in my search, a note from Manfred slipped under my door. It details that an SUV will be waiting for me outside the lobby at 7:00 a.m. for an 8:40 a.m. commuter flight from Liberia to San Juan airport, where a Cartier Black driver will be waiting to take me to Esterillos.

In the morning, after less than an hour's flight, a driver greets me, "Pura Vida," then whisks me into a Mercedes town car whose driver talks in Spanish the entire way, mentioning somewhere in between the island's history, the weather, and the recent murder. I tune him out and take in the difference between the landscape of Esterillos vs. Papagayo.

It's undoubtedly more rural than where I'm staying, and I guess people on this side of the island want to keep it that way with its lush green flora draping both sides of the road. Friendly residents, mostly biking and walking, wave as we pass and then return to engaging in lively conversation. Food vendors line the sides of the road, and their aroma causes a growling in my stomach. The driver mentions that there are directional signs for an upcoming soccer game. He makes it clear that since residents here live slower-paced lives, it has the highest number of centenarians. We even drive past an incredible mermaid statue coming out of the water. What I've noticed across both coasts of Costa Rica is its beautiful turquoise water, which I'd gladly trade in for the forever-falling snow of Park City.

Following a series of signs leading to the Black Sands Bungalows, the driver pulls off the main road and onto a winding unpaved road where the expectation is to see rundown shacks. I am pleasantly surprised when a large neon blue Bungalow marked HOME along with eight smaller Bungalows, four on each side, one of which I assume is where Isabella is staying comes into view. There's no press around, so they must not be aware of her whereabouts. The police officer who is supposed to be protecting her, sits on the hood of his car, scrolling through his phone. He gives us his full attention when my driver slows to a stop. Before he can reach us, Isabella Washington walks out of Bungalow 8.

Isabella is a sad version of the young woman I met many years ago. The closer she gets, her slumped shoulders and glazed-over eyes make me wonder if she's high, which would be a disaster to manage. The rubber band that holds back her braids isn't doing much good, seeing that those white streaks blended into her braids fall against her face. This reminds me of how sassy and cute a teenager she was, especially when she went through the phase of dyeing her hair a myriad of colors.

She hugs me as if I'm a stranger.

"You didn't have to come, Ms. Sasha. I really can handle this, so please don't pitch me why I need your services."

I can see she will be challenging.

"I came at Arshell's request, all the same, your bravado doesn't impress me. I know you're scared. You're also old enough to call me Sasha."

"Why would I be afraid?"

"These people may love you, but you're still an expatriate living in Costa Rica with a dead American who was under witness protection, and another man, a wealthy American businessman fighting for his life. If this were just a simple romantic rivalry between two men vying for the affection of the same woman, that would be straightforward. However, a murder-for-hire plot on foreign soil adds a sensational twist. Once the Associated Press catches wind of this narrative and learns your whereabouts, this location will be inundated with journalists."

"Sounds like you have it all figured out. First, you should know that Bryce isn't my lover. Considering you recently lost your husband under suspicious circumstances, you should understand."

Another phrase I've begun to hate. Trent isn't lost.

Her ungrateful attitude reminds me of Briana. I swallow the words I want to say and respond, "I can leave this place any time I want. What about you?"

"You're pretty direct, aren't you?"

"That way, my words don't get misinterpreted," I tell her, yet I find myself annoyed that Arshell would have a conversation with her about Trent's death. The only thing suspicious was his being at Teterboro.

"Fair enough. I'm headed to the hospital to visit *my client* now."

In my past life, as a publicist to celebrities and athletes, I know how easy it can be to move from client to lover, and my instincts tell me she's crossed the line.

"Can I suggest you ride with me instead of in the backseat of that police car? It makes you look guilty. He can follow behind us."

During the drive, we don't make small talk. She spends the 20 minutes texting, and I spend it wishing I hadn't come.

Trent never had a chance to make it to a hospital to be saved, and since he wore an organ donor bracelet, he was delivered into the hands of the surgical and transplant teams. I don't even want to think about which parts of his body now belong to other people or science. When they emailed the report, I refused to read it as I did with so many things sent to me. What was the point?

Arriving at Metropolitan Hospital-Quepos, we're greeted outside by a few members of the local press, who are nowhere near as aggressive as those in the States. Inside the lobby, Detective Edwin Mora wants to know who I am. I introduce myself as a family friend because that is the only reason I'm here, and not in a professional capacity.

Detective Mora informs us that Isabella is the only visitor allowed to see Mr. Goodman. She follows him through the lobby, where they disappear into the elevator.

Now I'm stuck in a coffee shop wondering what I'm doing here, so I google Isabella's client, Bryce Goodman. Before I can scroll through the numerous results, a man strolls into the lobby with the swagger of men I've known all my life, a gait that exudes a dip of confidence, as if they're moving to a beat only, they can hear, which means he's from my hometown of

Philadelphia. This brother sports a meticulously groomed Sunni beard, and his smooth bald head is stamped by a prostration mark on his forehead, indicating that he's a lifelong Muslim or that he served time in prison.

He asks the receptionist for Bryce Goodman's room. Frustrated when she tells him in broken English that Mr. Goodman isn't allowed visitors, rather than leave, he paces the lobby and then posts up outside the revolving doors yet takes the time to give me a look that hits the center of my hormones. Luckily, my ringing phone breaks my train of wandering thoughts, and when I don't answer the 800 number, the call is followed up with a text message.

I would ignore it. However, the message indicates it's from Lavery Labs, the company to whom Trent's tissues had been donated for science. Why are they calling?

> Lavery Labs: Please contact us regarding an unexpected toxin in case #42464237. Click the link to access the portal and approve further testing.

What are they talking about, unexpected findings? What was wrong with him? I ask the receptionist for the hospital's WIFI access and guest password. When I click the link from Lavery Labs, I'm instructed to create a login and password. I type in my email address, but the WIFI drops. I try it again, but the WIFI signal is too weak. When I approach the receptionist's desk to ask where I can get a stronger signal in the building, an emotional Isabella exits the elevator behind me.

Every Little Bit Hurts

Isabella

Sleep never came last night. I was too frightened of dreaming, so I lay curled up in the hammock, wrapped in a blanket, trying to sort out how my life had come to this moment. Who could've orchestrated Elijah and Bryce's simultaneous arrival, or was it a coincidence? Had I been home, could it have been avoided? If so, I might be dead, too. Either way, I'm stuck in the back of a town car with Sasha Borianni.

I'd been excited to meet her at my aunt and uncle's Juneteenth celebration years ago. She'd been an A-list celebrity publicist; foolishly, she'd given it all up when her husband went into politics. Now, here she is, mourning her own dead husband with sadness all over her face. How does she even have the wherewithal to be here for me, dressed as if she's on vacation and carrying an overpriced Birkin bag? I imagine she still has connections to the world of the privileged. To appease my aunt, I can put up with her if she doesn't delve too deeply into my personal affairs.

Detective Mora greets us in the hospital lobby, and my first question is, "Eddie, have you caught who did this yet?"

"I'm glad to see you have a lawyer."

"This is Sasha," I respond without offering an explanation. Her haughty demeanor suggests she's not from the island.

"Where's my husband?"

"Malcolm Moore's remains are with the coroner."

"When do I get to claim his body, and why haven't you found his killer? The island isn't that big."

"Ms. Isabella, I know this has been tough, but don't blame us. These are your people; these men came here for you."

"I didn't invite them here, nor did I invite someone to kill them."

"Isabella," is all Sasha says to redirect me.

"Ma'am, Captain Castro, and Special Agent Solano will meet us later at the bungalows with updates." Then he whispers, "Izzy, I'm doing my best to get answers. You have to understand things get complicated when the FEDS get involved."

"I'm sorry. Mr. Goodman, how's he doing?"

"The first bullet hit him in the shoulder, shattering his clavicle, and then when he tried to get to your husband, he was hit in the groin. That man lost a lotta blood. After two surgeries, the doctors say he'll make it. Lucky for him, the right doctor was here yesterday. I can take you to his room; your aunt, I assume, has gotta wait here."

Following behind Eddie, I pause at the colorful gift shop window, displaying stuffed animals, flower arrangements, and half-price Valentine's Day candy. It would be appropriate to take flowers, maybe a plant; that's what I'd do under normal circumstances. These circumstances aren't normal. I keep going.

When we reach the third floor, the hallway is busy with nurses pushing medication carts and dieticians removing food trays. Directly across from the nurse's station, a police officer stands when he sees us approaching. Eddie enters the room first, and when I hesitate, afraid of what I'll see, he beckons me inside. Before entering, I wipe away tears to appear strong for Bryce and myself. When he hears us enter, his eyes barely open, as if even the slightest movement pains him. The first thing I notice are cuts and bruises on his face from falling onto the broken glass. Then, to the right of the bed, two drip bags run from a pole and intravenously into his arm. To the left are a heart monitor and another machine with tubes that trail under his robe. In his nose are air plugs that assist in his breathing, and on his finger is a clip that tracks his blood pressure. Heavy bandages wrap around his left shoulder. If that isn't enough, bandages bulge from under his gown. I am so heartbroken that my knees give way, and Eddie helps me onto a chair. For the first time, Bryce is vulnerable.

The volume on the television is turned down, yet it shows coverage of how my life blew up overnight. As expected, Solano and Castro are holding a press conference where I see them downplaying the entire ordeal as an isolated domestic incident; I assume to not send the island into a panic that a contracted killer is on the loose.

Bending forward on the chair, I take his hand and whisper, "Bryce, it's me, Isabella."

He gives me a weak smile yet cuts hard eyes at Eddie.

"I can step out."

"Please."

Eddie exits the room.

"Sit me up," he requests. When I use the remote to adjust the bed, he uses the other to turn the television off.

"I'm so sorry."

"Not your fault."

"The doctor says," I hesitate, my words breaking up into tears, "That you're gonna be okay."

"I need to get off this island. Back to Philly."

"Not like this."

"They'll never catch him."

"Why do you say that?" I ask, having watched enough episodes of NCIS to know that professional killers are rarely caught.

His dark eyes cut me a look that answers my question.

"Did you see anything?"

"Elijah was there. The glass broke. He was white."

"A white man?"

He must recall some officers wearing white hazmat suits carrying him out of the house. Moving to the side of his bed, I kiss his dry lips and again apologize for his circumstances.

He closes his eyes, then presses a button dispensing pain medication into his IV.

"I found you."

"How?" I ask before remembering who he is and how far his reach is. "Do you think Lady Zoë or her boyfriend did this?"

He drifts off from the meds, and I can barely hear him when he says, "She's different; he was a puppet...I'll kill her."

"Please don't say that. Let the cops handle it."

His sweaty grip on my hand loosens. He nods off.

A knock on the door startles us both, and when it opens, a nurse enters the room, excusing herself to take his vitals, check his bandaging, and adjust the level of meds in his IV. Bryce tries to be strong in front of me but when the bite on his upper lip draws blood, I know he's in pain. He can't leave the island like this, especially when I see her check the half-filled catheter and what I'm sure is a tube leading to a colostomy bag. We don't speak until she exits the room.

"When you leaving here?"

"I'm staying with you."

"No! Get the fuck out."

There's a knock on the door for the second time, and when it opens, it's Special Agent Solano and Captain Castro. I first notice that she's dressed appropriately in black pants and a white button-down shirt, with her federal badge swinging around her neck.

"We need to speak to Mr. Goodman, alone," she says, her hard stare antagonizing me.

"Do you have an update?"

She directs her attention to Bryce, "Mr. Goodman?"

"Isabella, go."

As Eddie and I exit the elevator, we see Sasha in a frenzy, speaking urgently into her cell phone. All that fades when Sémile strides through the revolving doors. Nothing else matters as I rush into his embrace.

"You alright?"

I can't answer.

"Let's get outta here."

I turn to look for Sasha, who's right on my heels, her hand pulling back on my forearm, stopping us.

"You don't need to be seen by the press in the arms of another man."

"Don't tell me what to do!"

She looks from Sémile to Eddie for their confirmation.

Outside, additional press members have gathered in the hospital parking lot. Eddie goes first, with me in between, to insulate me, followed by Sasha and Sémile behind us. I duck back into the open door of the Mercedes with Sasha, and the others take up their respective vehicles. About this, Sasha was right.

Inside the car, Sasha and I sit opposite each other. I sense something different about her. She is focused on checking her voicemail, and her trembling fingers are sending text messages.

"Is everything okay?"

She turns her phone over before answering.

"I'm fine; how was the visit with Mr. Goodman? Did you learn anything new?"

"No, he's in bad shape."

"Will he live?"

This woman is so damn rude. Can I blame her? Her husband is also dead. If nothing else, what we have in common is that we're both widows. How daunting.

"Sasha, is something wrong?"

Her phone rings. She declines the call and ignores me.

When we arrive at Black Sands, Ms. Ana and a lanky, dreadlocked man in shorts and a One Love t-shirt are sitting on the steps of Bungalow 8.

Pushing him in front of her, Ms. Ana gets up and announces, "This is my nephew, Marley, Reggie Marley, and before you ask, he ain't no relation to the great Bob Marley. He's gonna be your lawyer!"

A distracted Marley is shouting at someone in Spanish on FaceTime.

"Marley, hang up the phone. Izzy's here."

"Marley?"

"Lemme give you the short story. His no-good Daddy was doing business here and fell in love with my little sister. But you can figure out the rest when her belly got full, she flew to your nation's capital, and you know the rest."

Sémile leans down and whispers in my ear, "Don't fuck with this clown."

Thankfully, Ms. Ana doesn't hear him. "Now, this *hombre podrido* broke my sistas heart. But oh, when he died, his *esposa fea* and the *otros niños* tried but couldn't touch the money he'd put up for Marley, and he used it to graduate from that Georgetown."

I'm trying to keep up with her; from what I can understand, her sister was Marley's father's mistress. She ended up with trust money that paid for his schooling—money that it sounds like his wife and other children couldn't touch.

Taking my hand in hers, she pulls me close to whisper, "I always thought he was a little slow with those white genes, took him three times to pass that bar, his *madre mi hermana* would be proud."

Looking at the unkempt Marley, I wonder what he can do for me.

"I know what you're thinking, he's good, real good."

Marley comes over to shake my hand while continuing to talk on the phone. He takes a moment to say, "Er'body call me Marley, give me a minute. Marley trying to get a client outta jail in Havana."

If he can make that happen, he can get me out of Costa Rica.

"Mr. Marley, thanks for coming. I don't think—"

"Nobody thinks they need a lawyer till they do, and that's why Marley's here."

Suspiciously eyeing Sémile, Ms. Ana tells me, "I'm going to let Marley take care of you. I left food in the room. Walk down if you need me."

"Mierda aquí vienen," Marley indicates, referring to the approaching police vehicle that I can see is carrying Solano and Castro. He hangs up his call and says, "I'll handle them."

"What do you need to know from me?"

"I already know everything. Relax, Marley got this."

Sémile then excuses himself and walks off to take a call. His eyes, though, are on what's unfolding.

When Solano steps out of the car, she again embodies Salma Hayek. Her hair is smoothed over one shoulder, and she wears a midriff shirt that shows off her perfectly toned abs peeking above a low-riding skirt. I'd seen the skirt on Vogue's Spring IG page, worn by one of the Hadid's. Her jewelry mixes Hermès bracelets and chunky David Yurman earrings, and her cross-body bag is Chanel. How much does this woman make, and when did she have time to change?

"Before we head off the island, I wanted to update you on the case. Can we go inside?"

I see Sémile take her in, and when she looks his way,

probably trying to determine who he is, he holds her stare. He isn't a man to be toyed with, married or not. I want to tell her that he belongs to me, or at least he used to.

Marley leads the way, making the bungalow, with its lack of air conditioning, stifling as it's now crowded with Solano, Castro, Marley, Sémile, and myself while an uninterested Sasha remains outside. Not to be closed in, Sémile steps out onto the back porch but leaves the door open to hear what they've come to report.

"Marley, I'm not sure why you're here. This case is too big for you. I'm guessing it'll get your name in the papers."

"Castro, I'm here, so let us hear what you got."

Salma pushes her sunglasses onto the top of her head and starts with her shit, "We discovered Malcolm Moore had a visitor before coming here, Sémile Brantley," she states, lifting her pointy chin toward the back porch.

"His God-given name is Elijah Moore."

"The name we gave him was Malcolm, and that's what I call him. Either way, can we move on? Now, why would he visit Malcolm and then turn up here?"

"You'd have to ask him. Wait, you can't be suggesting. They're like brothers. What motive would he have?"

"You maybe? He's a former lover, right?" she asks, already certain of the answer. Sémile and I were lovers long before I knew Elijah, and I was unaware they were friends until long after we were dating.

"Everyone is a suspect at this point," Castro adds, sounding like her puppet. "He's the only one who knew he was coming to see you. Maybe he had an opportunity to take over his business and his wife, and he wanted to ensure he was out of the way."

Sémile moves so fast I don't even see him come through the back door. "Mothafucka, are you outta your fucken mind?"

Castro eases his hand onto his gun. Foolishly, I step in between them.

"Sémile, don't."

Neither moves until Marley says, "All sounds circumstantial to me. This man is here to comfort his friend."

"I don't give a fuck what it sounds like; keep my name out ya bitch ass mouth."

"Sémile, please," I say to his back as he heads out the door, allowing Castro to sigh with relief.

"And what about the friendship between Malcolm and Mr. Goodman?" asks Solano.

I was struck by the irony of how Elijah introduced us. We bumped into Bryce at a restaurant, and Elijah invited him to join us for a drink. I felt a twinge of annoyance since it was our first night out in a while. The situation worsened as Elijah left me with him due to a work emergency. I couldn't fathom any emergency that would pull a CFO away from dinner. I later found out it was Ramon Morashou.

While he was gone, I tried to deny my attraction to a stranger who seemed to know so much about my forensic work and was interested in what he didn't know. By the time Elijah returned, I already knew I could never be alone with Bryce, and now, in his dying moments, Elijah knew it was Bryce who'd comforted me through his unfolding drama.

"Word back in the States is he has some shady clients. Maybe someone came after your Bryce, and Malcolm was collateral damage."

She's right. Bryce has clients who include wealthy businesspeople and people from the underworld whom I hoped never to meet.

"What about that car, the Mercedes coming out my driveway?"

"We interviewed the driver. Goodman used Cartier Black Limo service. The same one that's outside now. There's nothing there, and Malcolm rented his car from Enterprise. According to my timeline, they both arrived at your house within about 15 minutes of each other, and the shooter was probably already waiting."

Directing his question to Solano, Marley asks, "Wouldn't this woman's husband have to get approval to travel?"

"Do you really think he sought permission? He did this on his own. Like I said he did it for love."

Defeated, I ask, "What happens now?"

"His house is being packed up, and things will be sent to storage. You'll need to go there at some point and sort through it."

"Why would I go there if you've already handled everything?"

"Your call, we can ship it."

"And Elijah, where's he? Where's his body?"

"Your husband is being cremated."

Astounded at the thought of Elijah being cremated without even a simple prayer or goodbye spoken over him, almost like he was nobody, crushes me. I take a seat on the edge of the bed. Embarrassing tears break up my words. "What…are you talking…about? It's only been two days. Why would you do that without asking me?"

"As we told you before, he belongs to us, but we can send his ashes to you once you provide a forwarding address. We have a copy of his Will, and everything was left to you and his mother, and now that diverts to you, too. He doesn't own any property. There's money in his bank accounts, including the one he tried to keep hidden. Did you know about the money?"

Taking note of those in the small room, I wonder where Sasha went. Shouldn't she be in here defending me against this horrible woman?

"I don't know anything."

"You're the lone beneficiary on a million-dollar insurance policy, I'm sure he told you."

This time, jumping up I get close enough to Solano until I can smell her expensive perfume.

"What is your fucken problem with me, and why are you always strutting around here like this? When you come here on business, you need to dress like a fucken professional."

Marley intervenes, pulling me back from Solano, and then glancing down at his phone, he reads aloud, "Ballistics report, 9MM."

"You're crossing the line. How'd you get that?" an angered Castro asks.

"There is no line. My husband is dead, I'm trapped on this island, and Marley is my lawyer!"

"It doesn't matter. Ma'am, we've checked the flight logs in and out of the San Juan Airport before and after the murder, and you failed to mention you had visitors." He looks at his phone while Solano adds, "White Magic, the football player, and a woman? Or are they clients?"

My chest hurts, burning up to my throat, which makes me certain I'm either experiencing an anxiety attack or having a heart attack. "You don't fucken know me."

"I do. You Americans are all the same. You come here with your messy lives and think our sun and sand can solve your problems as if you could wash them away in the ocean. Maybe next time, you should leave the men back home."

"GET OUT! GET THE FUCK OUTTA HERE!"

"It was better when you couldn't talk. You don't seem to understand. We're here to keep you safe."

"Like you kept my husband safe. You're never gonna find out

who killed him, are you? You used him to put those men in jail, and now he's dead, and you could care less."

"No, he testified to keep *himself* out of federal prison and then risked his life to come see *you*, and now he's dead!"

Marley moves between Solano and me, practically pushing her and Castro out the door.

With the sweet scent of Solano's perfume lingering, I run the short distance to the bathroom and vomit what feels like the lining of my stomach. Afterward, with my head in my hands, I sit on the toilet and try to put some order to my thoughts. 48 hours ago, I was preparing for my Valentine's Day party, and now I'm sheltered in a bungalow with an uninterested publicist, an angry former lover, and a lawyer imposing on the name of Bob Marley. I wash my face, pull myself together, and walk out to see what's next.

Sémile has gone onto the back porch, where I see him in conversation with Sasha. I can't imagine a conversation between them, especially since she hasn't said a word to me since we left the hospital.

I sit across the small kitchen table from Marley, who's started eating the food Ms. Ana dropped off.

"You'll be okay. They playing tough, hey it's what they do. You need to eat."

I pinch off a piece of *pan casero*.

"There's no need for them to keep you here. Give Marley 24 hours, you can pack your bags."

"Are you sure?"

"I'm a Marley regardless of what Auntie says. Now you listen, you can't go fighting the police, especially Solano; she's a federal agent. The angry man outside, he's got to keep his cool."

"What's Solano's fucken problem, and why does she dress like that?"

"'Tween you and me," he looks around, "word is she and Castro got a thing. She came for a vacation with him, and you canceled that when she got the call about her witness. She's taking it out on you."

For the first time in two days, I hear myself laugh. My laughter is cut short when, through the screen door, I notice a woman stepping onto the porch of Bungalow 8. Before she can knock, I push the door open.

She flips me her identification and says, "Good afternoon. I'm Tara Torres from *Diario Extro,* and I was hoping to get a few comments about the events that took place at your home yesterday."

As requested, when I look out to the road, the officer is gone. Maybe that wasn't such a good idea.

"How'd you know I was here?"

Her eyebrows go up, reminding me that everybody knows everything in Esterillos.

Sasha suddenly appears behind me, almost knocking me out of the way. "Excuse me, Tara Torres, correct? I will reach out when Ms. Washington is ready to give a statement or interview. Until then, don't darken this door again."

"Are you her lawyer?"

"I'm her publicist."

Her words dangle in the air until the reporter can respond. Eyeing Sasha suspiciously, Tara says, "I didn't think she needed one."

"And I need you to spend more time researching the celebrity stories you chase. You never seem to get them right, and you should have the decency to retract those stories when you're wrong – case in point, Giselle."

The saucer-eyed Tara Torres isn't sure how to react to Sasha inserting herself.

"And your name?"

"Sasha Borianni."

She writes it down.

"Ms. Borianni, here's my card. I only report what I'm given and I'd hate to get her story wrong."

"I need you to understand; there is no story here. My husband is dead. I mean, her husband is dead, so take your questions to the agents that were supposed to be protecting him."

"I'm sorry."

"SORRY? EVERYONE IS ALWAYS FUCKEN SORRY. Now, please go hunting for stories elsewhere."

With my back against the closed door, I ask Sasha, "How much will this cost me?"

"You're my best friend's niece, so it's a courtesy. You can't give these reporters one soundbite. I probably said too much, but you need to decide which of these men you're going to claim."

"Excuse me? I didn't ask you to come here. I almost had it taken care of until you blew up."

"Almost? Isabella, you can't measure almost; the word doesn't even make sense. Either you have your shit together, or you don't. Now, I can spin this entire situation, but I guarantee you won't like it, so why don't you start by telling me the details you haven't told the police."

"I told them everything."

"I doubt it."

Entering the room, Sémile demands, "What the fuck is going on now?"

"It's time for me to take my leave. I hope this works out for you. You have my number when you tire of all these men coming to your rescue. Don't you have any female friends you can lean on?"

Her cruel words are so shocking that I don't know how to respond. Without waiting for me to tell her I have girlfriends, Sasha takes out her sunglasses, places her ridiculously overpriced purse on her wrist, and walks out.

Sémile's chin-up motion signals to Marley that it's also time for him to leave.

Marley grabs a paper plate, piles on fish, beans, and rice, and starts eating it on the way out the door, saying, "I'll be in touch with the details of your flight in 24 hours. Be ready."

"Thank you."

With everyone gone, I join Sémile on the back porch, and find his eyes lost in the ocean until he turns to say, "It's me and you, Izzy; now what the fuck happened? How the fuck is it possible for them niggas to show up on the same day, the same time?"

"I don't know. I swear I don't know how they knew I was here."

"I told Elijah."

"How?"

"We came here on vacation and saw you out riding your bike."

"What, and you didn't even try to see me? Who were you here with?"

"My wife."

"And she knows you're here now?"

"Yeah, that's why I can't stay. I gotta get back to Scottsdale, to Devyn and the kids."

"What do you mean, you just got here, and why are you in Arizona anyway?"

"I got an opportunity with the Cardinals, Special Assistant to the Coach."

I always knew Sémile would do anything to get back into football, but for him to leave Philadelphia is no small thing.

"I'm happy for you."

"Yeah, it's cool. You need to let that woman help you."

"Who, Sasha? I don't want her in my business."

"She knows her shit."

"I can take care of myself."

"Listen, you don't need more shit on you. And I don't have

all the facts yet but ain't no way my man got killed, and that nigga survived."

"What do you mean?

"Bryce got some shit he's hiding. You need to cut him loose."

"Cut him loose? He almost died coming to see me."

"That man doesn't love you. Elijah loved you. You should've taken your ass with him."

"I didn't tell them to come here."

"What do you have to drink around here?"

"Sémile, are you listening to me?"

"I got you. We'll figure this shit out, now what you got."

"Nothing to drink, there's two puro's in the dresser's top drawer."

He looks at me, not understanding, until I say, "Two joints."

Illuminating a flame on the stove, he joins me outside where I recline in the hammock and Sémile rests on the top step with his feet in the water. A serene silence envelops us as we share the puro, its calming effects soothing my unsettled stomach.

"Sémile?"

"What's up?"

"Tell me what Elijah's life was like."

Pura Vida

Sasha

On the short commuter flight back to Papagayo, where there is no Wi-Fi, I repeatedly read the computerized text message from Lavery Labs. My mind grapples at what they meant by the toxicology reports showing traces of an unidentified toxin in Trent's blood. Who cares about HIPPA laws? My husband is dead; they should've left a detailed voicemail.

Two years ago, Trent had a prostrate scare when he began having trouble urinating. After getting his numbers under control, he started keeping his annual appointments and followed a vitamin and supplement regimen, including yearly colonics and working out with a personal trainer. Despite this, the message from Lavery Labs and the call from Chase Bank make it feel like doomsday is lying ahead. I need to get home. Maybe I can get a flight out tonight.

By the time we deplane the small aircraft, my palpitating heart feels like it will burst through my chest. I rush through customs and realize I should've asked Manfred to ask him to reserve a car for my return. I pray there are taxis, Ubers, or anything else to get me back to my hotel. I'm about to text *My Travel Agent* for a flight when the unexpected happens.

Waiting for me at the Four Seasons kiosk is Azmar. I'm ashamed to say that seeing his freckled nose and open arms comforts me. I'm so sweaty and sticky that it feels like I've been fried in grease, yet I lean into him, lacking the energy to resist even if I wanted to. Sensing my needs, his arms tighten around my back until I am enveloped in his embrace. It's then that my knees give way, and I break down in tears – dramatic style, sobbing so hard it causes passersby to stare at us. A TSA agent wanders over and looks to see if I'm alright, and that's when Azmar lifts me off my feet and carries me outside to the waiting SUV. All I can think of is my God; this man must be strong. When he settles me into the backseat, he slides close and places his arm around my shoulders. In my attempt to regroup, the only thing I stupidly manage to blurt out is, "I need a haircut."

The hotel lobby is less busy now that all the wedding fanfare is over. The staff, as usual, and especially Manfred, are there to greet us.

"Pura Vida, Ms. Sasha!" his voice cheerful even at the sight of my distress.

Manfred and Azmar speak at the same time.

"Ms. Sasha, I will have dinner delivered to your room."

"Sasha, if you don't want to be alone, please text me."

"I'm not hungry, thank you, Manfred and Azmar I don't know how to thank you for being at the airport; you are a lifesaver."

"That's the one thing I've never been called."

In my room, while waiting for the Lavery Labs portal to load, I receive a text message.

Arshell: How was Izzy?

> Me: Doesn't need my help.

> Arshell: Explain??

I'm about to answer, but the text will be too long, and I don't feel like talking. Instead, I strip out of my sweaty clothes and sit on the bed, where I notice that the clothes I'd previously worn have been washed, pressed, and folded on the bench at the foot of my bed. The dresses hang in the closet.

Finally, after inputting the last four digits of Trent's social security number, my cell phone rings with a call from Lavery Labs.

"Good afternoon, Ms. Borianni. I'm Divya, the researcher processing your late husband's cells. I have his brain, lungs, and everything that remained except what was given to waiting donors. I was testing the blood platelets, and need to ask if he was on any prescription medicines, recreational or psychedelic drugs?"

I am stunned by her question, and the ease with which she speaks, Trent's body parts have been given away. How could he have agreed to give his heart away?

"Why would you ask me that?"

"I ran his bloodwork and found a combination of substances that weren't immediately identifiable."

"Are you saying my husband died from a drug overdose?"

"I'm not certain. With your permission, I'd like to send these samples to a colleague at the CDC. Would you allow me to do that?"

"How long will it take?"

"I'll try to have him rush it. I will send you a link via text for your approval."

"Is there anything else you can tell me?"

"Not until I'm certain."

The text comes through. I click where I'm told. The next page instructs me to sign electronically, and once the sand runs out of the hourglass, it reads that my request has been approved.

After being spoon-fed this information, to push back the tightening of what feels like a rope strangling my own organs, I take my Metoprolol, Lipitor, and Prempro, swallowing it all with a fresh glass of wine that Manfred continues to replenish. He must think I'm an alcoholic. Maybe I am.

I grab my iPad and search for everything that can be traced in the bloodstream that would cause a heart attack. It's overwhelming, making me lightheaded. After shaking two Ambiens into the palm of my hand, I do something I'll probably regret.

> Me: Dinner?

> Azmar: Pesce

I shower and moisturize my body, reminding myself to purchase some ocean-scented toiletry products from 44 Knots. With few options for clothes, I step into an awkward adult romper whose buttons and closures slightly pull against each other, even so, it's the only thing I have yet to wear.

When I get to the path leading to the restaurant, Manfred is waiting for me in the golf cart.

"Don't you ever go home?"

"I was told the lady required an escort."

The kindness of the Four Seasons staff, especially Manfred, is abnormal. I know it's not required to leave a tip, but for him, it would be disrespectful if I didn't.

"That's true. Thank you for the wine you keep replenishing."

"Ah, that bottle was courtesy of Mr. Azmar's private stock."

"How well do you know him?" I ask, not even having recognized the different label.

"We're not allowed to share guest information. Between us

and since you're a lady here alone, I will say that there are rumors that he's a *very wealthy* businessman who keeps a residence here and is a talented surfer who's often a guest instructor at our award-winning SurfX."

The way Manfred emphasizes wealth may indicate a different level of wealth.

"He'd happily tell you anything you want to know."

"As long as he's not a drug kingpin."

Manfred finds this so funny he can't even get his words out.

"Pura Vida, Ms. Sasha, and Ms. Sasha."

"Yes?"

"You smell amazing!"

"Thank you," I say, allowing his compliment to lift my spirits.

Before I reach the doorway, the aroma wafting from Pesce makes my mouth water. The gracious host shows me through a restaurant filled with well-tanned men and women. When we reach the screened outdoor patio, Azmar stands out amongst them, wearing ocean-gray linen pants and a matching button-down shirt. I would guess he has a closet full of linens in every color. The only jewelry he wears is a roped bracelet and a necklace from which hangs a chunk of gold.

Slightly bowing to greet me, he says, "Beautiful as the night."

The other diners glance a little too long our way, like me, probably wondering what this man is doing with this sad old widow.

"Hi Azmar," I stumble, which sounds ridiculous.

He pulls out my chair, and when my body brushes against his, my skin heats like fire, especially when his face lingers against my cheek while shaking the linen napkin out on my lap. That's when I look down and notice his manicured toes inside a pair of suede Bottega sandals. I should have had dinner in my room.

The waiter comes over and sets down the wine list, and

without giving Azmar a chance to respond, I nervously spout out, "Anetoro Brunello."

"That came easy. I sense you know the language?"

"A little."

"I'm even more impressed."

"Azmar, why are you spending all this time with me?"

"If your question is, am I married? No, and no girlfriend either. As for why I'm here with you, I've somehow been drawn to you by a greater force, and something tells me you feel the same."

Does that mean he really was reincarnated from Trent's ashes? There's no other way to explain it.

Anxious and not knowing what to say, I blurt out, "Tell me about your day."

"All day?"

"Sure, why not."

The waiter brings our wine and says, "Courtesy of the Four Seasons Papagayo." When he displays the bottle to Azmar, he defers to me.

We tap glasses without toasting, and when we sip our wine, his eyes never leave mine until he replies, "Surfing at sunrise, then I caught up on some reading, answered a few emails, had lunch poolside, rescued you from the airport, then took a nap before coming to dine with you."

"I really appreciate you being there, and I apologize for always being a damsel in distress."

"Distress, no, in need of a friend, yes."

I take another sip of wine, a big one this time, before asking, "Do you have any pet peeves?"

"Unkindness."

"M-m-m-m. What's something you haven't done?"

"I'd like to travel across the country, buy one of those recreational vehicles, visit small towns, and eat local food. I'm always flying everywhere, never on the ground."

"Didn't expect that. Is traveling indicative of the work you do?"

"Import Export."

The waiter returns to refill our glasses. Again, we touch glasses, and feeling relaxed I say, *"Ai nuovi amici, friend!"*

"Dame au beurre noisette."

I only understand two words in his response: lady and butter. It's an odd combination but sounds sexy coming from between his lips.

When the waiter asks if there will be appetizers, Azmar replies, "I'm going to let the lady choose for us."

"Anything you don't eat?"

His eyes close when he replies, "I have a varied palate."

Knowing exactly what that means, I take another sip of wine, then order our appetizers in Italian. The waiter and Azmar both smile at my familiar use of the language.

"Pura Vida!" he says, raising his glass to mine. "Sasha, was there a profession before the lodge?"

It appears he's looked me up online, just as I should have done with him. Unfortunately, there hasn't been an opportunity for that yet, and there's really no need, as I'll be heading home after tonight.

"For many years, I owned a PR firm called Platinum Images."

"Do you miss that work?"

I shrug my shoulders. "Not really. I use some of those skills to market the lodge."

"Celebrity PR is different?"

"You have done some research."

My phone chirps with a text that I see is from Briana. "Excuse me."

> Bree: Why are you ignoring my calls?

I turn the phone off.

"Have you spent time in Italy?"

"My mother died in childbirth, and I was raised by my father, whose mother was Italian. I learned the language at home and, of course, at my grandmother's house. That's all she would speak at family gatherings, so I had no choice."

He takes a deep breath before stating, "Which makes you even more enchanting. Wait, so that means Italian cuisine comes naturally to you."

My smile provides his answer.

Dinner lasts two hours; diners come and go, but we stay, sharing food and working on our third bottle of wine. I don't know what we're talking about or why I'm comfortable with him, maybe I'm a little drunk; whatever it is, I don't want it to end. When I look up, Azmar is gazing at me, and I don't shy away. Fortunately, our waiter arrives with a decanter of limoncello.

We sip the cold, sweet, lemony drink, and he catches me off guard with his next question.

"Still need a haircut?"

I finish off the glass. "That bad?"

"I'll do whatever it takes to keep you in this mood."

"And you can do that? Give me a haircut?"

"If you're finished, we can take the limoncello with us."

Neither of us speaks during the drive to his residence, allowing the warm breeze to settle around us on a black night sprinkled with a varying brightness of stars, some so close that I feel like I could reach out and touch them. For me, it's a moment of serenity, and when I gaze up, I wonder if Trent is in heaven, knowing that he's sent this man to ease my pain.

Azmar's residence is at the top of Papagayo's highest point. Its luxurious layout offers ocean views from every window as if we were standing in its midst. How is this even possible?

"Your place is amazing," I say, glancing around the spacious two-bedroom condo that feels more like a house.

"I'd have to selfishly agree."

"This has to be the best location on the island."

"By far, but it's good enough for me. Feel free to look around while I get my tools ready. I must tell you I can't take any credit for the décor."

In the primary suite, where I imagined he'd be neat, clothes are strewn across an oversized chair. On the perfectly tucked and made bed, I flip through a book titled *Barbarian Days, A Surfing Life*. A peek inside his open closet confirms my suspicions, as it's filled with colorful sets of linen pants and shirts, almost as if he might be OCD. His bathroom has French toiletries, a robe, slippers, and three electric toothbrushes.

Next, I wander into the kitchen, where magazines and a leather travel folder are engraved, Azmar. It holds a brochure for a June surf competition in the Maldives. There are more books on surfing, along with an itinerary from his trip to Esterillos, including a receipt for Cartier Black limo service. His MacBook sits open, displaying surfboards with price tags of $50K. I could never have imagined it to be such an expensive hobby.

Coming up behind me, he says, "Apologies for my untidiness. I did not expect company."

"How often are you here?"

"Maybe three times a year. Depending on the waves."

He hands me a half-filled champagne glass with limoncello, where in the living area, there's a freestanding chiller holding a bottle whose label reads, '*Methuselah Louis Roederer, Cristal Brut de 1990, cuvée millénium.*' Did he plan to entertain, or am I the entertainment?

"Are you ever on the East Coast?"

"Not my favorite place to visit; it's too cold, and the congestion is choking. I have a small place in the Hamptons you might like it."

"Sounds nice."

"No, it's small, I mean tiny, not even 1,000 square feet."

I join him in touching glasses without toasting.

"Are you ready?"

I am relieved that he hasn't asked me if I've ever let my hair grow long or what I look like with long hair. Those are the most foolish questions I've been asked. I've never asked anyone what they would look like with short hair. When you don't conform to the norm, I find people respond out of ignorance. However, he isn't American.

"I'll take excellent care of you."

Offering me his robe to put over my clothes, he then motions for me to sit on a vanity stool in the guest bathroom. I watch through the mirrors as he unbuttons and removes his linen shirt, leaving him in what the young people used to call a wife-beater. To refrain from staring, I close my eyes. As his hands make contact with my shoulders, causing me to visibly shudder, he reassures me, saying, "There's no need to be nervous."

To begin this process, Azmar first combs through my hair and then uses the trimmers to cut down my unwanted growth. He evens out the sides and then changes tools, buzzing the shape. Neither of us talk during the process, yet I notice the slight bulge in his pants that he tries to hide by moving to stand behind me. Within minutes he's tickling my neck with the duster to brush away the stray hairs. When he drips oil into his hands and begins massaging my scalp with slow, pressured strokes, I relax and lean back against him. With Trent having been the only man to massage my head, I imagine it's his hands, which is when I tense up, and he responds by moving his hands down to massage my shoulders.

"*J'ai envie de toi beurre noisette. Je ne peux pas croire que je peux te toucher ce soir.*"

Guilty with desire, tears gather in my eyes, and I can't stop them from sliding onto my cheeks.

"*Dio egizio di un uomo.*"

Sensing my sadness, he situates himself in front of me and then places his hands on my shoulders, blocking my reflection in the mirror.

"My task is completed. You will be the judge."

Unsure if I can speak or know what to say, I manage, "Thank you."

The air between us is heated. How do I exit? Do I shake his hand? I can't possibly hug him, but I've been in his arms several times. His cell phone ringing saves me, making it a perfect time to escape.

"I need to take this."

"Please go on. I need to pack," I say, knowing I don't have any luggage.

He looks disappointed, yet he kisses me on both cheeks and says, "*Bonne nuit, Sasha.*"

Feeling safe in my room, I turn on my phone to find a text message from *My Travel Agent* confirming my flight details for tomorrow afternoon.

There are also six voicemails, one from Arshell and two from Briana, demanding that I return her call.

To relieve myself from the lingering scent of Azmar on my skin, I shower, wash my hair, and then change the showerhead setting to massage. Using the handheld, I spray it across my breasts and circle my nipples, and then, in hopes of getting some relief, I open my legs and hold it close to my clitoris, begging, "Please, God tell me how to make it stop." When the desire only increases, I turn the showerhead to pulsating and allow my thoughts to run freely at the memory of Azmar's touch, his voice, and how he might feel inside me. When I reach down between my legs with my fingers, I notice that my Brazilian wax has become an overgrown bush.

Realizing there's only one way to relieve myself, I finish an open bottle of wine, slip back into his robe, and then take a chance that could prove disastrous. But at this moment in my life, I have nothing to lose.

With two fingers, I tap lightly on his door. When it opens, Azmar wears a towel tucked around his waist, his chest hair moist from the shower. Before he can react, I open his robe and say, "You missed a spot."

"S'il te plaît," he replies, taking my hand and leading me inside.

"Where'd you like me to sit?"

Before directing me to the bathroom, his lopsided grin gives me the obvious answer. Gently lifting my right leg onto the bathtub, he kneels between them, asking, "Have you ever had it shaved?"

"Long time ago."

"Regardez-moi êtes-vous prêt pour faire l'amour?"

I close my eyes to the one word I know he's spoken, love; at least, I think that's what he's said, but I can't fully concentrate as the motion of the razor has begun tickling me as it goes up, then down the outside the mound of my vagina, clearing it of any hairs.

"You have a beautiful peach, Sasha Borianni. I'll need to make sure I got it all."

"Peach, I like that."

Expecting him to use the back of his hand to check for stray hairs, he lays his cheek against my freshly shaved peach. Instinctively, I tug onto the top of his head full of thick hair, and that's when his tongue slips inside, tasting the nectar oozing from my peach.

Glancing down, it's hard to ignore that his towel has fallen off, and his blessing is fully engorged with two tones representative of a brand-new copper penny.

He stands up and brings me close to him; his tongue licks my lips, allowing me to taste my juices. Then he tilts my head back and begins planting kisses around my neck.

Without waiting for him, I shake the robe from my shoulders, and in turn, he fills his hands with my breasts, pushing them together and sliding his tongue in between them. I don't even realize I've wrapped my legs around him as again he picks me up, carrying me from the bathroom and placing me in the comfort of his down comforter.

Thoughts battle inside my head. What am I doing? I know what I'm doing. This is the first time in 15 years that a man other than my husband has touched me. I should feel guilty. This is Trent's fault for directing me to this island and sending me Azmar from his ashes.

Azmar lies next to me, his hands cupping and caressing my freshly cut hair, leaning in for deep kisses while speaking French and maybe even Arabic. *"Viens me faire goûter ton beurre noisette."*

While lost in my sexual fantasy, Azmar slows down, and when I open my eyes, he's watching me. Unable to hold his stare, I reach down to feel his blessing, which is hard, heavy, and dripping at its head. I circle it around my clit, and that's when he attempts to enter me. Either I'm too tight, or he's too big. To remedy that, he swipes his blessing back and forth across my wetness until my whimpering begs him to enter me, and when he does, I exhale.

My body is fraught with hunger for this man, my muscles clenching then releasing. I'm lost somewhere I've never been, and he makes me orgasm repeatedly from his blessing to his mouth until he stops, pulls out, stands, and stares down at me.

As I lay there panting, wanting more, wanting him to finish inside me, he pops the cork on the champagne, takes a drink from the bottle, and with his mouth full, he slides in between my legs and releases the cold liquid inside me. Again, another orgasm. My mind races back and forth from Trent to Azmar; I close my eyes and see Trent; I open them and see Azmar. It feels like I'm having sex with two men simultaneously, caught in some wicked threesome.

Speaking his language into my open mouth, when his hands bare down on my hips, I know he's coming, and while he speaks in French, I softly cry out Trent's name.

A closing door wakes me from my deepest sleep in the past few months. My body is too heavy to lift or even turn over. When I attempt to rise, I drift back to sleep. The smell of coffee stirs a hunger inside me that I hope is only for breakfast.

"Bonjour belle!"

Imagining how hungover I must look; I offer him a weak smile, then pull the covers up to my chin. He kisses my forehead.

"How are you feeling this morning?"

"Pura Vida."

Hours later, when I finally make it back to my room, it tickles me to see that my clothes have been packed into a new carry-on bag. Who are these people, the Four Seasons Fairies?

Anticipating that I will pay the price for my romp later, I turn on the faucet in the soaking tub and slip under the water since the soreness has already sneaked in.

As I'm leaving my room to meet Manfred at the golf cart, my phone chirps with an unexpected text from Isabella.

> IW: Need somewhere to go I've been cleared.

> Me: Meet me in Utah. Text My Travel Agent.

Between texting with Isabella, I give *My Travel Agent* a heads up that she will be reaching out.

IW: Thank you.

I then share the virtual card for *My Travel Agent*.

Me: You'll need a coat.

Dreams and Nightmares

Isabella

I hate that I had to reach out to Sasha, except I'm not ready to return to Philly. For some reason, maybe considering she's seasoned, I feel safe with her, almost as if she can somehow insulate me from the salacious story my life has become.

The news of what's happened in Costa Rica has made its way across the major networks. My cell phone won't stop ringing with calls from *CNN, MSNBC, The Houston Chronicle, New York Post,* and *Philadelphia Inquirer,* all requesting comments and interviews, and since I don't respond, they write stories from what they've dug up, which are filled with some truths and some not. I can only imagine Bryce's anger at the fact that parts of his life are tabloid fodder.

Marley stopped by the Bungalow last night to tell me that Castro and Solano have left the island for their vacation in Cartagena, which means the case for them is no longer a priority. As for the Russian oligarch, he will forever deny any involvement; hence, I am free to leave the island.

This morning, before leaving the Bungalow, I return a call to

White Magic, who, in response to my cryptic text messages, is threatening to come get me. I already know the Feds have questioned him; I hope it hasn't caused too much of a strain on his marriage or his career.

"Izzy, what the fuck is going? How'd that shit happen? Are you alright? I need you to talk to me. Are you gonna get through this?"

"Magic, I'm good. It was crazy. They both showed up not long after you and Lady Zoë left the island, and that's when, you know, I found them; it was awful."

"You must be fucked up. Do you need me to come back there?"

"I'll be alright. What's Hailey saying? Are you okay?"

"She gets us. She's more worried about how the league will react, but my agent said I'm locked in. I mean, the season's over, and I ain't done shit. I got a lawyer on standby for you."

"Thanks, I have a lawyer here. I'll call you when I return to the States, okay?"

"Alright, baby. Hang in there."

Hanging in is a true statement, knowing some questions will never be answered. Why had this contracted killer waited until Elijah came to Costa Rica to kill him? Why not go to his home in Colorado or his job at Home Depot? No, they followed him here, waited until he arrived, and took him out. More importantly, whether it be Lady Zoë or Ramon Morashu, I'm determined to find out who was responsible.

The Twins, who've been a blessing to me, dropped off my car, so I'm driving myself to the hospital. Each time I visit Bryce, Tara Torres from *Diatro Extro* is there, and as usual, she approaches me while I'm crossing the hospital parking lot.

"Ms. Isabella, don't you think you owe it to the people of Esterillos to at least apologize?"

She's right, and what would be the harm in saying a few words? With the microphone in my face, I offer an apology.

"Everyone knows I love Esterillos; it's my home, and I consider everyone family. I'm so sorry this has happened, but the tragedy at Casa La Paz was an isolated domestic incident. I beg you to bear with me as the police work to find whoever did this to my—"

Tara cuts me off, asking, "Were you planning on going into witness protection with your deceased husband? Why didn't you divorce him, or were you in love with Mr. Goodman?"

"Excuse me?" I ask, remembering this woman wants gossip, and not the real story.

Another reporter swoops in behind me, asking, "Will you sell Casa La Paz?"

Tara suddenly has her phone on video, asking, "What's your relationship with White Magic? Is he your client or another lover?"

The F in 'fuck you' has already left my lips, until I recall Sasha telling me not to react, that anything I say will be misconstrued, and I've already said too much.

"Call Sasha Borianni. You have her number."

When I open the door to Bryce's room, his bed is empty. Then I hear him giving angry orders to someone from the bathroom. "Does he not know I'll wipe him off this fucken earth? Nobody comes after my business, and I don't care about his net worth! Make it clear; I'm not after the shooter; it's who ordered the hit that I'm going to fucken kill myself!"

I don't want to hear what he's saying, but as a rule, Bryce refuses to deal with self-ingratiating people regardless of their net worth. When we met, he surpassed several financial goals, from a storefront business on Chestnut Street to a suite of offices in Liberty Place, including a penthouse at the Ritz Carlton Residences. If he's trying to manage all of that while recovering from gunshot wounds on a foreign island, I'd suffice it to say that Bryce is pissed off.

While waiting for him, I recall our first time together. After an argument with Elijah, I'd left the house to cool off and called the woman I considered a friend, Lady Zoë. Her solution was to have a driver bring me to Manhattan. I'd imagined we'd sit and talk over a bottle of wine, but unbeknownst to me, she was inviting me to one of her private parties, making it my first time seeing a Futanari in the flesh. I thought they were erotic anime designed to be watched online. I was wrong. Witnessing firsthand the unhinged sexuality of the wealthy and famous people in the room, I couldn't deny how much their interactions with the Futanari aroused me. Bryce's gaze caught me off guard, not on the show before us, but on me. He found the idea of me in a world where I didn't belong intriguing and suggested we walk to his hotel a few blocks away. That night, he allowed me to dominate him with sexual fantasies I'd only dreamed of. Those fragmented memories end when Bryce walks out of the bathroom, dragging the pole that carries his IV bag

"Is something wrong?"

"The vultures are circling."

"Was that about the shooting?"

"It's about a lot of things. Did you bring what I needed?"

Bryce, always impeccably groomed, has gone from a five o'clock shadow to an unkempt beard into which his top lip has disappeared. I like seeing him a little disheveled. Today though I've bought him razors, more toiletries, and clean pajamas to rid himself of his hospital gown.

He kisses me from dry lips before stating, "You don't look like you're eating."

"I can't keep anything down."

"The best thing about this place is the food, and I guess they saved my life."

"I'm sorry."

"Stop saying that shit."

"Are you still okay if I leave tomorrow?"

"I won't be far behind you."

"What's the doctor saying?"

"I'm good. When you get to Philly, stay at my place. I'll have the concierge let you into the building. You still have your code, right?

"I'm not going to Philly."

He sits down next to me on the side of the bed.

"You going to Houston, see your mother?"

"No, Utah."

"Why the fuck would you go there? If that's where Elijah was living, it's not safe."

"He was in Colorado Springs."

"Then why Utah?"

"Sasha lives there."

"The woman I saw you with on the news. I looked her up. You don't need a publicist. She's old school. And isn't she dealing with her dead husband?"

"Bryce, she's family."

"If it helps, then yes, take the time to process and grieve. That'll give me time to get my business in order so my clients don't think I'm dead. When all this is over, you will belong to me."

"Bryce, I won't belong to anyone."

"You're right, that's not what I meant."

"Yes, it is, but if there's any chance for us, you gotta work on that. I'm not a commodity."

"Isabella don't make the same mistake of not seeing us through again. You know how I feel about you."

"When did you become this person that cares so much?"

Disregarding the pain, he turns, grabbing a handful of my braids, and says, "When I decided to fly here and take a bullet, two bullets. And then there's this?" he adds, placing my hand on the rise under his gown. "Can I give you this when I get home?"

Cringing at the thought of having sex with a wounded man, I say, "As much as you want."

A young dietary aid knocks on the door, entering the room. She eyes us suspiciously when I snatch my hand from under Bryce's gown.

Once he's situated with his tray in front of him, savoring a delightful meal of baked fish and gallo pinto while deftly managing calls and text messages, it prompts me to take my leave.

"I need to get back to the Bungalow and pack. Are you sure you're fine with me leaving you?"

"The sooner you go, the sooner we can start what we never finished."

Outside his room, an unexpected flush of anger fills me at how easily Bryce assumes we'll be together now that Elijah is gone. I never told him to come, either of them for that matter, so he's right; it's not my fault, but if that's true, then why do I feel so damn guilty?

As for Elijah, even with his bad choices, I loved him, and over the past two years, I often regretted not having gone into witness protection with him, and now I must live with this unbearable load of guilt forever.

While convincing myself that it's their fault, my phone lights up with a FaceTime call from my mother.

"Mommy, hey, how was your trip?"

"Isabella Washington, what is going on? Where are you? What happened to Elijah, and why was he in Costa Rica? Who was that other man? You know your Aunt Ethel texted me the article. It was the first thing I saw when I turned on my phone."

I wouldn't have expected less.

"I'm still here," I bite the inside of my jaw to keep the emotions out of my voice, "In Esterillos."

"They're not blaming you, are they? I heard they won't let you come home. Why are you whispering, and why aren't you answering my questions?"

While I'm talking with Mommy, I receive a text from Sémile.

> Sémile: You still locked down?

> Me: No, leaving tomorrow

Then in response to my mother, I tell her, "I'm at the hospital visiting Bryce."

"Who is that, and why'd they kill Elijah? Wasn't that man supposed to be protected? I hope you didn't let him move to your island. I don't want those Russians looking for you."

There's so much my mother doesn't know.

"Mommy, nobody is looking for me. I'm fine."

Satisfied that I'm safe, she forces a weak smile, yet her eyes fill with tears that fall onto her cheeks like mine. At 68, her skin has gone from chestnut to walnut while on vacation, and her hair is a blend of gray and silver streaks. My mother is a beautiful woman.

"Right now, you tell me what happened. Wait, I don't wanna have to repeat it to Mr. Rich. Rich, come in here, Izzy on the phone!"

Mr. Rich, my mother's husband of three years, has planned and taken enough cruise vacations, to have made them Pinnacle Club Members of Royal Caribbean. I love it for them and would love to give her a grandchild, except that window has closed. A smiling Mr. Rich comes into view, his face close to my mother's, their cheeks touching. That's what I want, what they have.

I share with them what happened, and Mommy gets emotional. Mr. Rich puts his arm around her shoulders.

"Izzy baby, it's time for you to come home, and I mean home to Houston."

"I love you Mommy, and I promise to be home for Mother's Day."

When pulling up to the Bungalow, I know something is wrong when I see the Twins seated on the porch and Marley walking back and forth in the road, yelling at someone on the phone.

"What's everybody doing here? Did something happen?"

"We bought you some clothes to take on your trip," she says, pointing at my rolling suitcase.

"First, we gotta get those braids out your head; that's what's making you sick; you're all tied up in knots."

"You don't have to do that. I can get them done when I get home."

"Oh no, we not letting you leave like this. Sit, sit right here."

As if I were ten years old, I do what they say. With Tiana on one side and Trisha on the other, I sit on the steps while they begin unbraiding my hair. With every braid they unleash, I feel a little lighter. When I get in the shower to scrub my hair clean, I notice a few dried blood particles circling the drain.

In the kitchen, the Twins, who believe food will improve everything that ails you, uncover a platter of Arroz con frijoles served in a half coconut, one of my favorite dishes. To show my appreciation for all they've done, I push the food around on my plate, taking spoonsful until my stomach decides not to cooperate, causing me to dash to the bathroom to vomit. When I return to the room, they suggest a different approach. They light and pass me a puro; after a few puffs, my stomach settles down.

"What are you not telling me? What is it? Where's Marley?"

"Come, sit down; what we doing to this hair."

"Blow it out. I can't stand anything tight on my head right now."

"We take care of it."

"Here I am, here's Marley. You have my attention, and I need yours," he says, hopping up to sit on the dresser.

Trisha hands me a Ziploc bag containing a cigar. "We were cleaning up, you know, after everything, and outside in the bushes, I'm guessing Eddie, and his boys didn't see this."

"A cigar?"

"Our first clue," Marley states.

"It could belong to one of the groundskeepers. They were there the day before, right?" I ask of the Twins.

"They don't smoke, at least not this," Trisha chuckles.

"I checked it out. See the wrapper, the little skull head with a cigar in its mouth, Cigare 77—El Volcano. This was purchased on the island."

"And you think the killer dropped it?"

"Contract killers have weird habits. Some take pictures of their victims, others drink rare whiskeys, and some go home to their families and live like normal people. This one planned to smoke it, got spooked I guess when your Mr. Goodman showed up."

The idea of a killer being contracted to kill Elijah and the audacity to celebrate with a cigar is sickening. This again leads me back to Lady Zoë being the orchestrator in retaliation for Elijah's testimony and drawing me closer to her.

"And they don't know, Solano and Castro?" I ask over the noise of the blow dryer.

"No one."

"What about Eddie?"

"If the Policiza weren't smart enough to find it…"

"Won't we get in trouble for tampering with evidence?"

"We traced it to the Brown Pipe, meaning they had to have been on the island longer than a day cause you know that place has strange hours."

"Do you think the store has cameras?"

Trisha gives me a look that makes me feel stupid for asking the question.

"How are we gonna check for fingerprints without the FBI?"

"I got a guy," Marley says.

I begin to feel hopeful.

"Marley is going to tell it straight. We all know someone was keeping tabs on your husband, and when he made a move, they did, too."

"There has to be some record of the killer getting on and off the island."

"Depends on how he was traveling, but nothing so far."

Tiana chimes in when she says, "Cruise ships don't dock here. Fishing boats though are always in and out."

"You're saying they could've come in on a fishing boat?"

"Don't know, Marley is gonna track 'em like a hound dog 'til we find out who killed your husband."

"Thank you, Marley."

"Now, we must pack and take you to the airport."

"There's something I want to do before I leave."

The three of them stare at me in question.

"Take a walk on the beach."

The Lodge at Sugar Hill

Sasha

"Ms. Sasha! Welcome home," says an emotional Cosay, who greets me inside the arrival terminal, wrapping me in a sheepskin coat. Cosay, a 72-year-old Native American from the Navajo Nation and one of our longest-serving employees went from being a groundskeeper to a driver, to eventually becoming transportation manager, overseeing two sixteen-passenger vans, three Suburban SUVs, and two Lincoln town cars. Now, he primarily serves as our driver. What he doesn't want people to know is that he's 10% owner of The Lodge at Sugar Hill.

"Glad to be home," I respond, my tear-filled eyes happy to be heading to Sugar Hill, which, according to Forbes, is the only African American-owned and operated Five-Star Ski Resort and Spa in the country. Except for the slopes and the outdoor activities, the only African American resort close to ours is Sheila Johnson's Salamander in Maryland. I feel proud of what we've built, and now it's up to me to continue its legacy.

He hugs me again, and although he's wearing a hearing aid, he shouts in my ear, "My God, it's good to see you."

"Thank you, Cosay. I hope I'm ready."

"We're here for you, Ms. Sasha."

Cosay provides a weather update while loading my new carry-on into the back of the SUV.

"Snow coming, probably the last one of the season. The weather people say it's gonna be eight inches, my people say it's more like three."

"Are we prepared?" I ask, knowing that sometimes he's right, but most of the time, he's wrong.

"Yes, ma'am, the grounds crew and my drivers have everything gassed up and ready. I also learned from *My Travel Agent* that your friend, Ms. Isabella, will arrive on the last flight tonight. I'll send one of my drivers for her if that's okay with you."

Of course, she'd make it inconvenient for us. "That's fine. You should have them take a coat. I doubt if she'll have one."

"Already taken care of."

When Cosay pulls out of the lot, the emptiness of the backseat without Trent shadows my spirits. I pat his space and close my eyes to taste salty tears that I wipe away. Now I know what it means to feel empty.

"Let's climb the mountain," I say, repeating what Trent would tell him when we pulled away from Salt Lake airport.

By the time we reach Park City, the sky has darkened, and the moon lights our way. Driving through Guardsman Pass and up Royal to Bald Eagle, the lights of what is known as America's Winter Playground come into view. Originally home to a large Mormon community, it has since embraced the LGBTQ+ community, with the highlight of the winter being the Sundance Film Festival. Park City is filled with incredible restaurants of varied cuisines, breweries, ski lodges, and luxury boutiques. During the pandemic, California residents began buying property to get off their sinking land, and now they don't know whether to stay or go.

When we reach the foot of the driveway, the bright lights of our beautiful lodge welcome me home. Along with my building anxiety, I need to use the bathroom, but there's no way I can pass by Marquise, who awaits us in the carport.

Before Cosay can pull the vehicle to a complete stop, Marquise flings the rear door open, reaches in, pulls me in his arms, and hugs me so tight that I fear he might squeeze the pee out of me.

"Ms. Sasha, I've missed you! We've all missed you!"

"I'm home now," I reply, noticing a van with dinner guests pulling up behind the SUV. "Let's get inside."

About ten staff members are gathered inside the spacious yet cozy lobby to welcome me. The inviting atmosphere is created by oversized leather chairs, crackling fireplaces, and carefully chosen art. It feels like walking into my private living room. The fragrance in the air is a balanced blend of cedar, citrus, and hints of brown sugar, which I specifically created for Sugar Hill. Guests often inquire about purchasing it in our boutique, if they could, it wouldn't be special.

For those employees who could not travel to the funeral, Marquise and I agreed to allow them to host a celebration of life honoring Trent. They deserve a chance to say goodbye to the man who has been their boss for eleven years and treated them like his family. At this moment, I feel Trent's presence hovering over me and all that we have created.

"Everyone wanted to be here, but I didn't want to overwhelm you."

With Cosay and Marquise behind me, I approach and hug each employee, allowing us to feel each other's pain.

"I prepared a suite like you asked," whispers Juliet, the head housekeeper.

"Thank you."

"If you're hungry, I've set a place in The Grille with Peruvian chicken, mashed sweet potatoes, and sautéed Bok choy, prepared how you like 'em," says our Sous Chef Auguste.

I don't want to eat, nor do I want to sleep in a suite. I want to be home in bed with my husband. In my new reality, I am a woman with a business to run, and people depend on me. It would be rude not to eat what they've thoughtfully prepared.

Before I can reach the table where Trent and I often dined, a few guests come over to offer their condolences, and I offer another round of "thank you's" and "Yes, I'm okay." Others who don't know me personally yet know of my loss, smile my way, and place their hands on their hearts to acknowledge my pain. Marquise's pouted lips make it clear that he wants me away from everyone.

It satisfies me to see diners headed into our recently renovated two-star Michelin restaurant Bristeca Prime, where we'd been able to lure a world-renowned Chef and Sommelier, Tránsito Lupe. We also house an outstanding soul-infused Italian restaurant, In Vino Veritas, and a waitlisted Chef's Table, with rotating chefs nationwide. For those who prefer a less pricey eatery for breakfast through dinner, we have The Grille at Sugar Hill.

"That's perfect. I'm starved. I need you to excuse me for one moment," I tell them, then rush off to the lobby ladies' room, where, after relieving myself, I sit on the toilet crying into mounds of toilet paper while wondering if my tears will ever end.

Marquise pulls out a chair for me, and I tell him, "Join me, please."

One of our newer waiters, whose name I can't recall, fills our water glasses and then sets down an opened bottle of my favorite Sauvignon Blanc, Chateau d'Yquem.

Marquise approves the wine, and we touch glasses in an unspoken toast for Trent.

"How's the staff?"

"Worried about you and also concerned things might change."

"This is going to be a whole new way of life for me, for all of us. Nothing I promise will change."

"Exactly what I told them, but they needed to lay eyes on you."

"And how are you, Marquise?" I inquire, with genuine concern, knowing that he and Trent worked hand in hand.

His eyes begin to water, so he clears his throat before continuing; instead of answering, he shakes his head, which means he can't even bring himself to share his feelings because, like me, I know he's not okay.

"Is there anything I need to know tonight? Are any groups coming in?" I ask, knowing Trent would be requesting the run-of-house reports and a list of Signature Services guests, their special requests and any overall guest complaints.

"The L.O.U.D. writers retreat checks out tomorrow and the Real Estate Roundtable guests have already begun arriving for their four-day conference. United Football League's Executive Board Retreat and Mr. Rock are in the villa next to yours. We also have The National Trial Lawyers Summit checking in tomorrow, and your husband's friend, Judge Rasso, called inviting you to dinner."

Judge Rasso, a staunch Republican Pennsylvania circuit court judge with a reputation for being a hard ass on the bench, somehow managed to befriend my husband.

"Lunch is better; dinner goes on too long, and I don't have the patience for condolences."

"Understood."

"Hispanic Women Who Ski arrives in next month, and once we move into Spring season, we'll start prepping things for next year's X games."

When he refills my empty wine glass, I'm sure he's questioning my consumption.

"How were the numbers for the Super Bowl?" I ask, knowing our place is usually sold out for a big party hosted by retired players and their guests.

"The numbers were exceptional. We had a full house, and even our residences were booked. For the slopes, we had to bring in additional staff. Trent would be…I'm sorry," he states, shaking his head.

"Please, there's no need to apologize; you're right. Trent loved a full house."

"It pains me to say this…guests have offered condolences, and I've been stacking sympathy cards in your office. This reminds me that the custom-ordered thank you cards should arrive this week for you to sign."

I want to use my fingers but since people are watching I use my fork to peel away and eat the chicken's crispy skin. "Cosay says we're expecting snow."

"That man and his people. I want to know about the weather and the beaches of Costa Rica."

I pray he can't read the guilt on my face. "Beautiful. I might even consider buying a small place there."

"That would be a nice balance. Coldest of the cold and hottest of the hot."

"Now tell me, how's the baby? Show me some pictures."

A smile fills his face until it stretches around his eyes. "I never thought I could love someone so much." He opens his phone, and the home screen displays a photo of bright-eyed Rhyan.

"She's beautiful; look at those cheeks. I can't wait to hold her. Weren't you supposed to be taking some time off?"

"It wasn't the time."

"Ah yes, the unexpected happened and shifted all our lives.

Give me two days, and then you can take the week off and spend time with your daughter."

"But Ms. Sasha."

"Nope, that's final," I say, and then take a forkful of the bok choy.

"Do you know if we should expect Trent's daughter?"

"I haven't returned her calls, so I'm hoping she'll come to her senses; that lawyer she has is draining her for money."

"Probably her grief."

At some point, I will return Briana's calls to see if she's serious about challenging my ownership of Sugar Hill. Maybe I never saw her for who she was as an adult, and I still see her as the 15-year-old girl I met.

Marquise's cell phone buzzes, and his raised eyebrows indicate there's something he needs to handle.

"I'm fine, go. I'll see you in the morning."

Juliet has prepared a one-bedroom suite on the second floor of the main building, at the end of the hall, where I won't run into guests. It's much like the others except that it has two wood-burning fireplaces, one in the bedroom and the other in the living room, whose dancing flames fill the room with a warm glow. On the coffee table sits a bottle of Silver Oak Cabernet with a note that reads, "Welcome Home, from the Sugar Hill Gang," which is how Trent referred to our employees.

I pour myself a healthy glass of wine and head into the bathroom, where my toiletries have been neatly arranged. I glance into the closet, pleased to see some of my clothes hanging and others neatly folded in the drawers. It feels like home, yet it's not home. The thought of the deep grief that awaits me there is terrifying.

I turn on the water, pour lavender bath salts, strip out of my traveling clothes, and step into the warm bath. There's a window next to the tub, where the sparkling lights from the houses beyond our property and those outlining the ski slopes remind me of the bright stars of Costa Rica.

I can't leave Sugar Hill. I also can't imagine staying here without my husband. I still don't understand how Azmar appeared out of the ocean while I was scattering Trent's ashes. He became a source of comfort, and since returning to Utah, I no longer feel the need for physical intimacy. Maybe Azmar filled that emotional void, a void that no amount of condolences could have filled. For that, I am grateful.

An incoming text pauses my mood.

> Azmar: tu n'as pas quitté mes pensées

Before responding, I cut and paste his text into my app, which translates to, "I've been thinking about you." How could he not? I respond in Italian.

> Me: rilassarsi in un bagno caldo

I assume he also translates when he responds with a bubble bath emoji followed by, *"dors bien jusqu'à ce que je te revoie."*

My translation assures me that we will see each other again.

Later, when I'm tucked under the covers, I can't ignore another call from Owen. I glance at the clock on my nightstand, it's midnight here and 11:00 p.m. in Los Angeles.

"Hey, son, how are you?"

"Mom, you home yet?"

"I got in a few hours ago...I'm not at the house."

"Yeah, I know. I talked to Marquise, but I was thinking about flying in to see if you needed company to help you with the house."

"Don't you have to work?"

"Mom, with my laptop, I can work anywhere. Remember, I have employees."

All through school, Owen tested in the high percentile. He'd majored in computer science and held several IT positions at Google and Nvidia until he abruptly quit and decided to start Vesper, a cybersecurity company. I was skeptical, but when he reminded me that I'd built my own business, I gave him my full support.

Unlike me, he worked underground and never saw the people who hired him. The company's sole mission was to hack the hackers. His first year was slow, and as a mother, I panicked and sent him a check for $10K for fear he wouldn't make it. Within three years, he had hired eight employees and refunded my $10K, and last year, he shared that Vesper had grossed $10M. I was wrong. He knew exactly what he was doing.

"The kids been asking about you. They wanna come out and go skiing before the weather changes."

My grandkids, both Owen and Briana's children, love visiting Sugar Hill and learned how to ski as soon as we moved here. Trent insisted they get lessons during every visit. The five grandchildren insisted on sitting beside me like pillars at Trent's funeral, handing me tissues and taking turns switching seats, giving each a chance to hold my hand.

"I'm not sure it's a good time. Hey, you said you needed some advice; what's up?"

"Mom, its Deidre. She does an excellent job with the children, and I love her, but we haven't been right since she started that job."

My daughter-in-law had been an emergency room nurse at Cedars Sinai in Los Angeles. During the pandemic, when there was a shortage of nurses, she accepted a job as a traveling nurse for a much bigger paycheck although she continued after the threat was lifted. I knew her being away from Owen and the kids for three weeks every month would cause problems. Despite that, she insisted it would make her family financially secure.

I always believed her obsession for material possessions was because she wanted to compete with those LA women, she called friends, and all those damn housewives shows she watched. Whether it's a bigger house, the Porsche that she insisted on driving, or her goal of buying a home in Malibu, Deidre wanted more.

"I'm listening. Go on."

"I'm gonna keep it 100 with you, Mom. She met someone, stopped coming home, and then started talking about a divorce."

"Owen, that's terrible, who was he?" I ask yet knowing my son, I'm sure he did a ton of research on this man.

"She was seeing this white boy, a cardiologist from Connecticut, claiming they were in love. What she didn't tell me was he was married too, and she thought when she left me, he was gonna leave his wife, but that shit didn't happen, and now she's back home."

"Why'd you take her back?"

"The kids were having a tough time, and the shit was embarrassing; I mean, my wife cheating on me?"

"How long ago was this, and why didn't you tell me when all this was happening?"

"She was gone all summer. I talked to Trent. He was helping, kind of counseling us, well, me."

"Can you trust her?"

"Honestly, Mom, I can't."

"And what part did you play in all this?"

"I wasn't totally faithful either, that's why I accepted her back. Mom, nobody was worth me leaving my family."

"They never are," I say, briefly recalling the disastrous affair I'd had with a married man.

"Right now, things seem to be working, I guess."

"What does that mean?"

"We're both doing whatever it takes to get things right. It's like starting over."

I don't quite understand what that means.

"Are you happy?"

"I am, we're good, but how do I trust her."

"You don't."

My alarm goes off at 6:00 a.m. Monday morning, and as much as I don't want to get out of bed, if I choose to stay here, Marquise will be worried, and he's covered for me long enough. The struggle is lessened when I answer a knock at the door from room service delivering a breakfast tray. Ready or not, it's time to face my life as a widow.

Hesitant to start down the hallway where our administrative offices are located, I draw a deep breath and walk into Trent's office instead of going to my own. Having grown up so close to New York, his walls are filled with Giants, Knicks, and Brooklyn Nets paraphernalia. His most treasured among them are the framed and autographed picture of him and Derek Jeter, a basketball signed by Willis Reed, and his authentic 2012 Giants Super Bowl ring encased in a glass box. No matter how many ways I tried to persuade him, he never told me how he had secured that item.

Standing behind his desk, I flip through the neatly stacked papers on one side, then glide my fingers across the engraved lettering of his initials on a black leather portfolio, which held his daily reports. When the tears begin to form, I slide down into his tattered oversized leather chair, molded from his body, and imagine his arms wrapping around me. Before I can descend into my sadness, Marquise, Aunt Millie, our bookkeeper, and

Uncle Thomas's heart startle me when I hear someone clearing their throat.

Aunt Millie can barely look at me with her sad eyes as she pushes up her tortoiseshell glasses that sit so far down on the bridge of her nose; I can't imagine they even serve a real purpose. It doesn't stop her from handling our books, first via hand and then populating Excel, which she began adapting a few years ago. Trent always assured me her system worked, but our CFO has complained since we arrived.

"Sasha get in here," she says, pulling me up from the chair and into a big bosom hug.

"Just drifting, I'm good," I reply, moving to sit on the couch, where a folded New York Jets throw blanket fills me with the memory of our lovemaking the afternoon before we left for New Jersey.

For support, Aunt Millie leans against the back of Trent's chair. Marquise takes a seat across from me.

"Your friend arrived last night," she tells me.

"She's hardly a friend. Where is she?"

"Hasn't left her room. DND on the door."

"Good. I'm not ready for her shenanigans."

Arriving next at our impromptu morning meeting is Jordan Bridges, our Director of Marketing, who knocks on the door frame, alerting us to her presence. She and I work closely to promote Sugar Hill, along with a department of five young people who handle our social media, giving us an edge over the other resorts, especially during the high season. We've built a good alliance with resorts throughout Utah and Colorado, where Trent had been its president for two years. He stepped down with the plan that we could begin to have a life outside of work. We were too late; Costa Rica was supposed to be our first trip.

"Good morning, Jordan," I say, reaching up to hug her, averting her sorrow-filled eyes.

How do I get people to stop feeling sorry for me?

"Morning, Ms. Sasha, sorry to disturb. The sheriff's here to see you, and Marquise, the film crew, is ready to set up for the UFL Retreat."

"The Sheriff, for what? Condolences?"

"He's serving legal papers."

"I bet it's that fucken Briana."

I greet Sheriff Bronner in the lobby. After a hug and offering condolences, he apologizes when he hands over a packet of papers. As I suspected, it's the official notice that Briana is contesting the ownership of Sugar Hill. Thankfully, the properties we own in Philadelphia, New Jersey, and the condominium in Park City were purchased in my name.

My first instinct is to call Briana and curse her out; instead, I phone Adam, who suggests we meet in his office at 2:00 p.m. We met Adam and his wife, Parker, when they held a fundraiser at Sugar Hill. Parker comes from one of the wealthiest families in Utah and always told me that her marriage to Adam had been arranged. She sits on the board of the Sundance Institute and, along with her uber-wealthy friends, raised 2.5M for Sundance Institute High Schools.

Cosay is disappointed when I decline his offer to drive me into Park City. Comfort is not what I need today; I need to take control. There will be plenty of time for me to wallow in my grief.

Trent's oversized Chevy Suburban was his pride and joy. We bought it last summer in Salt Lake, and today, it's warmed up and ready for me to drive. My husband always kept his car spotless, except for the box of cigars on the passenger seat that he had bought and forgotten to bring with us to New Jersey. I turn the music off before it starts playing any of his favorite songs. It's baffling how easily I speak of him in the past tense.

Within 30 minutes, I'm pulling up to Seltzer & Associates on Prospector Avenue, where I'm shown to a small conference room. Before I can sit, Adam hurries into the room, hugging me and apologizing for being late. He's been our attorney for ten years and is the conduit between our accountant and investment banker.

While Adam and I make small talk, our Chief Financial Officer, H.R. Cranston, arrives, where I'm greeted with a hug and an, "I'm sorry about Trent." For the first time, he doesn't mention Aunt Millie's antiquated accounting.

Once we're seated at the table, the screen at the front of the room opens to a Zoom to include Clarice Valentine, our Financial Advisor. When everyone is finished with pleasantries, after only 15 minutes, I find myself drifting outside the room where I can see their mouths moving as they orchestrate the legalities of my life. Thank God, I trust them, or at least Trent did, but he's not here anymore, and for that reason, the knot in my stomach is tightening.

With my head moving back and forth, I try to figure out who is saying what. That's when I notice the split screen displaying a colorful waterfall chart of Sugar Hill's current net worth, its gains and losses over time, actual and budgeted amounts, and what will now be my net worth, including monies Trent has left me through insurance policies, real estate, and investments.

Clarice says, "You have financial safeguards to protect you."

"What are they?" I ask, drifting back into the meeting.

Adam places a folder in front of me with several yellow Post-it tags that read SIGN HERE.

"These are copies of the various deeds, titles, and mortgage transfer documents that need to be signed."

When I open it, the first thing I see is Trent's death certificate. I close the folder, wipe an escaped tear, and drink the bottled water set in front of me. Now I know why they offer water; it's a distraction.

H.R. leans across the table, touches my hand, and asks, "Are you okay, Sasha?"

I nod yes, but they know I am not.

They continue discussing my need for a new will and a living will, updating insurance beneficiaries and bank and credit union signatories, canceling credit cards, and reconfiguring a business from a partnership to a single owner.

I briefly considered telling them about Lavery Labs and the funds at Chase Bank, but I chose to withhold the information. Trent would have told Adam and the others if he wanted them to know.

To get my attention, H.R. taps the folder with his chubby fingers and states, "We've drafted a succession plan in case of your demise or inability to function."

Finally, I attempt to speak up, but my throat is so dry they can't understand me. I take another gulp of water and repeat myself.

"What about his pension checks and social security?"

"They were notified automatically once the funeral director filed the death certificate."

Adam then adds, "The other piece of business is Trent's daughter, Briana."

"Exactly what does she want?"

Clarice chimes in from the screen, "Half of everything left to you, specifically Sugar Hill."

"She also thinks you're hiding money; her lawyers are requesting that an independent accounting complete a forensic review, which is ridiculous," adds H.R.

"What she wants is to pressure you into settling outside of court, which would result in a payout," Adam says.

Insistent Clarice states, "I don't think that's it. She wants the lodge,"

Squeezing my hands together to hold back tears from my eyes and my voice, I speak up, "Briana and TJ were the beneficiaries of a million-dollar policy that her father took out long before I knew him, and she got the house she's living in. She's just fucken greedy."

Everyone takes a pause until Adam speaks up, "We'd like to suggest a mediator to resolve this."

"What the fuck are we mediating? Does she have legal grounds for any of this?"

"Anyone can initiate litigation, but your estate is iron-clad. I doubt if she'll have anything to stand on."

"Doubting doesn't make me feel good."

"Sasha, please, this isn't for you to worry about right now; that's why you have us," offers H.R.

The more they talk, the more the knot in my stomach twists. I look at Adam sitting at the head of the table in his $3,000 suit; H.R., who's across from me, has allowed spittle to gather at the corners of his mouth, and Clarice, who I once accused of flirting with my husband, bears her abundance of cleavage. Do these people even have my best interest at the forefront of their minds, or are they calculating their hourly rates for every minute I sit here?

Clarice butts in, offering her advice, "If you decide to remarry, I strongly urge you to allow us to draw up a prenup."

"Who would you suggest I marry?"

"She's right. You're a wealthy woman, Sasha, so you must be careful about who you date."

"That won't be necessary."

After the 90-minute meeting, Adam walks me to the elevator, reassuring me everything will be okay. It will not.

I barely reach the Suburban before breaking down in tears that freeze on my cheeks. Inside Trent's truck, I scream, pound on the steering wheel, and cry out, "God, I want my husband back. I can't do this. I can't."

I ignore the tapping on my window until I hear someone calling my name. Of all people, it's the woman I've named Park City Karen. She has annoyed me since Trent, and I arrived in Utah. Karen made it clear in her introduction that her family was one of the oldest residents and wealthiest in the valley.

When we'd entertained the idea of selling Sugar Hill, her family was the first to make an offer, and their overeagerness was reason enough to take it off the market. She's disliked me ever since, yet it didn't stop her from flying in her private jet to Trent's funeral.

Forcing a smile, I crack the window to hear her asking, "Sasha, Sasha, are you okay?"

Before I can repeat the standard response of a new widow, I blurt out, "No, I'm not okay. My husband is dead!"

"I'm sorry."

"Yea, get in line with all the other sorry motherfuckers."

Now, she is the one startled when I start the truck and screech out of the parking lot. Cosay was right; I should've allowed him to drive me.

Determined to finish this day of business, I drive the three blocks to Chase Bank, where Joe Thurmond walks up to greet me after I pass through the revolving doors.

"Ms. Sasha, let me again offer my condolences."

"Thank you, and yes, I'm okay! Mr. Thurmond, I'd like to get this over with?"

"Can I get you anything? Coffee, tea?"

"Would you have anything stronger than coffee?"

After passing by the row of tellers and glass-enclosed customer service offices, we enter an open vault filled with various-sized safe deposit boxes. Mr. Thurmond shows me into a private room to the side of the vault. We turn the locks on the first box using his key and mine, and then he hands me another key to turn the lock on the new box. I watch as he places them side by side on the table where I sit.

"If you'd allow me a moment before you begin."

While tapping on the metal boxes, he returns and places an 8-oz. juice glass and an unopened bottle of Macallan 18 on the table. I need to apologize to him for being rude, but I no longer have the energy for unwarranted niceties.

"Please push this buzzer when you're done or if you require assistance."

"Mr. Thurmond, when was the last time my husband was here?"

"Black Friday."

He exits the room and closes the door behind him. I fill the glass, and let it sit until I decide which box to open first. I check our original box, 4237. Everything appears to be in place. Deeds, Wills, and other miscellaneous papers soon will be replaced with updated versions. Inside a white envelope is $50K, which we stashed for an emergency. Three purple velvet pouches hold a three-carat diamond pendant necklace, matching drop earrings, and six loose diamonds given to me by someone who had been more than a client at another time in my life.

Before opening box 4246, fearful of what I may find, I swallow the full glass of Macallan, then shake my head to release the burn. I take out my phone and begin listing the items inside. The first item is a white envelope containing a State Farm Insurance policy for $500K with me as the beneficiary. I push it aside to remove a brown 11x12 envelope stuffed with three bank-banded stacks of money that read $10,000 each. I pour another half glass and drink it before picking up a tarnished 76ers key ring with a tag and a key engraved with 222. The final item is a rectangular white box engraved with *Expect Lace.* Inside, wrapped in black tissue paper, is a pair of silk women's G-string panties with pearls that match my Akoya necklace as its narrow strip, and underneath them is a business with the name Victoria.

My trembling hand pours another glass of Macallan. This time, the burn isn't as strong, yet I massage my chest and try to recall if I took my blood pressure medicine. Did Trent know he was going to die? He had to know I'd find these things. Did he leave them for me as a clue? If so, it only leaves me with more questions about the circumstances surrounding his death. Where would he get $172K in the savings and another $30K in this box?

Why was he hiding money from me? The third glass of whiskey causes my head to swim and the knot in my stomach to tighten and rise into my chest, making it hard for me to breathe. I ring the buzzer for Mr. Thurmond, then stuff all the items in my purse except the cash.

Drunk from the alcohol and rocked by what I've discovered, rather than risk driving, especially since it's started snowing, I call Cosay to pick me up, and he has one of his drivers take the Suburban.

When I return to the lodge, Marquise informs me Isabella is dining at The Grille. Unable to deal with anyone, I request a case of Macallan 18 be delivered to Mr. Thurmond.

Arshell is the first person I call, and I tell her everything: sex with Azmar, safe deposit box finding, insurance policies, Lavery Labs, and my greedy stepdaughter. She is silent for the first time in our 40 years of friendship. After our call, I swallow two Ambien.

Two days later, when I finally have the energy to face these new circumstances, without anyone to accompany me or giving it any real forethought, I tug my coat overtop my nightgown, slip into a pair of boots, and trudge through the blinding snow to our villa. Entering my passcode, I step into the mudroom where Trent's skis sit upright and his work boots stiff in the boot dryers. From there, I push my way into the butler's kitchen, where I'm afraid to take another step.

The house smells strange, or maybe it has no scent at all. Not Trent's, not mine, not a burning fireplace or food cooking in the kitchen. The auto temperature makes it warm, and when I peer into the living room, it happens: the sound of Robert Glasper's, *Better Than I Imagine*, begins to play on automatically.

Taking the wide staircase, I step into our bedroom, where

housekeeping has done its job of neatly putting everything in its place, not messy like when we'd rushed out to catch our flight three months ago. I can't imagine lying in this bed without my husband beside me.

In our bathroom, I remove my nightgown and slip into Trent's last pair of pajamas hanging behind the bathroom door. On his side are his razors, aftershave, deodorant, and cologne. Next, I go into our joint walk-in closet, where our luggage, even the empty one, has been stored. Dragging my suitcase into the bedroom, I sit on the floor at the foot of the bed, open it, and take out the bag I received from the morgue, Personal Belongings.

He wore jeans, a faded long-sleeve jazz cruise t-shirt, Nike sneakers, and a Patagonia jacket that day. A smaller Ziploc plastic bag contains his wallet, driver's license, credit cards, a receipt for the suitcase he purchased, and the $6,000 cash for our vacation. Hopeful of what his cell phone might reveal, I enter Briana's birthdate, 0508, where a text message from someone named Lee reads, "Don't be late."

Who the hell is Lee?

Startled by my cell phone ringing, the caller ID reads it's from Trent's doctor.

"Dr. DiBello, thank you for returning my call."

"I'm so sorry to hear about my friend. It was quite a shock."

"Is there anything you can tell me that would've caused him to have a heart attack?"

"Cardiac arrest is not something that was expected. Trent was in great physical shape."

"There had to be some indication that his heart was failing. A lab in New Jersey found a trace of some shit I don't even understand."

When he doesn't respond right away, it scares me. Maybe he does know something that Trent hadn't shared with me.

"Doctor, did you hear me?"

"Yes, why don't you have them send those results to me? I'll see what I can make of it."

"So, there was something wrong with him."

"Not that was known to me. He had his annual check-ups, and I sent him to a urologist about six months ago to get his prostate checked. Everything came back clean. Did the lab say anything else?"

"They were more than annual. I recall him seeing you every few months. Please don't lie to me."

"I would not. He saw me for his arthritic knees and some back pain. We adjusted his blood pressure meds to get his numbers down, and that was it."

"I wasn't aware he was on blood pressure medicine."

"You know how men are with their health. He probably didn't want to worry you. If you need anything else, please call my cell phone."

As I curl up on the floor, my mind races with the possibility that everyone has been deceiving me, or perhaps Trent has been withholding vital information from us. I return to his cell phone but find no definitive answers before the battery dies. As frustration surges through me, I hear a faint voice repeatedly calling my name.

"I'm up here," I say, certain Marquise has sent someone searching for me.

"Sasha, hey."

I turn to face Isabella.

"Wait, what are you doing in your husband's pajamas? You poor thing."

I want to answer her but again, I'm crying. She passes me a box of tissues off the dresser and sits cross-legged on the floor beside me with her arm wrapped around my shoulders. As much as I try, I can't hold back the big waves of grief, so I rest my head on her shoulder and let it out. She doesn't try to stop me or tell me it's gonna be okay.

Glancing around at the pile of papers and luggage surrounding me, she asks, "How long have you been up here?"

"There's so much shit I didn't know."

"Please don't tell me he had another family."

Through tears, I say, "I don't think so, maybe. But my God, there's money everywhere. I'm dealing with brokers, bankers, lawyers, employees."

"I can help you, Sasha; it's what I'm good at."

"They're good people, I trust them."

"It's also in your best interest to have an independent professional who can see things through a non-emotional lens."

I lean back against the foot of the bed, and she sits close beside me when I ask, "You're an accountant, right?"

"Forensics and we study more than the numbers; it's bigger than that. I analyze everything from lifestyles, personalities, and relationships, all to formulate a clear picture. In my mind, everything is deduced to a number."

"I promise you I'm not one of those women in the dark about their finances. I knew everything. Our finance team ran an audit every six months."

"Why not let me conduct a forensic audit across the board and see what turns up."

"It scares me that he has so much cash lying around, and I haven't even checked the safe here in the house. If something happens to me, it'll be a mess, especially with his greedy daughter, who's already contesting everything, she's even threatening to come here to confront me."

"If she's that greedy, I hope she doesn't show up while I'm here. I may be forced to push her down a mountain."

We both find that funny.

"I always tell people, especially those in your situation, not to let your finances get tangled up with your grief. More than men, women do it all the time regarding money."

"Do you really think you can help sort this all out?"

Isabella takes on a more serious tone when she states, "In Einstein's words, *"If you can't explain it simply, then you don't understand it well enough."*

"There are a lot of things I can't explain, starting with why my husband had a heart attack."

"I can't answer that. What I can do is create a financial profile for you to include a full inventory of all your assets, known and unknown. It's like puzzle pieces that I'll upload to my proprietary financial software. From there, we should be able to diversify your portfolio and reposition your investments, giving you more disposable income while I search for loopholes. I'll warn you though, your team will be pissed that I'm involved."

"As the kids say, I have zero fucks to give at this point. Now, what about you? What's going on with the investigation back in Esterillos?"

"You mean, why am I here?"

I nod yes.

"It's a dead end to hear the Feds tell it, but my lawyer is working on some things outside the Feds."

"You kept Marley?"

"He's good. He got me off the island."

"How are you handling all this? Emotionally, it's a lot."

"It's different for me. Once Elijah went into witness protection, we were no longer in contact, so I learned to bury my feelings for him, which probably wasn't a good idea. Still, with him being murdered in my home, I'm not sure of anything, so I came here 'cause I wasn't ready to return to Philly yet."

"What about the other guy?"

"I know what you're thinking. We're not lovers, at least not anymore. He was there for me when all the shit started with Elijah. He took it upon himself to have someone find me, then came to the island, and now it feels like I'm being guilted into a relationship."

"And the woman, another client I heard you mention, Lady something?"

"I'm unwinding myself from her, too."

"That bad?"

"She's evil, a unicorn."

"A what?"

"One day, I'll explain, until then let's get you up and into some clothes."

Sugar Hill Gang

Isabella

The staff has invited me to join an intimate gathering to celebrate the life of Sasha's husband. Following the sound of the jazz band, I reach the Trenton room, where, from the doorway, I can see a gathering of maybe 100 people. Inside, the friendly crowd begins introducing themselves to me as employees, former employees, friends, and a few hotel guests. No one appears sad; instead, the crowd is engaged in lively conversation and light-hearted laughter while partaking in an abundance of food. I pick up a plate and go down the chef-staffed buffet line.

Across the room, encircled by a group of people, is Sasha, casually dressed in an ankle-length black scoop neck sweater dress with a wide leather belt cinching her waist and black suede boots. Her hair is freshly cut, and she wears drop earrings to match the pearl necklace she's been wearing since she showed up at the Bungalow.

Everyone shares memories as if the guest of honor is about to enter the room at any moment, and he almost does when the screen over the stage lights up with a video montage from their life here at Sugar Hill. This must be incredibly hard on her; at least there's no audio, so she doesn't have to listen to his voice, which might be why she keeps her back to the screen. Sasha, I realize, is an incredibly strong and classy woman. That's the strength I want and the life Elijah and I'd planned, but neither has come to fruition and now Bryce is asking me to imagine having that life with him.

I'm drawn away when Aunt Millie pulls me into a group and introduces me to people, I've yet to meet who welcome me to Sugar Hill. One of those people is Millie's grandson, Viraj, who insists I try a concoction they've named the New Jersey Devil. Aware that I've traveled from Costa Rica, they tease me about being a surfer and unable to handle the cold weather. Their friendly banter ceases when Marquise takes Sasha's hand, leading her up to the podium.

"Good evening, everyone! It's my honor tonight to show love for my friend and our forever boss, Trent," he says, followed by applause.

Marquise clears his throat of tears and then extends his hand to Sasha to stand beside him. If this man is choking up, how will Sasha say anything?

"No one worked harder than my friend Trent. He learned every aspect of this business and brought with him so many ideas that helped our struggling Sugar Hill become a 5-star palace, as I like to call it. With this woman leading us, we will continue to expand and welcome the world through our doors. Trent's motto, '*Always treat your guests with decency.*'"

Another round of applause.

"Tonight, we will show that same love to his wife and our new boss, Ms. Sasha."

Sasha's trembling hands take hold of the microphone for support. The audience silences.

"Thank you for this beautiful celebration of my husband's

life and work. Three months is a long time to be away from my home, from Sugar Hill. If you bear with me, I'll eventually know what I'm doing because some days, I'll appear to have it all together, and other days, I may be too broken to come out of my office."

The applause is deafening. "I also want to acknowledge what you're feeling. I know that some days, it won't be easy for you either, but I pray that God will keep his arms around us, around Sugar Hill, as we hold each other up and mourn together until we can see our way through."

When she gets choked up, people encourage her to continue with words like, "We love you... Sasha, you got this...take your time...we got your back."

There are other murmurs in the audience.

"I don't know how she's gonna make it without him."
"Do you think she'll sell?"
"Makes sense. Why live in that big house alone?"

Sasha continues.

"When we showed up eleven years ago, we promised to continue Uncle Thomas' legacy, which now includes Trent's. We all must find—" she pauses in emotion, "Let's not make tonight a sad occasion. Let's celebrate the man I loved and still love, your boss and sometimes my boss, Mr. Trent."

Realizing there isn't a dry eye in the room, including mine, I text Aunt Arshell.

> Me: yr friend is incredibly resilient

> Auntie: Yup, you need to listen to her

> Me: sorry to have doubted you.

> Auntie: It ain't the first time – heart emoji

"Everyone knows my husband loved good food and a good party, so tonight, we better not let him down."

Then, surprisingly, Sasha turns to face the screen and kisses her handsome husband's smiling face.

Applause fills the room, along with cheers and cries for Sasha and themselves, and I'm not sure if I'm crying for Sasha's loss or my own. The shame of not having had a memorial service for Elijah bears down on me, but Agent Solano was right; who would've come? I promise I will do something special in his memory once I take possession of his things, specifically when his ashes arrive.

When Sasha steps off the stage, like any celebrity, the crowd closes in around her, me included. She graciously hugs those closest to her, allowing them to cry in her arms until Aunt Millie instructs everyone to give her space.

That's when the bartenders begin pouring drinks rapidly, and the band attempts to play *Before I Let Go*. The entire room breaks into the electric slide, making it the party that Sasha planned for it to be. In the middle of my cha-cha, I'm pinged with a text.

> Bryce: You make it to Utah??
>
> Me: Yes
>
> Bryce: leaving the island see you at home.

I don't have a chance to respond since Viraj is pulling me to the bar for a drink when I hear someone behind me ask, "Did you get yours?"

Another person adds, "Yes, can you believe it!"

The bartender, with more than a friendly eye on Sasha, chimes in, "That woman is a class act. She won't be on the market for long."

While Viraj goes behind the bar to line up shots of Tequila, which I decline, Cosay stands beside me, and I ask him what they're referring to.

He turns up his earpiece, and again, I repeat my question.

"Five hundred cash to each employee. How could she even think about doing something so kind for us?"

Taking a mental note for my forensic audit, I estimate the number of employees to run this place at about 200, making what she gave away at least $100k. Do they keep that kind of cash on the property?

At the bar, tequila shots are lined up, and the peer pressure is on so to avoid seeming wimpy, I take not one but two shots with the rest of the group.

Sasha rescues me from her employees, introducing me to the VP of Signature Services, Ginger Grant, whom I noticed at the bar earlier, throwing back excessive shots of her own.

Who am I to judge?

Ginger reaches in for a weak hug and says, "Isabella, welcome to The Lodge at Sugar Hill. If there's anything I can do to make your visit more comfortable, anything you need that you don't have, here's my number." She taps her cell against mine, and her number populates.

"What exactly is Signature Services?"

"It's for our elite guests. Mr. Trent never liked the term VIP, so if guests are willing to pay extra, I mean *extra*, they pay to get the VIP treatment. You get it. We service their needs."

Her response indicates that they might be paying in cash. Perhaps that's why she gave away the $100K. It also makes me wonder to what extent guests are serviced. Surely not like Lady Zoë services her clientele.

Sasha answers, "Her department, of three people, ensures that requests from our Signature guests are met, which sometimes can be quite challenging, but Ginger's team gets it done."

"So, if you need anything, let me know, and if we don't have it, we can get it."

While I'm still wondering if Ginger is her real name, I can't wait to ask Sasha if records are kept on these payments and what they include that isn't listed on the brochures.

Ginger turns to Sasha, almost too close, grabbing hold of Sasha's hands, where she attempts to whisper, "Sasha, all our signature guests miss Mr. Trent so much, including myself, and now I have no idea how we're gonna *get right*. Are we gonna still be able to offer that?" Ginger exclaims with a lift and a weird wiggle of her hips.

Sasha, taken aback by her conspiratorial tone, asks, "What are we offering?"

My ears perk up, as does Aunt Millie's, who places one hand on her hip.

"You know what I mean, Trent took care of me."

Sasha's voice changes from friendly to authoritative. "Tell me exactly what you mean."

"What I meant, Sasha, I mean what I'm saying, it's not like that."

Aunt Millie, who has positioned herself between Sasha and Ginger, tells her, "*Ms. Sasha* is asking you to clarify."

Realizing she's said too much, Ginger loudly exclaims, "I'm sorry *Ms. Sasha*, I'm so sorry I was outta line. I was only saying that Mr. Trent was always willing to put our guests' needs first."

"I'd be careful with how you speak of my husband," Sasha tells her before walking away from us.

"Girl, you are stupid!" exclaims Aunt Millie.

I quicken my pace to catch up to Sasha, approaching the elevator bank, "What was that about?"

With her thumb, she dabs the tears at the corner of her eyes. "My husband, it seems, was having an affair."

"With her?"

"Why not? She's young, beautiful and you heard what she said."

"Yea, about taking care of your guests and you think your husband had an affair with the help. What is that girl, like 25?"

"She's 32, the guests love her, and you can see why, with that manufactured body."

"I didn't know your husband, but from everything I've heard about him, he wouldn't disrespect you like that."

"Respect or not, he's still a man. I mean was a man, was, is, past, present, I don't even know how to refer to him. Can you tell me how to do that?"

I can't.

If there ever was a morning after, this is it. I stayed at the party way too long and drank way too much, and now I'm paying an awful price. The closed drapes don't even allow a sliver of light, and I'm unsure what time it is. I need to pee, but lifting my head off the pillow causes the room to tilt. Instead of attempting to get up, I turn over, crushing a roll of toilet paper. What the hell happened last night? The last thing I remember is eating a gummy.

I feel my cell phone jabbing into my ribs, and when I squint my eyes to see the last number dialed, I was on a call with White Magic that lasted 40 minutes. Was I crying to him about Elijah and Bryce? I can't even remember. What makes it worse is there's a seven-minute call with Lady Zoë. Why'd I allow myself to get so drunk? I reach for the light on the nightstand, and my head spins; the phone falls on the floor, and when I reach for it, the bitter taste of vomit rises to the back of my throat.

Once I clean myself up, with a cold bottle of water, I curl under a blanket on the chaise lounge, where I further scroll through my phone; I see that I also called Sémile. Thankfully, he didn't answer, and why would he? He's built a life with his wife and family. Maybe if I had a family, I wouldn't be so consumed with myself. I'd have someone to care for, to love without judging me, it's too late unless I decide to become one of those women who raise a child alone. But can I keep a child safe?

My head pounds, a steady throb, as my phone blares a FaceTime call from an unknown number. I slide to answer, greeted by an excited Viraj and my other new friends from last night, their voices a cacophony of shrieking and chatter. They've somehow nicknamed me *Baywatch*, a name that echoes in my ears. Viraj claims I made a $100 bet when they challenged me to take a ski lesson. The memory is fuzzy, yet I feel compelled to honor the best to avoid their relentless teasing.

It's 10:00 a.m. when I make it to the staff dining room, which is filled with a cast of characters, some of whom were at the party last night and on the call this morning. Over the clatter from the kitchen, many languages are spoken Spanish, French, and English, all seemingly blending into one. A server sets a cup of black coffee in front of me, along with brioche toast to soak up last night's Tequila and two Excedrin to clear this morning's hangover.

I've barely finished eating when Viraj directs me to a dressing room where he hands me a pair of long johns, then assists me in donning a bright orange one-piece snowsuit, oversized ski boots that come up to my knees, goggles, a skullcap, and a helmet. It feels like I'm about to walk on the moon.

Outside, the freezing temperatures and blinding snow clear up my hangover better than the aspirin. How is it that I've gone from 89 degrees with a view of the ocean to what must be 15 degrees below zero on the side of a snow-packed mountain?

While Viraj steadies a passing lift chair, my cell rings with a call from Marley.

"Marley, what's going on?" I scream into my phone, fumbling to remove my helmet and then ski cap so I can hear.

"We pulled prints off that cigar, no match. Eh and one more thing."

"What's that?"

"Marley need to poke around in Colorado."

"Did you find out something?"

"No, I need to see what he was doing there. All the Feds tell me is he worked at Home Depot and did taxes for his neighbors. Gotta be more to it. Thinking maybe someone was hanging around there, followed him to you."

"You need to be careful. These people are dangerous."

"No fun in being careful but hey Marley did find out something. You recall Eddie telling us that the Chief and Solano were a thing?"

"Yeah."

"Solano was one of your husbands' handlers, so it's kinda the Feds' fault for not keeping tabs on him. Them handlers got a history of falling back once they get what they want; that's when these guys start getting the itch to return to their former life."

Feeling the heat building up under my multiple layers of clothing, I can sense sweat rolling down my back. "What do you mean?"

"Solano and her underling, another woman, were the ones who checked in on him and made sure he got to court; they were his main point of contact."

"That bitch never mentioned that. It's her fault!"

"Could be the underling got flipped which would be bad for Solano cause she's in line to head a field office."

"Both of them should be fired, put in jail!"

"Eh, Marley, gonna find out. Pretty interesting right, and she gotta feel responsible for what happened. I know the bureau ain't liking that. Might take her a little longer to make her next move. I'll call once I get to Colorado Springs."

"Like I said, please be careful."

Viraj situates me on the chair lift and informs me that a Ranger Johnson will be waiting at the other end.

Before he closes the gate, I ask, "Who?"

"He's the one that dared you."

"I'm not built for this. He can have the $100."

"Awe c'mon *Baywatch*, you can do it. He'll wear a microphone, and you have an earpiece built into your helmet. Listen to his instructions when you get up there."

I try to make another excuse, but he's already waving me off.

As I ride the swaying lift chair up the mountain, I realize that the snow on Sugar Hill is equivalent to the sand in Esterillos. The sky is a deep, cold blue and everything below me looks miniature — the houses and the people. Other lifts pass me by, and I feel like we're birds on a wire, going further into the sky. I wonder how far above sea level I am. My thoughts turn to Elijah, wondering if he learned to ski in Colorado. He had to have been exercising; it was apparent he'd lost weight, and Sémile had confirmed as much. Again, I wonder what would have happened if there hadn't been a shooting and if I had been faced with choosing between Elijah and Bryce that day.

"*Baywatch*! Let's go!" a voice screams into my earpiece.

When I look up, a hulking figure stands in front of my chair, waiting to release the bar across my lap. Annoyed, I'm about to tell him to stop calling me Baywatch. Instead, I do the most embarrassing thing, I fall onto my knees at his feet. With one arm, he lifts me, and I instantly notice how fresh he smells, like the cold snow itself.

"You okay *Baywatch*? This ain't the beach, you know."

Being so close, it's unsettling how much he towers over me.

"I know where I am and why I'm here, so let's get it over with since you need your hundred dollars."

"Listen up, Baywatch, I'm Ranger Johnson; you're on Pennypack Overlook, better known as Bunny Hill. If you listen to me for the next hour, maybe I'll take it easy on you."

His condescending tone irks me.

"I thought I was going to ski down a mountain. This is a hill."

"Like I said, Bunny Hill, *Baywatch*."

"My name is—"

Cutting me off, he continues, "The fact that you're wobbling tells me you don't even know how to stand up straight, so let's start with that."

Without asking, he grabs me by the hips, and like a drill sergeant, he barks out commands in my earpiece, "Stand tall, tilt your shins forward, center your weight over your feet."

What is he talking about, shins forward?

"Poles get pointed backward. Now glide back and forth to get the feel of it, take small steps, then push off with your poles on the *little hill*."

Using the analytical side of my brain, I know I can figure this out. I recall all the people I've read about who've had accidents on ski slopes, so I do as he tells me, only managing to fall three times. Finally, I get some traction and can glide a few feet. We repeat this until a slight smile shows his approval when I go about 10 feet, then 20 without falling.

When it feels like all my senses are firing and I understand the trick is to glide by feel as much as by sight, his annoying voice barks into my earpiece that the lesson is over, causing me to again fall flat on my face. Amused, he picks me up and sets me back on the ski lift. I don't even bother to thank him.

Hours later, my ringing cell phone wakes me from my best sleep in weeks. It's Sasha. I also see that I've missed two calls from her. This can't be good news.

"Sasha?"

"I know you had a long day, but I promised the gang we'd go to the Wooden Floor."

"Where? Who?"

"It's a supper club in Park City."

I sit up against my pillows, pull the comforter up around my neck, and ask, "You wanna go to a club?"

She laughs, telling me, "Before you use the excuse of not having anything to wear, there should be a garment bag hanging in your closet."

"You bought clothes for me?"

"Aunt Millie noticed you didn't have much luggage, and it's not exactly 90 degrees here, so she sent Ginger to pick up a few things."

"Signature Services," I whisper to myself.

"By the way, I hear you were impressive on Bunny Hill today."

"That Ranger, he was so rude."

"He's a good guy."

"You really wanna go to a nightclub?"

"Trent and I used to hang out at the Wooden Floor once a month to see some of our employees perform. Our front desk manager is performing tonight in a cover band that sings Adele, Beyoncé, and Lady Gaga, which he calls the Three Queens Routine. If you're too tired, I understand."

How can I turn her down? "No, it's fine, I'd love to go."

Unzipping the Gorsuch garment bag is a rich suede dress with a price tag that tells me I'm reimbursing Signature Services. There's also a large box from Kemo Sabe that holds a beautiful pair of cowboy boots. Since I'm going Cowgirl Carter, I slick my hair back in a high ponytail, allowing the gray streaks to outline my face freely. I apply minimal make-up to hide my tired eyes.

Cosay is waiting in the carport to drive us, and when I slide in the back seat, surprisingly, Sasha looks refreshed. Her close-cut hair gives her a sexy edge. From what I can see, she's wearing a close-fitting black knit dress, over-the-knee red suede boots, and a fur poncho tossed over one shoulder.

"You really know how to put it on!"

"Thank you."

"No, thank you for the clothes. I'm repaying you for every penny you spent."

"Don't do that; I'm the one that asked you to come out. Truthfully, I needed you with me."

"You're good, right?"

She smiles unconvincingly, deflecting by pointing out her favorite restaurants and shopping spots as we travel down Main Street. Despite the cold night, the streets of Park City are bustling. Late-night bars, restaurants, art galleries, and theaters are open, and people walk around as if it were a warm summer day.

"Usually around the holidays, the moneyed go to St. Bart's or Aspen. We get a good showing, but we haven't yet been able to convince them that they should be here, specifically at Sugar Hill."

Park City reminds me of a scene from a Charles Dickens movie. The town is as colorful as Costa Rica, except it's covered with snow that continues to fall, yet people move about like it's nothing. I can't imagine how the Sundance Film Festival landed here in January. Robert Redford must really love this place.

"Are there many Black-owned businesses in Park City?"

"Not enough."

When she goes quiet, and I see her staring out the window, laying my hand over hers, I say, "You got this."

The Wooden Floor parking lot is packed with vehicles, yet there's a spot reserved for Cosay, who delivers us right to the front entrance. Inside the low-lit club, Sasha is greeted with hugs, condolences, and apologies for not attending her husband's funeral. Of course, for her, all drinks are on the house. Her smiling face shows me how comforting the attention makes her feel.

When people go on too long, Sasha politely cuts them short by introducing me as her niece, and for once, I don't mind. Some people even congratulate me on winning a bet I haven't collected yet. It seems in Park City, as in Esterillos, everyone knows everyone's business.

While Sasha is in conversation with someone, I turn upon hearing a familiar voice call out, "*Baywatch?*"

I'm dumbfounded to see a man in uniform, badge hanging around his neck, with a cheesy smile.

"Excuse me?"

I can't see his face clearly in the dark club, yet his gruff voice is undeniable.

"Ranger Johnson, you're a cop; no wonder you're so mean."

"Full time Park Ranger, part-time ski instructor."

"I believe you owe me a hundred dollars."

"Indeed, I do."

I put my hand on my hip and give him a teasing pout until he finishes counting out five twenty-dollar bills. Holding them out to me, he asks, "Are you up for some night skiing?"

"Are you crazy? I barely made it through the morning."

"We'd be in a snowmobile; I think you'd like it."

Sasha, having overheard our conversation, says, "You should go."

"Like this?"

"I can get you out of those clothes at the station."

"Go for it Izzy! Have some fun!"

Oddly, Sasha kisses my cheek and whispers, "He's one of the good guys if that's worth anything."

She's obviously had too many drinks.

Sasha gets distracted when a woman saunters up. They both exclaim how happy they are to see each other. When they finally break apart, Sasha introduces me.

"Isabella, meet my friend Parker Selzer."

I extend my hand, but Parker pulls me in for a hug, captivating me with the rich scent of whatever perfume she's wearing.

"Pleasure to meet you, Parker," I respond, recalling Selzer as Sasha's lawyer.

"Are you taking care of my friend here," she asks, bringing a smiling Sasha in for a side hug.

"I think we're taking care of each other."

"Right, you're the one she rescued. Looks to me like you both got out of your mourning clothes," says the woman wearing a Chanel jacket and suede pants tucked into 5-inch leather boots, and clutching a Balmain embroidered purse.

"Either way, I love you, and I'm a horrible friend for not remaining in New Jersey with you."

"Stop that. I know how much you hate the cold weather."

Her apology seems sincere; I wonder why she's here if she hates the cold.

"I'm gonna call you, I have the best getaway for us, but I have to get home; Adam's dreadful family is visiting." She kisses Sasha on the mouth, and after they say their goodbyes, the room practically divides to make way for her exit.

Sasha tucks her arm through mine and leads me toward a reserved table near the front of the room. Before I can look around to see where Ranger Johnson went, a server appears with bourbon for Sasha, and since I'm keeping it light, I ask for a glass of white wine. That should keep me from making bets or going off at night with a stranger.

Flashing lights indicate that the show is about to begin. It doesn't stop a couple from rushing over to tell Sasha what a good man Trent was. I can tell by Sasha's shifting from one foot to another that she's getting annoyed and wants a moment to enjoy herself. That is until the wife says, "Your husband always knew how to get us right."

"And who's getting you right now?" I ask.

Sasha cuts in. "Thanks for your condolences; the show is about to start."

"But we—"

When we take our seats, Sasha leans over and says, "You'd think my husband was the damn mayor, the way he took care of everybody."

I've never experienced a live drag show. I have had the pleasure of attending Lady Zoë's parties with their vibrant characters, making this an event to remember. As the MC introduces the Three Queens, the crowd erupts in applause at the rhythm of the band. Three talented performers, dressed as Destiny's Child, take the stage and start singing *Say My Name*. The audience, including myself, joins in between their singing and comedic acts. When they slow down to perform, *I Will Always Love You*, Sasha wipes away tears. When they switch to their Tina Turner routine, donning body suits and corsets, the energy escalates, and Sasha and I, like everyone else, enthusiastically shout along to *Proud Mary*.

While going to the ladies' room during a much-needed intermission, I bump into Ranger Johnson, who is exiting the men's room.

"You ready?"

I'm about to tell him hell no, I'm not skiing at night, but that's when the opening of the men's room door behind him casts a light across his face. I'm suddenly unsure if it's his untucked uniform shirt or those broad shoulders, but when he tilts his head back to get a good look at me, my excuse weakens to, "I can't leave Sasha."

He glances toward the room where Sasha is on stage practicing a country/western two-step routine to the Three Queens rendition of Beyoncé's *Texas Hold 'Em*."

"She'll be alright; she's with the Sugar Hill Gang."

After taking off in his oversized white pick-up truck, we begin rounding the dark mountain roads where the only lights are those stamped on the trees. Concerned for my safety, I ask, "How can you see where you're going out here?"

"Mountains are similar to a woman's body, gotta know your way around the curves even with your eyes closed."

"You're such a smart ass. Anyway, how long have you been a ranger?"

"About 12 years, full-time ranger, part-time ski instructor. Don't worry, Baywatch, I ain't gonna let nothing happen to your curves," he says, bumping his thigh against mine.

"Do you have the authority to lock people up?"

"Mostly bears and mountain lions. What you do, *Baywatch*?"

"Count other people's money. Not exciting at all."

When I see lights up ahead, he pulls to a stop in front of a building with a sign marked Sugar Hill Ranger Station.

"Lemme run inside to see if there's any snowmobiles available."

"You were serious?"

"You weren't?"

Observing the SUVs and pickup trucks with snow removal equipment attached, I ask him, "How do you survive out here?"

"Your tank always has to be full, your safety gear up to code, and I always keep water and food in my truck, so yeah, you ride around, and sometimes I use my legs and walk."

"You think you're a comedian but listen I'm not dressed for this."

"Hold tight, Baywatch, I told you I'd take care of you," he states before hopping out of the truck.

Alone in the warm truck, the only thing visible is my reflection in the window, and that's when I look closely at the woman staring back at me. Lately, my life has been shrouded in darkness, but tonight, it's providing a peacefulness that makes me want to step out into it. I'm about to open the truck door when Ranger Johnson climbs back in and tells me, "No riding for us tonight. I can drop you at the lodge."

"Not yet."

In silence, we drive deeper into the mountains until he turns into a driveway practically covered by trees. When the path opens, we pull close to the garage door, next to which sits a log cabin.

"Hot chocolate?" he says, jumping out.

"Does that mean you don't have heat?"

"Now, who's being funny?"

He helps me remove my boots in the mudroom and then steps out of his. Once we're inside his cozy house, he drops a pair of Ugg slippers in front of me and then invites me to make myself comfortable in the living room. When I sit down, my feet sink into what I'm sure is a bear rug without the head. I watch as the Ranger throws logs into the fireplace, and when it lights up, he stokes it until the warmth permeates throughout the cabin.

"Give me a minute. I need to wash the day off."

I pick up the remote but change my mind, preferring the crackling of the fire. It's so relaxing sitting here, like nothing else exists outside this cabin, no Elijah, Bryce, Lady Zoë, or anything else weighing me down.

When Ranger Johnson returns, he bends down and kisses me on the forehead, and that's when I notice that he again smells fresh like snow, the same way he did on the mountain. I wouldn't dare tell him that he reminds me of the brawny actor who played Thor.

"Tell me, Baywatch, what you doing at Sugar Hill, 'cause you sure didn't get that golden skin from around these parts."

"I was on vacation in Costa Rica, and I'm guessing you're not gonna stop calling me that."

From the kitchen, he yells, "Once you get a nickname in these parts, it sticks. How long you here for?"

"What you got there?" I ask when he enters the room with two steaming cups.

"It's my special blend of hot chocolate. Here, try it."

Eager to drink whatever concoction he's fixed; I burn the tip of my tongue. "This is delicious. What's in it?"

"Slow down Baywatch, I can't tell ya, 'cause I'd have to kill ya."

"You're so corny."

Before sitting at my feet, he leans forward and frees my hair from its ponytail. "I like this," he says, threading his hands through my gray streaks.

"You don't believe in boundaries, do you?"

He shrugs his shoulders before asking, "Where's home for you?"

"Can we keep our personal lives out of this?"

"Easy for me."

"Can answer the question of what the hell am I doing here with you in a log cabin?"

"Why do you women always do that? Play that innocent role, like someone lured them against their will. We connected on the mountain, and tonight at Wooden Floor, you couldn't stay away from me. Plus, I don't pose any threat to your personal life."

"Fair enough, but I was not all over you."

"I tell you, though, if you were my woman, you definitely wouldn't be traveling alone, anywhere."

"Maybe I like traveling alone."

He shrugs his shoulders and then, in a surprising move, he pulls me down from the chair and onto his lap.

"You need some home training."

"Awe, you haven't complained."

"What's it like here in the summer?"

"Green with snowcaps. You'd like it."

I finish off my chocolate and say, "This really tastes good."

He puts his hand under my chin and lifts my head until our lips meet. "Let me see."

Abruptly pushing back, I ask, "Wait, do you have a girlfriend or someone who might stop by?"

"No personal stories, remember."

"Yeah, c'mon really."

Showing his pearly white teeth through a wide grin, he reassures me, "No one is coming, except maybe…"

He lifts my hair and places it on one shoulder where he nestles his face. There's nothing gentle about this man.

"You wanna sleep over?"

Why did I go off with this strange man to his cabin? The answer is simple; I got here the same way I always wind up in a man's arms, needing to be rescued from another man. This time, though, I needed rescuing from my recent past. So, I do what I always do. I turn my face toward his only to find his tongue too anxious to search my mouth while his hands fumble with my breasts with too much haste.

Taking hold of his hands, I kiss the palms, whispering, "Slow down, Ranger, I'm sleeping over."

"You don't understand."

"What's that?" I ask, then follow up with a few light kisses on his lips.

"It's been three months since I let myself get this close to a woman."

"Why?"

"Personal choice, but when I saw you at the memorial and then this morning when you kept falling, and tonight in this get-up, I knew you'd be worth breaking my promise. Now listen, I'm gonna slow down, but you won't get much sleep."

"A man who hasn't had sex in three months, I'm intrigued, and I never said I wanted to sleep."

With care, his eyes follow his hands as he unbuttons the front of my dress, and when my breasts break free of my unsnapped bra, he takes one in each hand and gently massages them, his thumbs encircling their nipples. That's when I feel him rise beneath me. Anxious, I pull his wife beater over his head, and the glint of the fireplace reflects off a chest that must be bench-pressing snowmobiles. Where I delight in rubbing my face against him, he delights in licking and sucking my nipples until they're firm enough to burst.

"I wanna see what you taste like so bad but if you think I'm moving too fast."

"Have at me, Ranger Johnson."

After three months, his desire is laid bare when he removes what's left of my clothes, placing wet kisses across my belly, allowing me to guide his freshly shaved head to meet the heat between my thighs. When I hear him groaning, I move my hips enough to give him an orgasm he can taste.

Lifting his head, he tells me, "I gotta get inside you."

Without waiting for me to respond, as if I could get any words out, he lifts his long body, pulling me with him, then wraps my legs around his waist, driving himself so deep it feels like he's coming through the other side and while I gasp for air, he explodes inside me.

Late the next afternoon, Ranger Johnson drops me off at Sugar Hill, making me feel like a teen sneaking into the house. Since I've already showered with the Ranger, I change in my suite, grab a cup of hot chocolate from the staff kitchen that tastes nothing like Ranger Johnson's freshly melted chocolate, and then head to Sasha's office.

Her office, stacked with boxes and gifts from guests, also has framed photos of her son and his family, her stepdaughter and her wife and children, and stepson TJ spread across the credenza. On the corner of her desk sits a picture of her and Trent at what appears to have been his election night celebration. Somehow, the photos seem forced as they are the only personal décor in the room, making me wonder about her life before Sugar Hill and before she married Trent.

I face a daunting task as I confront a pile of black and white composition books labeled "Sugar Hill Accounts." The penciled entries are strewn haphazardly across the pages of a chaotic ledger. Upon opening my laptop, I click on the attached Excel spreadsheets sent by Aunt Millie in my email. I promptly create a "Sugar Hill" file on my computer and meticulously organize and cross-reference the handwritten files spanning a decade with the recent entries in the current NetSuite financial software. The numerous erased and rewritten entries suggest that Aunt Millie is concealing something significant.

Talking aloud to myself through each entry assures me that I won't miss anything until I see Sasha standing in the doorway.

"How did that walk of shame feel?"

"No shame at all."

"Ranger Johnson's a nice guy. He owns the Naked Bakery. I'm guessing you didn't make it there."

"He never mentioned the bakery, but we did get naked."

Pushing aside folded towel samples, Sasha sits in the chair opposite her desk. Her eyes tired from last night's partying, she asks, "Do you always talk to yourself when you're working?"

"It helps me sort things out. As if I'm explaining my findings to someone to see if they make sense."

"Do they?"

"Aunt Millie is good, and your husband's initials are on everything."

"He stayed on top of the quarterly review of the hotel and our finances. I spoke to Joe Thurman from the bank; his files should be in your email by now. You know you were right. Our CFO and Financial Advisor gave me some pushback, but their files will be here by the end of the day."

"Who is *My Travel Agent*? Is that a person or an actual travel agency?"

"That's the agency we use for our travel plans."

"Interesting."

"Is there a problem?"

"Not sure. Are you and Trent their only clients? I see lots of entries, payments, and activity between your accounting and theirs."

"He was using them before we met; now, we use them for business and personal trips. Even the kids and some of our Signature Services clients have retained them."

"Here's the thing; everyone hides money, or they should as long as it's legal. So far, everything is on point, but I still have a lot to cover," I tell her, as I'm nowhere close to confirming my suspicions.

"If you have everything you need, I'm heading to The Grille to meet a guest for a late lunch; by the way, she knows you."

"Knows me?"

"Yes, the Unicorn, Lady Zoë."

Float

Sasha

Every day at the house gets more manageable, and every night gets harder. There's no getting over it; Trent is never coming home. I feel his presence throughout the house, so I talk to him and listen to what he expects of me. This means filling the house with his music, whether it's Gary Taylor, Danielle Ponder, or any of the many musicians on his playlists, which, at moments, I embrace, and at other moments, when his presence is unbearable, I shut everything down and crawl into my empty bed.

Last night, when I walked into the house after my night at the Wooden Floor, I opened a bottle of Trent's Pappy Van Winkle and intentionally texted Azmar. Nothing salacious, nevertheless he never texted back. I contacted Isabella, who offered to stay with me at the house, but she was caught up with Ranger Johnson. I'm unsure where that will lead because she doesn't have good luck with men. Like me with Azmar, maybe she needed the comfort of a man with no emotional attachment.

As hard as I've been trying, the items from Trent's safe

deposit box still lie scattered over our bedroom floor, but nothing has added up. The only thing that does make sense is the money he's been dumping into upgrades at Sugar Hill, except for the ridiculous idea he had to build a restaurant at the top of one of our highest peaks. The other ridiculous purchase was the Delancey Street house on Rittenhouse Square in Philadelphia.

The one thing I have been putting off is turning on Trent's now fully charged cell phone. Realizing there could be a lot of pain hidden there with messages from women he may have been involved with would scorch me. It could also do the opposite and confirm that there wasn't another woman. Seated at the dining room table with Jarrod Lawson crooning *All That Surrounds Me*, I take my chances.

When the screen lights up, I cover my mouth to contain a scream when I see his favorite picture of us dressed in full ski gear, our faces bright from being out in the cold, with him planting a wet kiss that I can still feel on my cheek. He loved that picture.

Scrolling through his text messages, so far, nothing is indicating a mistress; when I try to read all of ours, it hurts so badly. I scream out, "What did I to deserve this suffering?" Since there are no answers, I pop an Ambien and pass out under a blanket on the couch.

Missing the morning meeting, I arrive in time to meet Isabella's friend, Lady Zoë, for lunch. Isabella was surprised when I told her, but she didn't suggest that I not go. I couldn't have done that to a Signature Services guest, so I'm heading to The Grille to meet the mysterious woman Isabella calls a Unicorn.

Lady Zoë approaches me purposefully and greets me with a hug, appearing familiar or perhaps offering condolences. In some ways, she reminds me of Parker with her recognizable designer clothing and an exquisite Chanel bag. Unlike my friend, who cares less about others' opinions, this woman not only needs people to recognize her wealth but also desires for them to feel her exuding sexuality. This may be why she unnerves Isabella.

"Ms. Borianni, thank you for accepting my invitation. I know you are a busy woman."

"My pleasure. Sasha is fine."

I let go of her fragrant hug and notice her simple fitted slate gray cashmere dress and gold rush sling-back pumps. Everyone in the restaurant, including me, is captivated by her numerous diamond strands, ranging from a choker to a long necklace that catches the light in the room.

Our server arrives to pour from a bottle of 2013 Dom Perignon that we upsell for triple the price; for that reason, I feel compelled to taste a glass. Trent and I always agreed that the best part of working in the hotel industry is that you can drink on the job.

"I invited you to lunch as a thank you for welcoming my group to your resort on such short notice."

"We do our best to accommodate. Is everything to your liking?" I ask, not having any forewarning that she's a guest.

"I've hosted many private affairs, but your staff has gone far beyond to please us, and their discretion is appreciated. You have trained them well."

"If there's anyone specific, you'd like to recognize, that would be nice. We like to add that to their file."

"We've recognized their excellent service. They even suggested I book future events here or purchase a property."

"Ginger from Signature Services can assist with your dates for future events. Regarding residences, we have a realtor who handles whatever we have on the market."

"Oh yes, I've met Ginger. She is the perfect person for the role. I would love to spend time with her."

Something tells me that's not all she'd like to do. I'm sure I'm reading too much into the mysterious woman Isabella refers to as a Unicorn.

"How'd you find out about Sugar Hill?"

"I stayed here once with an old friend, but your niece called the other night and said so many wonderful things I made my way here with haste. Now that I'm here, I don't want to leave."

When our salads arrive, Lady Zoë eats as if she's famished. On the other hand, I pick at mine and sip my champagne.

"Do you ski?"

"I'd never take that chance, but I understand it's exhilarating. Most people can't imagine what I take pleasure in. Would you agree that most people deny themselves pleasure in life?"

"Participating in what one imagines is a pleasure is not always good."

"We differ there, but I appreciate you stepping in to assist *My Love* through that awful business in Costa Rica."

My Love? Is she another one of Isabella's lovers?

"A murder in one's home would be tough on anyone."

"Knowing her intimately, I make it my responsibility to replace that bad space with things that make her feel good. I'm sure you understand we all need something to make us feel good."

Changing the subject, I ask, "Is your accent Russian?"

"No, Greek, a Greek Goddess is how I chose to be referred to. Men are intrigued by a woman bold enough to own her goddess form, and for that, I've elevated myself with complete strength and zero vulnerability. You know, like yourself."

This woman and I hardly have anything in common, but something tells me I need to listen more than talk with this woman. She invited me to lunch for a reason she has yet to divulge.

While pouring another glass of champagne, I respond, "We all have someone or something that makes us vulnerable."

She fingers her hands through her hair, which reflects off the sunlight, as does the large turquoise stone on her ring finger.

"Was there something specific you wanted to discuss?"

"I wanted to meet the woman taking over this lodge."

"I'm not taking over; my husband and I managed this place together."

"What I'd like is a customized Signature Services package for my clients or rather, my friends. We could benefit Sugar Hill's bottom line."

That was no slip; she meant clients. What has Isabella gotten herself into?

"It would be my pleasure to recommend your place as an alternative to those who choose St. Bart's and Cannes during the holidays. My friends could give Sugar Hill the gold seal of approval. Are you interested?"

Isabella had to tell her that was one of my goals. Now that I know what she wants, I stand up and say, "I tell you what. Put what you're offering in an email for me to review with Marquise, our general manager, and we'll see if we can meet your and your *friends' needs*."

"*My Love* has assured me you have the capability. Expect my proposal before I depart."

"Thank you, and if you'll excuse me, I have to prepare for a meeting."

"The pleasure of your company has certainly been mine, and Sasha, when you're ready to be vulnerable, I invite you to attend one of my private parties."

"Have a pleasant stay, Lady Zoë."

Later that evening, after meeting with guests and sitting through two business meetings, before going home, I stop in the lobby bar, where I see Lady Zoë and Isabella at a table in what appears to be a contentious conversation. I don't have the energy to figure it out, but something is odd about that relationship. If their behavior doesn't negatively affect the lodge, it's none of my business. Even so, I tell the bartender to keep an eye on them.

By Tuesday, I hadn't seen or heard from Isabella since I saw her with Lady Zoë. I tried calling and texting her, but there was no response. Initially, I suspected she'd gone to see Ranger Johnson to avoid further interaction with Lady Zoë. When I checked with the front desk manager, I was told Isabella checked out. I cannot wait to talk to Arshell and see how well she knows her husband's niece, who's constantly running from something or someone. If the reason for her urgent departure was Lady Zoë's arrival, according to that woman, Isabella invited her here. What's worse is she didn't even complete the audit of my books before she left. I'm done with trusting her.

Before the afternoon marketing meeting, I encounter Ginger outside Trent's office. She was still trying to redeem herself.

"Ginger, I need you to tell me what you meant by Trent getting you right?"

"Nothing. I had too much to drink that night. It'll never happen again."

"Was my husband selling drugs?"

"That's a hard no, Ms. Sasha, but he did allow me to bring in weed for Signature guests."

"So, then he was offering marijuana to our guests, and as we both know, it's illegal in Utah," I respond, realizing now what the couple at the Wooden Floor was referring to. It makes sense, but weed wouldn't garner the money Trent had been hiding.

"Would you like me to stop?"

"Is that even a question? I cannot afford to have the cops arrest you or me for having it on the premises. If guests bring it with them, that's not our problem, but you can't allow yourself to be labeled a drug dealer."

"Yes, Ms. Sasha."

"Another thing, what do you know about this, Lady Zoë."

"She paid upfront in cash for the villa and the rooms. She also required round-the-clock catering and bar replenishment. The staff isn't complaining, besides the built-in gratuities, from what I'm told, her guests are free flowing with cash tips and that it was a pretty risqué party."

"Anything else?"

"White Magic showed up and signed autographs for a few staff members."

"He was here, at the party?"

Her stupid grin says yes.

I'm about to delve deeper when I receive a call from Adam, who has spoken with Briana's lawyer. I step away to my office to take the call, where all the files Isabella was supposed to review are neatly stacked in piles on the floor.

"Your stepdaughter doesn't want to mediate, but she will consider settling."

"That's bullshit! I'm not giving away what's rightfully mine; tell her lawyer we're going to court."

"Maybe you could try talking to her first."

"Adam, when did you become so fucken soft?"

"You're right, I'll let them know."

My next reluctant order of business is lunch with 72-year-old Judge Rasso, who always babbles on about his two ex-wives and what they took from him in their divorces. What I don't want to talk about is Trent. I've already asked Marquise to text me in an hour, giving me an excuse to escape from him.

When I walk into The Grille, he stands to hug me longer than necessary.

"Sasha, you look radiant!"

"Thanks for being kind."

He dismisses the waiter and pulls out my chair. "Please, let's sit. I've been dying to have lunch with you."

I hope this man isn't trying to come onto me. If we weren't in the dining room, I'd be skeptical about him pouring me a glass of wine.

"How've you been, Your Honor?"

"Your husband, my friend, was a good man. Many people will miss him, but I'm sure you already know that."

"Everyone has shared those sentiments."

"He left a beautiful wife behind, and I can't imagine you'll stay single for long. Is returning to Philadelphia and your former business a consideration?"

"Judge, this is my home. I won't be leaving. And I think it's a little early to discuss my personal life, or is that why you asked me here?"

He covers my hand with his, "Sasha, I'm trying to stay right, and with Trent gone, I want to make sure you're alright too."

"What did you say?"

He repeats himself, but a text from an 800 number distracts me.

Excusing myself from the table, I tell him, "I need to take this."

> 800: we need to meet.

> Me: Who is this? Who are you?

> 800: It is better to discuss in person.

> Me: WHERE ARE YOU? PLEASE CALL ME!

> 800: NJ, text when you arrive to get the adz.
> Come alone.

Barren Hill

Isabella

The first-class flight felt meaningless as I was surrounded by a noisy family of seven. To make matters worse, a teenager beside me was mindlessly scrolling through TikTok videos with her Air Pods, disturbing my peace. The chaos made the four-hour flight to Philly seem interminable.

Inviting Lady Zoë to Sugar Hill added to the misery of the pleasure she provided. I willingly succumbed to her influence, not because she coerced or tempted me, but when White Magic arrived, I felt the irresistible pull to engage. The original plan was to have dinner and drinks, as he wanted to ensure I was coping after the tragedy. Who was I fooling? I've grown so accustomed to the other side of my life that I crave it as an escape from my thoughts. The combination of the two has become my undeniable fixation.

Lady Zoë possesses a unique talent that few people know about and employs others with similar talents. If you're lucky enough to be in her favor, you'll have the pleasure and, ultimately, the satisfaction of her rising hormones, transitioning her womanhood into a Futanari. When that happens, the three of us partake in hours of what some might call freakish lovemaking. This time, at Sugar Hill, she was different. It was one of the few times she allowed me to pleasure her in ways that I never had before; she became the submissive, and I the dominant with her confessing an unrequited love for me. Leaving me wondering if I feel the same. For his part, White Magic was only allowed to watch until he forced his way between us.

While riding the shuttle bus to Enterprise, I text the person who can help me organize the final steps to get Lady Zoë out of my life.

> Me: Will be in Houston for Mother's Day & need your help

> Betty: call me when you arrive

Traveling along I-76, passing by Center City, I notice the increasing number of skyscrapers compared to two years ago. It was right after Elijah had been taken into custody. To avoid a federal prison sentence, he had agreed to wear a wire and participate in a sting operation a week after our wedding. The whole experience was incredibly distressing, especially when he confessed to being the middleman in a billion-dollar weapons operation led by Russian oligarch Ramon Morashou. It was later revealed that Lady Zoë, who was supposedly Ramon's girlfriend, was the mastermind behind the operation. By then, I had already become intimately involved with her, and she used this to blackmail me into becoming her accomplice.

Pulling the SUV to a stop in front of our beautiful 18th-century Victorian, now an award-winning Bed and Breakfast, I couldn't be happier to have decided to let Synearra and her husband, Corey, be its innkeepers. Synearra came into my life when I was going through a difficult time, and now, she claims I saved her from a life of mundane work as a night manager at the Loews hotel.

My car is barely parked when the front door swings open. With her belly swollen with seven months of baby, Synearra waddles down the steps with Corey, trying to keep pace, shaking his head at our excited embrace.

"Izzy, I missed you! Are you alright? I'm so glad you're home!"

"My God, look at you!" I say, rubbing her belly. "How you feeling?"

"Fat and ready."

We're both talking through tears of joy when Corey chimes in, "Ladies, can we please go in the house?"

"Oh, Corey, I'm sorry." I hug him, too. "You been taking care my little sister?"

"She doesn't let nobody do nothing for her," Corey tells me as he removes my suitcase from the trunk, with Synearra insisting on carrying my backpack.

"Izzy, you good? That shit was crazy. What you do to them boys?"

"It ain't her fault, Corey!"

Synearra holds onto the railing, and I follow behind her, wondering what it might feel like to have a baby nesting inside me.

"Yo, that's not what I'm saying."

"You better not blame her 'cause I don't want her feeling guilty."

"Do I need to send the brothers to Costa Rica?"

"Negro that's not what you do anymore, you got a family now."

"Guys, I'm good," I reassure them, realizing that they are my family, and this is my home.

I am completely unprepared for the overwhelming sinking

sensation in my belly as I step into the house and proceed down the hallway.

"Sit down. I know you're hungry. I fried up some chicken, baked mac, and cabbage. I know you weren't getting that in Costa Rica."

"You're right. It smells so good."

"And the chef baked a butter pound cake."

My mouth waters for that crispy rim around the borders of the cake that I can see sitting under a glass dome on the counter.

While Corey carries my suitcase into the first-floor rear bedroom, Synearra sits my backpack on the scratched-up chair in the far corner of the kitchen, the same chair Elijah used to set his briefcase. The only change in the large kitchen is the fireplace, which has been converted into a coal oven.

"Sis, it's time for a new backpack. You been carrying this thing since we met."

"Like I've had time to go shopping. Plus," I pat the tattered bag, "We been through a lot together."

Synearra collapses onto a kitchen chair, panting for breath, and teasingly rolls her eyes at me. At that moment, I can't help but notice the radiant glow that her pregnancy has bestowed upon her, making her look remarkably younger than 27.

"Like you ain't never heard of Amazon."

"Alright, I'll get a new one, but I'm not getting rid of this. Now, what can I get you? Cause while I'm here, I plan to wait on you."

"Corey does enough of that. That man is a pain in my fat ass."

"You'd be complaining if I didn't," comments Corey when he reenters the kitchen.

"Oh, Cousin Anderson says hello. He's still talking about the time him and his wife spent at Casa La Paz. Now, what do you wanna do first?"

Standing behind Synearra, Corey plays in her thick hair, making it the first time I've seen her without braids.

"Elijah's boxes came from Colorado, two from Costa Rica."

"I gave them this address. Is that okay?"

"Sis, this your house, what you talkin' about, is it okay?"

Corey grabs a bottle of water from the refrigerator and tells us, "I'm going to the barbershop then Wegman's; text me your list, and stay off your feet, please."

"Trust me; the farthest she's going is to the couch."

He kisses her on the forehead, then her belly. "I'm out," he tells us, then heads down the hallway to the front door.

"What you mean, while you're here? Please tell me you won't run off before the baby is born."

"I don't wanna get in the way of your guests."

"How many times do I need to remind you this is your house? Plus, there ain't no guests this week," she says, trying to hide a suspicious smile. "There is something I wanna tell you."

I brace myself.

"You know we love managing Barren Hill. We got this down like clockwork and like you suggested, we hired housekeepers and a chef to prepare meals. Corey tries to handle the maintenance, and he got someone for what he can't handle, which is usually everything."

Holding onto her back, Synearra stands up and fixes me a plate. I know not to stop her.

"You already know this place is a gold mine, especially since we started offering it as a wedding venue. Brides will drop a bag to get married at Barren Hill, especially when I show them your pictures."

She's right; Elijah and I had a beautiful wedding until I ran away from the new life he tried to offer me.

"What are you telling me, Synearra?"

When she sets a hearty plate down in front of me, my stomach growls, and I say a quick prayer before digging in.

"There's a house one block over, 1101 Strahle Avenue. It's small, with three nice size bedrooms, a backyard, and a finished basement for Corey's caveman shit. Oh shoot, I'm trying not to curse, sorry baby," she says, apologizing as she pats her belly.

"You're moving?"

"Yes and no, lemme show you."

Turning over her phone, she shares with me the MLS listing for a picture-perfect, 1,200-square-foot house with an asking price of $375K.

"I know what you doing. Izzy, you trying to count that money."

Through a mouthful of mac and cheese, I manage to say, "It's none of my business, but can you afford that?"

"Listen, I never told you this, really, we never told anybody. About a year before the pandemic hit, Corey had this white man whose hair he cut who was big into that IT shit. Sorry baby," another pat on the belly. "Anyway, he was moving to San Jose, so he told Corey and the other barbers to buy stock in Zoom, which made no sense to me. I mean, what the hell was Zoom? Corey was the only one who listened cause he'd already taken his advice on a few other low-key investments that paid off, and sis, you know what happened, the bag dropped."

"Are you fucken kidding me? You own stock in Zoom?" Now I reach over and pat her belly, apologizing.

"I know, right."

"I'm so proud of you both and you're right, don't tell anyone! Now, this makes my offer seem so small."

"Whatever the offer, we're in cause this white man done gave Corey a consultant job. Now what's this you talking about?"

I set down my fork long enough to tell her my offer. "You've cared for Barren Hill more than I ever could, so I'd like to make you and Corey my partners. We'd split the profits 50/50. What do you think?"

"Sis, you gone make me drop this baby right now. Are you serious?" she asks, bouncing to get up from the chair.

"Whoa, slow down; I don't want you having that baby early."

"Wait, why would you do that? This is your home."

"Elijah and his mother are gone—"

"Wait, the mother died too?"

I wave my hand, not ready to get into the details. "And who knows where I'll end up? If something were to happen to me, it would go to you," I pat her belly, "and this guy, generational wealth, that's what I want for you and your baby."

She starts tearing up. "You mean your godson."

"Are you serious?"

"Corey decided before I could tell him it's what I wanted, and now you come here with all this good news."

"So, what do you say? You want to talk it over with Corey."

"You know I run this. Of course, he'll say yes. My husband is a legitimate businessman."

"It's settled. I'll have my lawyer draw up the papers, and if you'd like me to, I'll review the contract for the house."

"Okay, help me off this chair 'cause I gotta pee."

She turns before leaving the kitchen, hugs me, and says, "Sis, I don't know how to thank you. You've been so good to us. I love you."

"The love is mutual."

After dinner, we get comfortable in the living room, where I sit beside her on the couch to be close to my godson. We talk about baby names while watching *Madea Goes to Jail*. When my godson starts moving around, Synearra places my hands on her belly bringing forth unexpected emotions.

In bed that night, feeling more empty than lonely in yet another strange bed, unable to sleep, instead of mulling over my regrets, climbing out of bed, fix a cup of chamomile tea, and eat another slice of pound cake. I wander into what was once

Elijah's office to review the contract for the Strahle Avenue house. After a few minor markups and suggesting a negotiation on the price, it feels as if I've done them justice.

Sitting cross-legged on the floor, I peel back the tape from one of the smaller boxes. Inside is a clear bag marked PERSONAL BELONGINGS, which holds the items that weren't cut from him that day, including Gucci loafers, a MacBook, his wallet, prescription sunglasses, an Apple watch, and a cell phone.

From a second larger box, I remove and unzip his duffle bag, which I recall was sitting on the floor of the rental car. Inside I remove, a pink gift box, once tied with a ribbon, has been resealed with duct tape; this, I imagine, was my Valentine's gift. After cutting the tape away, I find a rich brown leather-bound book nestled inside. Gently turning the gold-trimmed parchment pages, I am brought to tears to see that interspersed between color photos of Elijah and me are black-and-white photos of our parents. In calligraphy on the last of the almost 60 pages, he wrote, *"These are the people on whom our love is built; I want our future to mirror it; love, your husband, Elijah."*

Over the next few days, I relished the valuable time spent with Synearra and Corey. Together, we devised a comprehensive punch list of upgrades for Barren Hill while Corey diligently liaised with the contractor to construct a timeline for the completion of the projects. To equip myself for overseeing the house during Synearra's postpartum recovery, I fully immersed myself in the day-to-day activities. In addition to signing off as owners of Barren Hill, they boldly extended an offer for the Strahle Avenue house, and the thrill was unmatched when their offer was accepted. It was a moment of pure excitement and joy as we celebrated our successful house transactions with champagne for Corey and me and sparkling cider for Synearra.

As my family enjoys a Saturday night out, I delve into my Sugar Hill findings on my computer. An unexpected email dump from Aunt Millie reveals troubling information. Upon scrutinizing the numbers linked to Trent's business account, it becomes evident that Sasha's husband was the true owner of *My Travel Agent*. This revelation points to potential money laundering orchestrated by Aunt Millie and Cranston, their CFO, who attempted to conceal the illicit activities by labeling transactions as building materials for their various properties. Moreover, clients seemed to have overpaid for trips in cash. This discovery mirrors my previous encounter with money laundering for Lady Zoë. While an email could suffice, I feel compelled to contact Sasha via text. Unfortunately, there is no response.

My curiosity then leads me back to Elijah's boxes from his house in Colorado. I plug in his phone and sit on the floor next to the outlet, and when the screen lights up, I'm disappointed to see the factory setting and not a picture of us. Since there is no passcode when I tap on his messages app, the folder is empty, his voicemail folder is empty, and so are his email account and photos. There aren't even names in his contact list. The Feds had to have wiped it clean. What did they think I would find, or what were they looking for? It's almost as if he didn't exist.

Finally, mustering the courage to open the box from the morgue, taped on top of the box is an envelope with his death certificate under the name of Malcolm Moore. Inside, where I expect to find an urn, there's a wooden box holding a plastic bag filled with gray ashes. This is my breaking point.

Needing an escape, a search through the kitchen cabinets results in a bottle of Don Julio. Taking a water glass and the bottle to my room, I pour myself a drink and take a big gulp of the burning liquid. After the third glass, I pull out my phone to call Lady Zoë.

"*My Love*, I'm so glad you called. Come to Manhattan tonight!"

"I can't do this anymore; you're draining me. Your parties, us, moving your money; I can't do it."

"*My Love* we're good together. We know how to make money and we know how to make love.

The tears fall, and I don't care if she hears the choking in my voice. "It's over. It's me and Bryce now."

"I will not allow you to be with him! You belong to me, I love…" is the last thing I hear before I disconnect the phone and spend the rest of the night drinking and crying until I pass out.

Two days later, I go to the Ritz Carlton residences in Center City, where Bryce casually waits for me in the open doorway of his penthouse, wearing sweatpants and a long-sleeved tee.

I hug him lightly and plant a kiss on his cheek.

"I'm not going to break."

"How you feeling?"

He pulls up his shirt to show me a discolored, bruised, and still swollen wound. "Pretty much healed up. Therapy at NovaCare for the next few weeks."

We step inside, and I sit at the dining room table where he's set out a bottle of Jordan. He pours me a glass.

"I was concerned when you weren't responding to my calls or text messages. When did you get back?"

It starts with a lie. "Yesterday but I wanted to spend some time with Synearra." Noticing he hasn't poured a glass for himself, I ask, "You're not drinking?"

"Still on meds. Have you decided where you're going to live?"

"Barren Hill for now."

"You should be staying here."

The doorbell interrupts our conversation. "I ordered pizza from Joe's and made a salad with my mother's homemade dressing."

"I didn't think you were the type of man that cooked."

"My mother told me long ago that if I could cook, clean, and wash my own clothes, I'd only need a woman for one thing."

"I'm not sure that makes me feel good," I respond, questioning why a mother would give her son that advice. "You've never mentioned your mother or your family."

Not turning to look at me, he states, "Mother died last year; family been gone."

He places slices of pizza on our plates, dishes a beautifully layered green salad into bowls, and drizzles them with dressing before taking a seat at the head of the table.

"Sometimes I feel like I don't even know you, the real you, under the business persona," I say, anxious to bite into the gooey pizza while he sits at the head of the table.

"I'm a man who's managed to amass large sums of money for myself and my clients. You already know that, so what question do you really want answered?"

"Have you slept with Lady Zoë?"

Not even pausing in his reply, he answers, "I would never sleep with that freak."

I stop myself from telling him not to refer to her in that way, it isn't her fault with how she was born. But this isn't the time to defend the woman I'm trying to break away from.

"Then how did you get involved with her," I ask, now on my second slice of pizza and second glass of wine.

"One of her clients introduced me to her a few months before I met you."

"You were part of the Russian gun trafficking?"

"I was aware of it."

"Why didn't you stop it, stop Elijah? Maybe if you had, he'd be here."

Focused on eating his salad, without looking up, he tells me, "Say what you wanna say."

"Why is Elijah dead and—"

"And I'm alive?"

"I didn't mean that."

"Yes, you did, and it's a fair question. Contract killers only kill who they're paid to kill. I was in the way. You're also asking because you think I was involved, which I'm sure is an idea Sémile suggested."

"No, you're wrong, but you must be suspicious of Lady Zoë."

"You don't need to worry about her. She's indebted to me now. What you need to come to terms with is that she's in love with you."

Ignoring what I know is true, I ask, "How is she indebted to you?"

"She was in a bad situation with the wrong people, and I bailed her out. What I don't understand is why you're still involved with Sémile. I'm sure he has an opinion about me."

He has no idea I haven't talked to Sémile, which seems to irritate him more than my sexual trysts.

"He told me not to trust you," I admit while pulling cheese away from the crust of my pizza.

"I didn't have Elijah murdered, nor did Lady Zoë."

We eat silently, me picking at the salad and him folding his pizza. Meanwhile, on my own I'm halfway through the bottle of wine.

"Tell me about the women who've been in your life."

"I was engaged once, in love, and when I broke from corporate, she couldn't wait until the dust settled."

"That's it?"

"There were some habits of mine which you weren't privy to."

"What kind of habits?"

"I like to watch women. A voyeur, I was a voyeur."

I'm sure my squinted eyes show my confusion. "You're a peeping tom?"

"That's perverted. What I do, or what used to turn me on, was watching women engage in intimate behaviors, which doesn't always mean sexual. The simplest gestures can turn a man on. For that reason, I invested in women who could satisfy my sexual appetite. How's that for getting to know me?"

"And where do I fit in? Have you watched me? We've only had sex two, maybe three times. How do you know it's not sex driving you this time?"

"Isabella, you haven't been happy for a long time, and I plan to change that. I can set you up in a lifestyle you deserve and one that will make you happy."

"We both know happily ever after doesn't exist and I certainly don't need your money."

"Doesn't mean you don't deserve it. Listen, Elijah's actions put you in a bad situation, and now that you're mine, I plan to change that."

"So, I'm the prize now that Elijah's dead?"

"You're a prize to me; obviously, you were to him too. Is anything wrong with that?"

"Who killed my husband? That's what I want to know."

"Your husband, knowing the consequences of being a federal informant, risked his life for you, and I took the chance of making a fucken fool of myself for the same reason, love."

Startling me, he knocks over my glass of wine, reaches across the table, and pulls my face toward his, kissing me with more force than necessary. In return, I stand up and go to him, allowing his face to rest against my stomach, to which he mumbles, "I know I can satisfy you."

His hands slide under my skirt and begin to slide down my panties. Tilting his chin up, I find his lips, while at the same time, I gasp when he inserts two fingers inside me. Our passionate kiss brings back memories of our sinful lovemaking when I'd allowed him to manipulate my body to his satisfaction. The difference between what I did with Bryce and what I've done with Lady Zoë and White Magic is that one is a performance, and with Bryce, it could be love. To block out these jumbled thoughts, I drop to my knees, grab hold of and swallow his hardness that, within moments, softens inside my mouth. Violently, he pushes me away.

"Fuck! Get up!"

"What is it? What's wrong?"

"This is what's wrong," he says, holding his limp dick. "I can't believe this shit is happening."

Shocked and confused, I fall back against the table, mumbling, "It happens."

Angered, he stands up, his chair falling to the floor when he yells, "Not the fuck to me! If I can't satisfy you, what the fuck kind of man does that make me?"

Instead of pouring a glass of wine, which he's not supposed to drink, he swigs from the bottle.

"Your sexual performance doesn't define your manhood."

"Only a woman would say that."

"Maybe it's too soon. I'm okay," I lie, not sure how to handle the orgasms, fighting to be set free.

"I've never left a woman unsatisfied. That's not who I am."

"Tonight, I'm afraid I'll be your first."

Mother's Day

Sasha

Filled with memories of the last time Trent and I boarded this flight from Salt Lake to JFK and tormented by what lay ahead, I swallow an Ambien from my freshly refilled prescription.

The ride through rush hour traffic is sobering as if I'm in a funeral procession. That's when subconsciously I realize I've returned to dressing in all black. Maybe that's the Italian in me, feeling as if I must appear to be in mourning forever.

Until I get further direction from the stranger who texted me, my plan is to call Briana to see if we can resolve her issues. I'm willing to write her a check, maybe even turn over another property, anything except relinquishing Sugar Hill. Regardless of what she gets, it won't bring her father back. There is the option of telling her and TJ about the scavenger hunt Trent has me on, but I'll wait until I know more.

While huddled in the back seat of the town car, lost in my thoughts, my phone rings.

"Azmar?"

"Sasha, I'm calling to beg your forgiveness for being unresponsive. I was fasting for Ramadan and then went with my brothers to Mecca."

"You truly don't need to apologize."

"I must. I promised you I'd stay in touch, and no man should make a promise that's not within his power to keep."

Until now, we'd been texting infrequently, then, as the kids say, 'he ghosted me.' To deflect from his promise and the quiet he brings to my uneasiness, I ask, "How was your pilgrimage?"

"Alhamdulillah! It was the first time in years I made the pilgrimage with my brothers."

"Then that was a blessing."

"I thought of you often. Please don't be offended; I picked up something for you during my trip. I considered shipping it to The Lodge at Sugar Hill, but I did not want to make you uncomfortable or be disrespectful."

"Why would you do that?"

"It reminded me of you, and if you have a postal box, I can have my assistant pop it in the mail."

"I'm not in Utah, I just landed at JFK."

The line goes quiet as I wait for him to respond.

"Azmar?"

"Sasha, I'm in the Hamptons, and it would be an honor to see you again. I'm sure it's not easy returning to New Jersey."

"Give me a few days to handle some never-ending business, and I'll call you; will that work?"

"Perfect. *beurre noisette parfait.*"

After I hang up, I promise myself that the next time we speak, I'll get his last name so I can at least google the man.

When the driver slows to a stop in front of The Sandora, Rahim rushes outside to open the car door, greeting me with eyes that convey pity.

"Ms. Sasha, I missed you!" he hugs me, pulls back, and

continues, "We're so glad you're here, that you're home. Are you good?" he asks before hugging me again.

I've learned that as a grieving widow, it's my job to comfort others. "Yes, I'm good."

He reaches to take my carry-on bag from the driver. "Allow me to assist you."

"How've you been, Rahim? How's your family?" I ask, recalling how humbled he was to serve as one of Trent's pallbearers.

"We're good, we miss you and Mister…. I'm sorry."

"No, don't, don't ever be sorry. I know Mr. Trent was your *main man*," I tease as that's how they referred to each other.

Rahim updates me on the condo gossip, yet he doesn't tell me that someone is waiting for me inside.

When we step off the elevator on my floor, the door to my condo unexpectedly swings open. I almost anticipate seeing Trent, instead, I'm greeted by Arshell and the aroma of whatever food she's cooking.

After we cry and talk incoherently over each other, she says, "I hope you're hungry. And why the hell are you still wearing black?"

I shrug my shoulders. "I guess it felt appropriate coming back here."

"First, you gotta change out of this black shit cause we got some eating, drinking, and catching up to do."

Changing into a pair of black tights and one of Trent's NY Giants sweatshirts fills me with sadness as it still holds the faint scent of his deodorant.

Removing the lid from a pot of her infamous 15-bean soup, I ask, "Whatcha cooking?"

"Cornbread in the oven. Now sit down and tell me how it's going at the house."

"Painful, let's not talk about it."

"You're right. Let's talk about why you're here. What's with all the cloak and dagger? Did you find out anything more? Wait, I hope you didn't discover that Negro had another family hiding out in Jersey?"

"Not yet, but I feel better having you here."

"Where else would I be?"

Arshell serves our bowls while I head to the liquor cabinet and uncork a $900 bottle of Rothschild that Trent had saved for a special occasion. This is that occasion.

We say grace over our meal, and I immediately dip my buttery cornbread into the steaming bean bowl.

"Gurl, you was hungry."

"We should start serving beans at Sugar Hill. Wait, shouldn't you be home getting ready for vacation? I mean South Africa for a month; you must be excited."

"Don't remind me. I mean I'm excited, a month though is a long time to be away from home and from you, especially now. You could come with us."

I shake my head at the thought of traveling so far and being away for a month.

We tap glasses, and I toast, "To friendship that never ends."

"Now, let's get to the good stuff. Tell me about you and this gigolo in Costa Rica."

"I thought you wanted to hear about your niece," I tease.

"That can wait."

"You promise not to get all judgy?"

"That's what I came for, now who is he? I mean, where'd he come from?"

"Like I told you, the ocean, Trent's ashes, I don't know."

"That's some crazy shit. Go on, how was he, the sex, I wanna know?"

I scoop out a spoonful of beans, then press my slice of cornbread into the delicious broth.

"I told you all that on the phone."

"Yea, sis you were crying and shit, I need to hear it again."

I share the details about him picking me up from the airport, cutting my hair, and spending the night with him. I refrain from telling her he's in New York.

"Damn, I haven't been with another man in a hundred years."

She refills our glasses.

"Excuse me; what about that mechanic you were fooling around with a few years back."

"That was some risky shit and it was exciting until you made me shut it down."

"It's my job to let you know when your slip is hanging," I remind her, referring to our way of looking out for each other. "Honestly though, what's up with your niece?"

"She's always been a bit different, so don't expect her to listen until she needs to hear."

"That lil bitch left the lodge without saying goodbye, and she was supposed to give my finances some kind of forensic overview; all I got was an email saying she wanted to schedule a Zoom."

"Isabella does her own thing, and to hear my mother-in-law tell it, she doesn't even need to work. She received a payout from her job when she left Houston and picks up clients when she feels like it."

"If she weren't so unreliable, I'd probably like her."

"Yeah, well, you're stuck with me, oh, and your *friend* Parker."

"Be nice. C'mon, let's go to bed. I need to be ready for tomorrow."

"Gurl, we are not sleeping until we crack this bottle of bourbon," she tells me, motioning to a bottle of Widow Jane, "and what is it 8:30? Stop acting like an ole lady."

"I can't drink that shit. We just drank a bottle of wine."

"If we ain't drinking bourbon, then we're smoking this," she says, pulling a joint from her purse.

In the morning, while Arshell fixes a full breakfast, as directed, I text the anonymous number to receive the address to where I'm supposed to arrive by 11:00 a.m.

We book an Uber Black for the day and drive down I-95 to Middlesex, New Jersey. While on the way, I make unnecessary calls to check on things at Sugar Hill. When the driver arrives at the Middlesex Medical Complex parking lot, we head to building 645 at the rear, with an overhead sign that reads Lavery Labs.

The driver opens our door, I hesitate, saying to Arshell, "Maybe it's better if I don't know."

Squeezing my hand, she promises, "If there's a woman in there trying to claim Trent, I'm not too old to beat a bitch down."

Me, I'm too tired. I want to grieve like a normal widow.

We clear lobby security and are directed to the fifth floor. When the elevator door opens, I brace myself to meet a woman who may have been Trent's mistress. Coming toward us is a petite Asian-American woman, probably in her 30s, dressed in pink scrubs, with strands of black hair falling from under her mesh cap. Could she be the sender of the cryptic text messages and possibly the one he was meeting the day he died? I cannot put another foot forward. I hate her.

The woman's eyes land on Arshell, whose stance dares her to question my not being alone. Finally, she extends her hand and says, "Ms. Sasha, I'm Dr. Lee's assistant. I'm so sorry to hear about Mr. Trent. Please come this way."

Following behind the assistant, I sigh with relief.

"R. Lee Jian Chemist," Arshell reads aloud from the nameplate on the closed glass door.

Inside, I'm at least satisfied to see that Dr. Lee is a balding Asian man of average height with a slight paunch under his lab coat. He wears glasses barely covering his eyes and stares past me to Arshell.

He greets me with a more than generous handshake, pressing both my hands into his as if this were a friendly visit. Then, he turns as I introduce him to Arshell.

"Please have a seat."

The assistant stands behind us, offering the usual beverages.

"We're not thirsty," Arshell quips, her eyes reviewing Dr. Lee's credentials filling the wall behind his desk.

Uninterested in his backstory, I ask, "What was your business with my husband?"

"Let me start by saying your husband was my dearest friend. In high school, I was the immigrant who became the brunt of all bullies' jokes and pranks. Trent defended me and helped me learn the language. After high school, he went onto Seton Hall, and I went to Princeton."

He ignores my rolling eyes.

"Throughout your husband's career as an electrician and then as President of the IBEW and mine as a chemist for NIH, we shared many meals discussing our work. When Trent transitioned into politics, my wife and I attended one of his fundraisers. I remember you clearly; as the publicist, you had to leave early that night for your athlete client, Phoenix Carter. I recall your beautiful dreadlocks."

I try to remember him. We met so many people during that time that it's impossible to recall them all, clearly, he remembers me.

"During Trent's second run for senator, I was lobbying for him behind the scenes, offering a slush fund and contributing the max to his pact. Then the rumors started circulating, and that's when the bottom fell out for him. By then, I'd opened this place, and my research was gaining traction and getting early approvals in its patient testing phase."

I do not like this squirrely man, and I hate that he's about to reveal secrets my husband kept from me.

I let out a breath I've been holding to ask, "Did you know about him selling drugs in college?"

"I begged him to tell the truth, to admit that I was the one supplying the drugs, but he simply wouldn't allow me to accept the blame. Your husband felt it was more important that I not lose my license and patents. You see, the work I'm doing is groundbreaking, and it will help many people."

Arshell chimes in, "What are you working on? It's not as if you've cured cancer."

"Bringing a new drug to the market isn't an easy feat, and while Senator, your husband worked with pharmaceutical lobbyists to push my project through. Then, about three years ago, when he was in town for Father's Day, we met at the lab to discuss my long-awaited project, and since he trusted me, he offered to try it."

I distinctly remember not traveling with Trent during that year. Instead, I went to LA to see Owen while he came to Jersey to visit Briana and TJ.

"Are you saying you had him try a chemical you made in your lab? If so, then you poisoned my husband," I tell him, my voice rising at the very thought of it.

"Sasha, please calm down, let him finish."

"For the past decade, I've dedicated myself to developing what I firmly believe is a remedy for thousands of men who struggle with erectile dysfunction. What sets this breakthrough apart is its remarkable duality as both a cure and a sexual enhancement drug."

"How does it differ from Viagra and Cialis," Arshell asks, her pharmaceutical background on the ready.

"The components are mostly the same, as it also sends a signal to the brain. However, the enzymes I've integrated go further in regulating not only the blood flow to a man's penis but also center on a woman's hormones. I like to say it works on the human emotion called desire. For a woman, that means a controlled heightening of woman's hormones and an increased blood flow to the clitoris with time-released ease. For both sexes, it can last 8-10 days in the bloodstream without causing priapism, which would send a man to the hospital."

Arshell and I are stunned into silence.

"It has excelled in all clinical trials, and the only reason the FDA hasn't granted its approval for market release is their current challenge in establishing regulations for it."

"What's the name of this drug?" Arshell asks.

"Eluvient will bring billions to the pharma industry, hence the reason why the project has been frozen."

"Why would Trent take this? He wasn't impotent. His doctor told me he was in perfect shape."

"After your husband's prostrate scare, he began using it, and the reason why it's been such a success is that you probably never even noticed a difference in him or yourself."

I ponder the possibility that my heightened sexual drive after Trent's death was a result of the drug still in my system. How long and how frequently had Trent been administering it to me? Had he given it to me the night before he died?

Deflated, I ask, "How would he have given it to me without my noticing?"

"It's liquid, an eyedropper. It's tasteless and time-released according to a person's biological makeup. Two drops for men, one drop for women."

"Is that what killed him? What were the side effects?" Arshell asks.

"No, my friend died of a heart attack, not due to Eluvient. I've perfected it, so there are no side effects."

I can see through his carefully chosen words and the sly grin he's trying to conceal that he's proud of what he's created.

"And how much do these drops, cost?" Arshell asks.

"It became a business quite by accident, yet it's been very lucrative for all of us. For the individual looking to purchase, $1,250 for 0.5 oz."

It's beginning to add up; Trent wasn't having an affair. He was selling unlicensed drugs. That's how he could afford this $13K Birken bag in my lap, the house he's having refurbished near Rittenhouse Square, the pearls, a Richard Hunt sculpture, the cash, and whatever else I haven't found.

"Allow me to show you."

He beckons for the assistant, who glides into the office with a tray cradling a dozen vials containing a pale-yellow substance filled halfway.

He smiles when he says, "The street name Trent gave it was, 'Get Right.'"

"Is this shit why he was at Teterboro?"

The assistant speaks up, "Mr. Trent was arranging a private flight for the two of you to Costa Rica."

"That's a lie! We have a travel agent. Now, who else was distributing this poison?"

"I don't know. We kept that separate."

"I could send you to jail for this."

"You could. But it would implicate your husband, yourself, and possibly your lodge and, sorry to say, your daughter-in-law."

"That bitch," I mumble, realizing that Deidre understands the value of the product as does Arshell when she asks, "If you're Lavery Labs, then why'd you have someone call Sasha for further testing of his tissues?"

"It was a test to see how much she knew."

Unable to stomach another question or answer from him, I tell Arshell, "Let's go, I can't sit here any longer."

"You will have to visit the P.O. Box in Italy. He told me he wanted to keep something safe for you."

That's when I recall the key.

"We haven't been to Italy since our honeymoon."

"I can't answer that question. Before you decide how you feel about our work here, calm your emotions and think through the implications."

Arshell and I exchange glances.

"And take these too," the assistant urgently insists, thrusting three neatly packaged vials into my hands. "Have someone run tests, and you'll see."

Back in the car, my anger explodes, screaming and crying incoherently. I spit on my ring finger, twisting and turning to release my wedding rings. Next, I unclasp the Akoya pearl necklace and drop it onto Arshell's lap. Every item he's gifted me, I'm sure, was purchased with drug money.

"Sasha what are you doing, don't be foolish; I know you're angry, but like he said we have to think this through."

"Angry? I'm hurt and I'm pissed the fuck off! He betrayed me. I'm turning them in, I don't care who it affects."

"At least he didn't have another family."

"Arshell this is serious! I need to see a doctor, get blood work done. All that fucking we did; it wasn't even real. How could he leave me with all this?"

"What about the PO Box?"

"I think I've discovered enough. My husband was pushing sex-enhancement drugs and using them on me without my permission. What kind of man does that? We're not in fucken high school."

"Give me one of the vials; I know a urologist in Philly, Cynthia Lampley. I went to college with her, and she's known all over the country for her work with men who have erectile dysfunctions. Maybe we could reach out to her; she'd be discreet."

"Take it! I'm not reaching out to anyone else. It ends here. I'm done with Trent and that fucken Deidre! How could he involve her, that's my grandchildren's mother; what if she'd gone to jail, Owen would never forgive me."

My fuzzy brain tries to figure out who besides Deidre was pushing his Get Right drug. It hits me, the other person is Ginger. If Isabella had ever gotten back to me, maybe she could've followed the money trail and discovered something, but she, too, failed me.

"Please don't do anything crazy. Wait until I get back. We'll figure it out."

Knowing that Arshell has a train to catch and, subsequently, a flight in the morning to the Ivory Coast, I text *My Travel Agent* requesting travel arrangements back to Sugar Hill to ensure I won't do anything crazy.

For two days, maybe three, I stay in bed, ordering take-out that I barely eat yet drink whatever alcoholic beverage left in the condo. Then, one morning, the shrill ring of the house phone wakes me up.

When I answer, a frantic Arshell yells, "Sasha, why haven't you been answering the phone? Where are you?"

"I'm in bed, in Jersey." I try to sound coherent. "I need to sleep."

"You need to get back to the lodge and get on with your life."

"What life?" I ask, then disconnect the call.

Sometime later, or maybe it's been another day, I hear someone calling my name, "Sasha! Sasha, where are you? What the hell is all this shit, and why is it so damn dark in here?"

Having no idea how much time has passed, I squint in the darkened room to see Briana standing at the foot of my bed.

"What do *you* want?" I ask, pulling the covers up to my chin.

"Arshell is worried about you."

"And she sent you? YOU KNOW WHAT, BRIANA, TAKE WHATEVER YOU WANT, TAKE IT, AND GET OUT!"

Instead of leaving, she sits on the bed too close to me. I consider kicking her, but I don't have the energy to lift my legs.

"Sasha, I'm sorry, I swear I am. When my dad died, I was hurting so bad, and you were the only person I could blame. He'd be so disappointed to know I was hurting you. I'm so sorry; you've always been good to me. Please forgive me. I love you, Sasha."

When we both start crying, Briana uses the corner of the bed sheet to wipe my tears and snotty nose.

"Your father he, he left us with all this stuff—"

"We can get rid of everything, whatever you wanna do, but you gotta get outta this bed."

She stands up, offering me her hand, "And please I'm begging you, please take a shower."

Through my blur, I see Briana as the 16-year-old teenager I met who worshipped her father and with whom she shared a matching birthmark on the right side of their eyes.

"What's today?"

"Saturday."

The shower's sensation jolts me awake, and I stand there for close to 30 minutes, letting the steaming water soothe my body and wash away the tears streaming down my cheeks. I hear Briana entering the bathroom, and through the semi-transparent doors, I witness her clutching my bottle of Ambien. "I'm getting rid of these," she declares.

Rather than convincing her not to, I watch as swirl down the toilet bowl, knowing I can call CVS and get a refill.

While I get dressed in black jeans and a white button-down shirt, Briana catches me up on her life as a newly married woman and, the recent activities of children. Briana has also made coffee, and I watch as she searches the cabinets and refrigerator for food she won't find.

"What do you think about me turning the condo over to TJ?"

"That'll keep him off my couch, but he might have other plans. He's traveling back from Bali and has informed me he's found a woman whose as adventurous as he is."

"A real relationship? Your Dad would be ecstatic to hear that."

"You're right; he'd be asking for more grandkids. I know it's only been a few months, but do you think you'll date again? My Dad wouldn't want you to be lonely. Seeing you today, I don't think you can survive being alone."

"I'm shocked to hear *you* say that. It's way too early even to consider dating. I mean, I'm not going on a dating site."

"Maybe not, but you have to level up a little bit cause I've never seen you look so beat down."

"Thanks, Bree, and by the way, this is the worst coffee ever."

"My wife tells me the same thing. Let's get outta here. It's like being in a tomb."

"Where are we going?"

"It might be time for a new look," she says, rubbing her hands through my hair, "These naps, I mean curls, are a little tight."

"A makeover is not gonna solve my problems," I say without sharing her father's secrets which are now mine to keep.

"You don't have problems. You're mourning the loss of your husband; now let's get outta here 'cause you can't be walking around with a vagina neck."

Clueless about what she means I can only shake my head.

"You know, when your neck starts stretching from fat and you get all that loose skin until it hangs like a vagina. I'm not about to let that happen to you."

"Oh shit, that's one I'll have to tell Arshell about."

As Briana takes the wheel, I ensure everything is in order with Marquise and then inform Adam that Briana will relinquish her contest to the Will. In addition, I text Arshell offering a sincere apology for my rudeness and to let her know that I am currently with Briana.

Our first stop on the road to my makeover is Vtox Intimate Health and Wellness, where we indulge in microneedling facials and a Loni Loni massage. It doesn't stop there; I'm also treated to a Vtox spa and Brazilian wax.

As much as I'm ready for a nap, our next stop is her wife's salon, *Scissor Sisters*, where we are warmly welcomed with champagne, chocolates, and a spread of appetizers. All of this to convince me to straighten and color my hair. Reluctantly, I agree. Little did I know that while I was being pampered, Briana was out shopping for five new pieces of clothing that weren't black, one of which was a stunning Off-White leather shirtdress that she insisted I change into.

By now, I'm starved so Briana suggests we head to her place in Ft. Lee for some leftovers. Upon arriving, I am greeted by a heartwarming surprise – Owen, Deidre, my grandchildren, TJ, and his new girlfriend are all here.

On Sunday morning, which happens to be a sunny Mother's Day, I find Deidre in the kitchen making breakfast. When they were dating, my son nicknamed her 'Black Beauty,' referring to her blemish-free smooth skin and her hourglass figure, which she has maintained even after having children. Given her appearance and the addition of Get Right, it's no wonder she won my son back after her infidelities.

Sidling up next to her while she's putting potatoes in the pan for home fries, I whisper in her ear, "Got a minute to talk?"

"Sure, Sasha," she says, then yells for Owen to keep an eye on the food.

"You okay," she asks.

"Not really."

She follows me outside, but we're only a few steps from the house when I get to the point of asking, "Were you selling drugs for Trent, *Get Right*? For him and Dr. Lee?"

She stops, I keep walking. From behind, I hear, "Sasha, I won't lie; I didn't know how to tell you."

"Why would you risk your license and your freedom to sell drugs?"

"It wasn't like that. We weren't hustling on the streets. Trent came to me and wanted me to meet Dr. Lee to see if it was safe, and I promise you there were no side effects; that drug is the perfect solution."

"Solution to what, your marriage? You couldn't have been selling it for financial gain because when I asked Owen, he always said the two of you were solid."

"And you believed him? Of course you did, he's your son."

"How'd you two devise a plan to sell it."

"We had a few people test it and it took off."

"Were you using it too? Is that why you were fucking outside of your marriage? Couldn't get enough?"

"Sasha, don't do that."

"I stay out of you, and Owen's business, but this is affecting my life, and I need answers."

"I'll tell you whatever you wanna know."

"Have you been feeding it to Owen?"

"Once or twice. He knew what he was taking but I didn't share where it came from."

We walk in silence as I try to decide what's next. "I want it to stop. I warned Dr. Lee that I would go to the police, the DEA, or whatever department handles that kind of crime."

"I know, he called me, you can't get in the middle of this, too many people would be implicated, including Sugar Hill."

"You both keep threatening me with that."

"It's not a threat, but if the cops find out, they'll investigate your finances with a fine-tooth comb. You don't want that."

"Who else is in your network?"

"I don't know. Trent would never tell me. I'm sure someone

at Sugar Hill was handling it, and maybe someone in Philly. He never sold it directly to anyone."

"So, you're going to continue being a drug dealer around my grandchildren and my son? Is that the life you want to settle into?"

"No! Dr. Lee put a hold on things until he speaks with you again."

"I have no reason to speak to that man ever again, but I'm warning you, and you can tell Dr. Lee that this ends now, the manufacturing and the selling, all of it! Whatever batch you have left or whatever's cooking, I give you one month to get rid of it, or I go to the police regardless of the consequences."

"I get it."

When we return to the house, the kids are running around, and the adults are in the kitchen. Owen, of course, is pleased that Deidre and I have spoken, thinking I'm sure that we're shoring up their marriage. How can I tell him the truth? While they all sit down to play UNO, I sneak off and call Azmar.

Operation Unicorn

Houston, TX

Isabella

After leaving Hobby Airport, I first stop at the Lucid Building in Tanglewood. It's been two years since I visited The Source Foundation's office.

Betty Geffen and I had never been friends. Yet, in the last two years, we built a foundation to provide young mothers with the necessities to raise children in healthy environments, including housing, proper medical care, and a fully stocked food pantry in the heart of the 4th Ward. The Source also donates money to charities that align with our business model. We can only offer our services in Houston, and currently, we have four townhouses under renovation, which will be filled with families once they pass a screening process. We plan to grow until we build the same model in Philadelphia and Costa Rica. In addition to government funding, most of our funds come from ultra-wealthy donors. Betty refers to them as Limousine Liberals, who are willing to donate all the money you need as long as you don't move next door to them. She would know since she is one of them.

"Welcome home," greets my unlikely partner, who, at 69, has no plans of embracing her gray hair, yet she does appear to be spending time with a personal trainer, which is more than I can say for myself.

"This is nice, Betty."

"It's not much, but we're growing."

"Slow growth is better than none."

Betty rises behind her desk, and we sit at the small conference table. There are two iPads, and she passes one to me.

"How are you after that awful tragedy?"

"Glad to be home. Thanks for offering to help," I say, having not responded to her text message asking if I needed an attorney who could practice in Costa Rica.

"Before you tell me why you're *really* here, I need to share a few significant financial updates."

"I pray they're good."

"Turn on the iPad, and you'll notice that we've seen an uptick in donations from multiple sources, some identifiable, others anonymous. If it keeps up, in another year, maybe even six months, we could begin getting people in place to search for opportunities in Philadelphia or Costa Rica."

Looking at the spreadsheet, it's obvious what she's referring to.

"What's this first one here? I ask, pointing to a recurring donation for $4,999."

"We've been receiving that since January. I'm surprised you hadn't asked about it but you had a lot on your plate."

We glance up when the receptionist taps on the door, then enters with a tray of Aperol spritzes, t-cut sandwiches, and diced fruit. Although Betty is managing a nonprofit, her privilege still shows through.

"I guess I didn't pay attention. Could it be someone in your circle?"

"And not take the credit?" she asks, amused that her friends would even consider such a thing.

"What about this one? Moore or Less Foundation. Seven hundred and fifty thousand dollars? That's not anonymous."

"You're right. It came through two weeks ago and is in a revocable trust, with accompanying documentation stating that if we don't use it in five years, we'll lose it. Client privilege doesn't allow the law firm to divulge the benefactor. Maybe it was someone you know, one of your clients."

"It sounds familiar, and honestly, I don't have that many clients, so I need to start paying closer attention to our business. Did they stipulate how the money should be used?"

"No, only that it be used in five years. I've been checking out a few nonprofits in Philadelphia to see who could use our assistance; it won't be hard, especially if we go the housing route. What do you suggest?"

"Let me think about it. I'll be here for a week."

"The other thing you might want to think about along with the disbursement of our funds, is considering what we're bringing in, we should probably start taking a salary, albeit a small one. You should also consider leasing an apartment in the area in case we need justification for state funding."

"Thanks, Betty, it's exactly what I'll do, and you can expect me to be more involved since my client list is nil."

"It'll be nice to have you involved again. Now why don't you tell me what brought you to our offices? You mentioned on the phone that there was a situation. Who are we ending?"

"I'm calling it Operation Unicorn. I don't want you involved, but I need to talk with someone who understands finances and its legalities."

"Either way, I'm in."

"Zoë Inc.! is the name of my client's business; from what I've seen and handled, she's guilty of money laundering, tax evasion, and wire fraud."

"What's the business?"

"Her clients pay cash to attend her exclusive parties."

"She provides prostitutes, like a madam?"

"No, she only charges to attend. Anything beyond that is out of her control."

"I don't see where she's breaking the law."

"Cash, no taxes. Money is washed through her legal businesses."

"I'm assuming you've witnessed these transactions and how significant is the fee?"

"$5,000 per person. The limit is 20 people who all have to sign an NDA."

"We could set a few traps to expose her. I've used a black-market company called Vesper, who can access her computers and phones and may even be able to access her bank accounts. First, I need to ask what your role is in all this."

"When I started with her, my role was to collect money at her parties, bag it, and hand it off to her assistant, Lemuel. I've never met him in person; all our communications are via email and text, and the drop is at a PO Box. Later, I discovered she owns a chain of vending machines and coin-operated laundry services in privately owned federal halfway houses across the East and West Coast. Like I said, it's messy, and I purposely kept it that way."

"Drugs?"

"No, she could be connected to the sale of illegal guns. At least her previous partner was."

"You keep going and she could get hit with a RICO. I can tell you this, when the Feds begin tracking the landmines you've placed, the IRS will immediately run an audit of all her businesses. I'm not sure how we can keep you clean. I mean what do you want out of it?"

"I want to be free of her."

"Does this have to do with your husband's murder?"

"I think she's responsible."

"Isabella, you may be going about it the wrong way."

"Explain."

Relieved to finally be able to tell someone my plan, while Betty talks, I eat the delicate sandwiches and delicious spritz.

"Think about this. What if you pick up one of those trap phones from a convenience store and periodically send her and this Lemuel messages threatening to expose them? Maybe you even threaten to publicly identify her clients if she doesn't shut down her parties. Start slow, build the tension that should lead to paranoia. This way, you stay clean. It's important you keep changing phones."

"How do you know about trap phones?"

"I may be white, but I'm no Karen, at least not anymore."

Before heading to Knowles Estate in Beaumont on the I-10, I stopped at Uptown Convenience to purchase an untraceable phone.

> To Lemuel: the feds will pursue when the numbers don't add up

> To LZ: your days as a Greek goddess will end soon

It's 98 degrees in Houston but knowing it's one of my favorite dishes, I find my mother at the stove seasoning a bubbling pot of chili. Before she notices me, I take pride in watching her petite body movements and listening to her hum to Gladys Knight's *Midnight Train to Georgia*. If not for the age difference, we could pass for twins. Unlike me, Mommy maintains her overall health by attending church on Sundays, taking daily walks, and traveling constantly. God, I miss this woman.

With both arms, I hug her from behind so tight that she's unable to turn around. When she does, she buries her face in my neck and cries, "Isabella Washington, I've you had me so worried about you."

She pushes me away, then dries her hands on her apron to get a good look.

"Come here, give me another hug, do you realize you could've been killed over there."

"Mommy don't even think like that. I made it home."

To provide her with some hope, I suggest, "What do you think about me getting a place here?"

"Here? Houston? Izzy, that would make me so happy. We can look tomorrow, or you can live here with me and Mr. Rich."

"Whatever you want, it's easier if we start online," I say, having committed myself to what might be the perfect investment property.

"RICH GET IN HERE, Izzy's home," she calls to Mr. Rich, who has already entered the kitchen and is hugging me.

"Welcome home, Isabella. You okay, 'cause I got some friends who could go down there and take care things."

I reassure him, but not myself when I reply, "The Feds are working it out."

"Alright, you two, no more violence. Let's get this food on the table."

Mommy removes a tray of buttery homemade rolls from the oven, and Mr. Rich pulls Caesar salad from the refrigerator. Meanwhile, I set the dining room table and pour sweet tea while Mommy scoops what I know is spicy chili into our bowls, topped with chopped onions, peppers, and shredded cheese.

Even with all the questions Mommy has for me, sharing dinner with them is a comfort I didn't realize I was missing. There are no lies to be told today. The media has reported on every aspect of my life. Her most pressing question is, who is Bryce Goodman?

"Izzy, I never heard you mention that man. Were you dating him? Is that why he was there?"

"I was seeing him after Elijah went away, but I'd cut him off. I never would've imagined him showing up to Esterillos."

"A man's got to be in love to search that far for a woman."

I wonder if Mr. Rich is right, could Bryce sincerely love me?

"I'm glad you weren't home. If something would've happened to you."

When she starts tearing up, Mr. Rich gives her his handkerchief and calms her down by saying, "Baby, don't get yourself agitated; your daughter is fine; she's right here."

I lean over and kiss her on the cheek. "It's okay, Mr. Rich is right, and tomorrow we're gonna look for me a place to live, at least part-time."

This makes her smile. It also makes her mention the one thing I haven't been able to produce that would bring her joy.

"Do you think you and this Bryce will be able to give me a grandchild before I leave this earth?"

"Mommy, I'm not even sure what our relationship will look like or if it's possible."

"You're still young, don't close down shop yet."

After dinner, while she and Mr. Rich go for their evening stroll, I clean up the kitchen, then retreat to my bedroom to shower and relax. Laying across the bed, scrolling through my phone without reading them, I delete two text messages from Ranger Johnson. I don't even want to entertain a friendship with that man.

My thoughts instead turn to Sasha, who, once again, I reach out to, leaving her a voice message. Since there's been no response, I can only assume that she's still pissed at me for leaving Sugar Hill so abruptly.

I've dozed off to sleep, but over the noise of the television, the phone buzzes with a call from White Magic.

"Izzy, where you at? I haven't heard from you."

"I'm in Houston. Is everything alright?"

"Yeah, I want you at the white party next weekend."

"Not happening. I mean, it wouldn't look right, and don't you think I've caused enough problems in your life?"

"That's bullshit, we grown folks, and ain't nobody gonna fuck with you up here. Plus, Hailey wants to see you, you know, make sure things are cool."

"Another bad idea."

"Look, you know training camp is coming up, and I wanna have some fun. Shit we ain't got nothing to hide."

We do have something to hide. It's one thing for it to be discovered that White Magic is cheating on his wife, but with me and Lady Zoë, that would be scandalous especially if people knew her true sexual identity.

"Alright, I'm not coming alone."

"Whatever you want, just be here and wear something to get my dick hard."

Over the next few days, amidst browsing MLS listings and visiting family, I am surrounded by love. On days when Mommy doesn't cook, Mr. Rich barbecues, and they even let me take charge of the kitchen for one night. After viewing several places and virtual tours, we both decide on a two-bedroom condo in the gated community of River Oaks. Parting ways with her the day after Mother's Day leaves us both sad until I perk up her spirits by suggesting she go shopping to decorate the condo.

On Monday morning, instead of having a driver pick me up, Bryce pulls up to the arrivals at PHL in a Graphite Gray S Class Mercedes. I assume his new toy is a way to boost his manhood. Either way, he's in a lighter mood than when I left him. When he steps out to get my luggage, his gait is more vigorous, and I'm pleased to see that he looks like his old self, wearing a crisp button-down white shirt, jeans, which he rarely wears, and a pair of Gucci loafers. More telling is him holding my hand during the drive, making me hopeful that tonight he will be able to satisfy me.

"How was your mother?"

"She misses me, and she's worried, of course. She asked about you."

"What did you tell her that I'm a stand-up guy?"

"That and a few other things. She's funny. I'm over 40, and she's still asking about a grandchild."

"Is that what you want?"

"It doesn't matter, I told her it was too late anyway."

When he doesn't respond I assume he has no interest in children. It's not as if we ever discussed the subject. Before I can ask how he feels about having children he asks, "Where am I taking you, Barren Hill or the Ritz?"

"You can take me anywhere in this car, but I'm going home with you for now."

"Good choice cause we have things to talk about. First, on the chopping block, I'm selling the concierge side of my business."

"How long has that been in the works? Wasn't that your first business, even before Wall Street?"

"The game keeps shifting, and I'm tired of the bullshit dealing with Ticketmaster, StubHub; there's too many options; shits not clean anymore."

"You offer more than tickets."

"Yeah, and I don't feel like managing all those requests anymore either."

"Who are you selling to?"

"I'm in talks with a local PR firm, Platinum Images. I don't want to talk business."

He squeezes my thigh and that's when I see the glint of a sparkly big face watch I've never seen before.

"Thinking maybe we could take a trip."

With Lady Zoë on the verge of erupting in outrage, now is the ideal time for us to embark on a journey, hopefully outside of the U.S.

"That's not what I expected. Where are we going? Please don't tell me Jamaica."

His hand makes it further up my thigh when he tells me, "I'm talking about an adult vacation, like touring the South of France or seeing the Northern Lights in Iceland."

"Damn, you put some thought into this."

"Shit, what's the point of having money if all you do is count it? And as for what I thought about every day was you, and how I could keep you satisfied."

"Since you wanna go places, I have a small ask."

"I'm listening."

"Accompany me to a party in the Hamptons."

His welcoming attitude goes dark, and he snatches his hand from my thigh.

"That's not my kind of fun."

"What is your kind of fun? Wait, you already knew about it."

"I received the same text you did."

I don't dare tell him White Magic called me, which makes me wonder how much he knows about my relationship with him and Lady Zoë. He alluded to it, but now I need to know the truth.

"Aren't some of those people your clients?"

"You've never seen me socialize with them, and I certainly don't succumb to their narcissistic dress codes."

"He's my client," I say, looking away from him and at the crowded Dilworth Plaza in front of us.

"Do you understand that you're asking me to socialize with a man you've been fucking. I mean, had he stayed any longer on the island, he might be dead too."

"That's a horrible thing to say, and his being on the island doesn't mean I was fucking him. And what about you? I don't remember you talking about your personal life. Do you think I believe all you did was watch women? How many women have you fucked like you used to fuck me?"

"All of 'em! I fucked 'em all if that's what you wanna know."

"And what about Lady Zoë? Did you fuck her too?"

"No, I leave that to you!"

The screeching car jerks to a stop in the carport. With both his hands gripping the steering wheel through tight lips, he tells me, "You fucken think the best way to start this relationship is with lies. And while we're speaking of the men in your life, I'm curious to know if you fucked Sémile when he came to your rescue."

It's evident to the valet that we're in a heated discussion, and he backs away from opening my door.

"Fuck you, Bryce, maybe you don't wanna go 'cause you know White Magic and Sémile can satisfy me, and you can't."

That strikes a chord.

With the car door open, he turns to me, warning, "You will regret saying that shit, now get out my fucken car."

Ditch Plains

Sasha

With music playing, emotions swinging high, laughter in the air, and periodic tears, together with Briana and TJ, we begin packing up the condo for TJ to move in. I've put aside a few items to ship back to Sugar Hill, and what TJ and Briana don't want, we donate to a local charity. The plan is for TJ to move in at the end of the summer once he meets his girlfriend's parents, which means this relationship is serious. Briana has managed to convince him to hire her as his decorator since, as of late, her new career is staging houses.

In our condo safe, we'd tucked away $5,000 in cash, and from that, I put $1,000 in an envelope for Rahim as a gesture of my gratitude for his assistance over the years, along with a pair of vintage Jordans Trent never wore. Owen reached out on FaceTime, putting in his bid for Trent's ridiculous number of hoodies. It seems there's a part of my husband for everybody.

Every time I consider broaching the subject of their father's deceit and illegal activities, I'm stopped by the fact that it will do neither of them any good. There's still the question of whether I was enough for Trent. If he was taking this liquid sex enhancer, maybe he needed more sex than I was giving him. There were times when I honestly was tired, especially when I was going through menopause. I didn't feel sexy and lost interest for months, then my libido woke up. Or maybe the *Get Right* changed my hormones. Could I have been the reason we were taking it?

Deciding to forego dining out and gather at the dining room table with wine, pizza, wings, celery sticks, and fries. The TV is tuned to an UFL game as we share heartfelt memories of Trent, reminisce about the unique characters at his funeral, and reflect on the void his absence leaves.

"You should start dating; don't wait," suggests Briana, breaking our momentary sadness.

"Slow down, B. Let Sash get her bearings. I mean, who would she date after Dad?"

"I doubt either of you would be ready to see me hanging out with another man."

"Yeah, we don't want to see you turn into Coretta or Betty, never marrying again, and keeping it 100, never having sex again. I mean, I see you more as a Jackie O. What you think, TJ?"

"I think I don't wanna hear this shit. Where's the remote?"

"I don't know why he's acting so squeamish."

Briana starts scrolling through her cell phone. "Seriously, look at all these dating sites for people over 50. I can build your profile," she offers, while displaying apps for Silver Singles, Elite Singles, and Senior Sizzle.

"I'm with TJ."

Two days before I'm scheduled to meet Azmar in the Hamptons and attend a party he's invited me to; panic sets in on what I should wear. With nothing suitable in my closet and no desire to go shopping, I call my former stylist at 4Sisters Styling. A bubbly young girl on the other end of the phone tells me my stylist is on vacation in Milan. Sensing my disappointment, she offers to help.

Precious, the youngest of the four sisters, pulls up my outdated file and updates it with my current weight, age, and requested attire for the party I'm attending. With her excitement pouring through the phone at the opportunity to dress me, I fear she'll suggest something that isn't age-appropriate, but I give her a chance. After sending about a dozen pictures back and forth, I know she's on the right track when the last two she sends are a Schiaparelli Palazzo pantsuit and a Valentino swing dress. She even offers to send a skin-toned bra and thong, which I'd stopped wearing when it no longer made sense to have a string up my ass all day for the sake of sexy. This brings me back to the thong I found in the safe deposit box, and Veronica's business card, both are tucked into my overnight bag.

As for accessories, Precious insists on including a classic Chanel purse, Tiffany earrings, and, of course, shoes and a few sets of casual outfits. Along with her commission, I don't even care about the cost; I have it, so why not spend it? With that, my account is reactivated. Afterward, I go online and order what I consider a unique gift for Azmar.

The next day, when the courier delivers the two garment bags, I'm surprised to find that in addition to the clothes we agreed on, there are additional items I explicitly told her were too young for me. Admittedly, though, it's an incredibly sexy white sleeveless dress, held together by ties in the front, and so as not to show off all my goods, there's a nude lace body suit. As beautiful as it is, it's too much skin for me to reveal on a date with a man I barely know and one who is Muslim.

At 8:00 a.m. on Saturday, I dress in soft yellow linen pants, a matching sleeveless vest, and taupe sandals. When the driver arrives, instead of jumping on the Long Island Expressway, he takes me to a helipad in Manhattan. Feeling anxious about seeing him again, I try to push aside my fear and thoughts of past helicopter tragedies. I pray and board the chopper, realizing this would be the perfect time for an Ambien.

Forty-five minutes later, we're settling on the tarmac at East Hamptons Airport, and when the door slides back, Azmar is standing beside a dirty, uncovered Jeep Wrangler. We meet halfway, and it's easy to see his skin has been bathed in sunshine against his unshaven face and the highlights in his hair. Holding me away, he exlaims, "Sasha Borianni, you are stunning! How was your flight?"

Noticing his casual attire of linen drawstring knee-length cargo shorts, a matching short-sleeved shirt, and slides, I respond, "I'm a bit wobbly."

Wrapping his arm around my waist, he says, "I'll hold you up."

After placing my garment and overnight bags in the backseat, he helps me into the Jeep, locking my seatbelt around me.

"I like the hair."

"Thank you, and you look like you've been in the sun."

We don't talk much during the drive, as it's too noisy in the open Jeep to have a conversation. It feels good to have the warm breeze practically taking my breath away. My gaze settles on the ocean, where surfers are riding the white caps of the waves, and I imagine what Azmar might look like in swim trunks on a surfboard. That's when we pass a sign that reads, *Welcome to Ditch Plains.*"

Azmar's cozy white cottage with shutters trimmed in foam green contrasts the luxury of his Four Seasons condo. Taking me on a tour of the small space, he shows me my room, which is the larger of the two bedrooms. Through the kitchen door is a small yard with a rack that holds several surfboards. What he points out that I didn't notice is an outdoor shower.

He shares the cottage's history which he purchased from a politician whose wife moved to Paris, and the only things he upgraded were the bathrooms. I mostly watch him move about the kitchen, uncorking a bottle of Sassicaia while continuing to chat about nothing significant. When offered a taste, the wine moves like silk across my tongue with a hint of black fruit and mint. I want to tell him to have another bottle on standby.

"You look comfortable here."

"It's one of my favorite places, and I welcome you to make it yours, too. Are you ready to eat!"

For our lunch, he's prepared a tantalizing dish of lump crab cakes layered with avocado, mozzarella, tomato, and arugula. I compliment him on the meal. Instead of engaging in small talk, we relax in comfortable silence and observe the bustling scene outside the window, with people cycling, strolling, and transporting surfboards on their trucks.

"Is it always like this?"

"All summer, but when I visit in the winter, the cold breeze from the ocean clears my head."

"And when do I get the pleasure of watching you surf?"

"Cape Town, come with me."

"South Africa?"

"Have you ever been?"

Trent and I rarely went on vacation, and we certainly couldn't take that extensive a trip.

"Sadly, no. I plan to travel once my husband's estate is settled. By the way, I never asked you whose party we were attending."

"White Magic, the football player."

After chasing the lump in my throat with a sip of wine, I ask, "And you invited me?"

He sees my expression. "We'll stay as long as you want to."

"I'm not who you want there."

"Why not?"

Besides White Magic being Isabella's lover, I want to respond with the truth that I'm a tired widow. I'm sure his guests are young athletes and celebrities and someone like Briana would better appreciate this invite.

Sensing my hesitancy, he leans across the table, blending the taste of the wine with a sweet kiss on my lips. When he pulls away, I say, "Thank you for inviting me. I have something for you."

"*Why would you do that*?" he teases, mimicking me.

"I'll allow the lady to open her gift first," he says, offering me a black box with lettering that reads, House of Moussaieff. Inside the cushioned box lays a necklace made of what I pray isn't small white and pink circular-shaped diamonds, suspending a circular-shaped detachable pendant that holds a sand dial filled with sparkling sand.

"I wanted you to remember how we met. It may not have been the happiest moment, but it brought us together."

As Azmar speaks, my mind and heart sink at the thought of the Akoya pearl necklace Trent gave me and how hastily I discarded it when I found out he was drugging me just a few days ago.

"Sasha?"

"I don't know what to say. Please tell me these are rhinestones."

"I could never even think to gift a woman of your stature rhinestones, it is what it appears to be."

Imagining how much he must've spent on this piece, I reach out, my hand on the back of his neck, bringing him down for a kiss.

"Thank you, Azmar. I really am at a loss, except you're not the only one giving gifts," I tell him while handing over my black gift box.

Surprise lights up his face when he opens the box to an

engraved mahogany and gold navigator compass inscribed with the words, 'May Allah always be your guide.'

His freckled nose turns red, making me reach out and trace it with my fingers. He takes my fingers, kisses each one, and tells me, "This is special. Thank you for respecting and being unafraid of my beliefs."

"Azmar, in the very short time we've known each other, you've been so kind to me."

"You are a classy woman, and sometimes, most times, with women, you never know what you're getting. On this occasion, my older brother would say that women can be like cars; the new ones are shiny with all the electronic gadgets, yet the classics have the highest value. You, Sasha, are a classic, and like a classic, you will not be easy to maintain."

My eyes swell with tears, and I pray they don't make it past my lashes. I'm saved by the buzzing of his cell phone.

A few hours later I'm excited to get dressed in something other than black. Once I've showered, applied bronzing crème to my body, put makeup on my face, and spritzed all the right spots with perfume, I slip into the white Palazzo pants and top. When I look in the full-length mirror, my excitement wanes at the reflection of a sad woman masking her pain behind beautiful clothes. Who am I fooling? Stepping out of that outfit, I try on the ultra-feminine Stella Jean dress, somehow, it would be more appropriate for the afternoon. That's when I decide to try on the bare bodysuit, then slip on the Alexander Wang dress with tie closures down the front. Sliding my hands over my curves and seeing the perfect way my breasts hug the front of the dress, this time, when I reflect in the mirror, I'm awestruck at my beauty. Why wouldn't a man be proud to have me on his arm? I'm still that woman on top, Sasha Borianni!

Walking out of the bedroom, a stunned Azmar jumps up from his chair and breaks into a broad smile, stating, "Alhamdulillah, Sasha, you are beautiful!"

"Thank you. Can you help me with this?" I ask, handing him the necklace to place around my neck. Pressing his body against mine from behind, he can barely contain himself or the rise in his pants.

After clasping the necklace, he kisses me and says, "C'mon, brown butter, you're with me."

"Brown butter?"

"At Papagayo, the first time I touched your brown, buttery skin, on the beach, I knew if you allowed me the opportunity, I would give my all to please you. Now, let us go before I'm unable to control myself."

Outside, behind Azmar's Jeep, is an idling Mercedes-Benz town car whose driver is waiting to take us to the party.

We arrive at a security checkpoint, where guests swap out their vehicles in exchange for golf carts. At the edge of the property, a gaggle of media and paparazzi have gathered to snap pictures of the arriving guests; even helicopters are flying overhead. When our driver displays the screen on Azmar's phone, the security person waves us in another direction.

Upon exiting the vehicle, Azmar takes my hand, threading his fingers through mine. What I don't expect from his comforting gesture is for my body to go stiff, my sweaty hand unwrapping itself from his. This is the wrong hand. This man isn't my husband, and I should not be here with him. What if I see someone I know? What if someone takes our picture? Am I making a fool of myself? Intuitively, Azmar senses my hesitancy and gently places his hand on the curve of my back, guiding me toward the sound of the music.

After passing over a white garden bridge, in the distance, an all-glass house sits back off a meticulously landscaped property centered around an Olympic-sized swimming pool, complete with synchronized swimmers who appear more like mermaids in the glossy light of the water.

Our arrival at the party garners an interesting reaction from guests. I notice people acknowledging Azmar with a nod or stare, but no one comes up to greet him until White Magic and his wife approach us.

"Thanks, brother, for coming. It's an honor to have you here," says White Magic, shaking his hand yet offering what appears to be a slight bow.

It's one thing to have seen this man covered in a football uniform with pads and a helmet, but in person, especially in all white, it's easy to see why Isabella or any woman would be attracted to him. He has the kind of face and physique that stops you in your tracks, making it impossible not to desire him. Hopefully, Azmar doesn't notice the slight gasp in my breath.

"White Magic and Hailey allow me to introduce a special friend, Sasha Borianni."

"Thank you for having us."

"You staying on the island?" White Magic asks Azmar.

"It depends on Sasha's desires."

"Sasha, please stay. We can go to Nick & Toni's for lunch."

I politely decline their brunch invitation, which paparazzi usually attend. First, gazing at Azmar to ensure we agree, I respond, "Thank you, we may have plans for tomorrow."

"We're not gonna hold y'all up. Let me have someone show you to your section."

A stunning model strides ahead, leading our way past a stage where live entertainment is expected, with various seating options and multiple bar setups. This is the work of a professional set designer. It might be my perception, but even the air is scented.

We follow her to one of several reserved areas resembling a living room where a waiter stands nearby, ready to pour from a bottle of Sassicaia.

"You think of everything."

"I saw you liked it, so I requested they have it available. Here, let's sit a moment before we're forced to mingle."

We sit on one of the couches, indulging in a delicious assortment of hors d'oeuvres as we watch the arrival of Hollywood A-listers, entertainment elite, media personalities, and sports figures, including Jalen Hurts and his beautiful bride. The presence of these celebrities serves as a dramatic backdrop to the electrifying music that pulsates through the air. The DJ remains unknown to me, but her performance lyrics over the music generates an ecstatic reaction from the crowd. It feels akin to being in a concert attended by the elite. As I observe Azmar, it's evident that he is at ease, nodding along to the music and tapping my thigh.

For a moment, I imagine if this crowd had access to Trent's *Get Right*, I could charge them way over $1250 per vial. Based on my personal experience, when it comes to wealthy people, the higher the price, the more they purchase, especially when you tell them it's exclusive. Who knows, maybe they already have it. Perhaps that's why I'm here.

My mind races with wild thoughts until Azmar rises to introduce me to the talented Misty Copeland, whose beauty and grace truly leave me breathless. That classy moment is followed by the crowd going wild repeating the lyrics of the evening's first performer.

When I notice Azmar patting his foot and bobbing his head to GloRilla, rapping about showing off her moose knuckle, I wonder if rap is his preference of music, anything I pray except jazz.

"What's your genre of music?"

He hesitates, then says, "Marvin Gaye."

"That's it?"

"You can experience the magic of Marvin for every occasion, whether it's love, family, or the state of society. From *Aint No*

Mountain High Enough to *Sexual Healing* to *What's Going On*, and even the iconic *Star-Spangled Banner* – Marvin's got you covered."

"You sound very passionate about that. I love Marvin, too, but if you like R&B, we can find plenty of artists to add to that list."

"Marvin is the only one, but I'll listen to what you have."

When Azmar suggests we move through the crowd, I allow him to lead. He somehow finds a group of fellow surfers in awe of meeting him. Watching and listening allows me to see his love for the sport, as they use terminology as foreign to me as his language. Still, I wonder why he never became a professional competitor.

Feeling safe beside Azmar and tingly from the wine and star-filled sky, I notice when the parade of Kardashian women enters the party led by Momager. The only white party I've heard to be bigger than this is Michael Rubin's. This evening, he is a guest conversing with Meek Mill and Wallo. Briana would love to hear about this night, but I don't dare tell her I was here, especially when I see Vanessa Bryant walking across the grounds with Kelly Rowland.

I am trying to take in so much it's dizzying until I see someone who certainly shouldn't be here, Isabella, who's entering the house with Bryce Goodman. This woman is too much! According to Sugar Hill gossip, she was wrapped up in a threesome with White Magic and Lady Zoë. While I'm lost in the utter disrespect of it all, I hear a familiar voice over the music. Turning slightly and hoping my instincts are wrong, with outstretched long arms, he exclaims, "Sasha Borianni, that you?"

Standing before me is the last person I expected or ever wanted to see again. My former client and, unfortunately, lover, Phoenix Carter, a former NBA All-Star point guard legend turned team owner.

This young man possessed an irresistible magnetism that

drew me in for almost five years while I managed him. Our affair had to come to an end as it grew increasingly reckless, and now, all these years later, he's still able to send the same shutter through my body.

Without asking, he grabs me by the waist and kisses me directly on the lips. Pulling away, but with him still holding onto my hips, he asks, "Damn, what you doing here? If you working I need you."

I would never work for this man again nor trust myself to be alone with him. However, it's easy to see that even with the few lines that have etched themselves into his face, his good looks and muscled body are still intact and, I'm sure, virile, without the need for *Get Right*. Freeing myself from him, I ask, "Phoenix, how are you?"

"Damn Sash, look at you, still sexy as shit! You cut your dreads; I like this," he says, his hand reaching in to toss my hair. "Who you here with?"

Slightly nervous that he will mention Trent, I reply, "I'm here with a friend."

When I feel a hand resting on my curve, I relax, especially when I hear Azmar say, "Phoenix Carter."

"Azmar, yo man what's up? You got a good one here."

"This lady is to be cherished and, need I say, respected."

In defense, he throws up his hands. "No disrespect, I've known this fine woman a long time, right Sasha? Oh yeah, I'm sorry to hear about Trent. I wanted to attend the funeral but was outta the country. You got my gift."

"Yes," I say, having no idea what he sent.

Once again, sensing my discomfort and dismissing him, Azmar says, "Good to see you, Phoenix." He then guides me away, speaking more truth than he knows, "Stay close; there are vultures among this crowd."

Heartless

Isabella

On Saturday evening, Bruce suggested that I get behind the wheel of his new car to take what turned into a six-hour drive to the Hamptons. During that time, with music playing softly, I half-listened while he was on the phone with his lawyer, discussing the dissolution and sale of another business entity.

Since our argument the day I returned from Houston, there have been apologies, but they seem insincere. They only serve as a cover for his continuous attempts to assert his manhood, which have not proven successful.

After last night I'm not sure I could be faithful in this relationship, and I think he knows that. We've tried everything, even Viagra and Cialis, to make his hard-on last, yet nothing has worked. And his providing oral sex is unfulfilling. I get more than that from Lady Zoë with her special talent, but I can't allow that to be my only recourse, especially now.

The drive helped ease my worries about the information I suspect Vesper is acquiring. Determined not to let up, before leaving Philly, I picked up my second trap phone from Wawa, and while Bryce was pumping gas, I sent my second set of text messages.

> To Lemuel: you're slipping

> To Lady Zoë: every NDA isn't sealed

Nonetheless, I was caught off guard when he showed up at Barren Hill, happily conversing with Corey and greeting arriving guests while I finished packing for the trip. There was no way he would allow me to attend this party alone.

After arriving at the charming East Hampton Art House, I change into my bathing suit and relax by the pool in the warm sun. The 92-degree temperature is reminiscent of the heat I miss from Esterillos, where I used to swim every day and enjoy a leisurely pace. I hope to return there eventually.

My mind wanders to the recent men in my life, starting with Sémile, whom I met about seven months after moving to Philly. He was an intentional lover whose physical endurance in the bedroom was a pleasure to match. As a man of Islamic faith, he never tried to impose his religion on me. Still, he wanted me to consider adhering to their beliefs regarding women and relationships, which meant being married and dressing modestly. It wasn't the worst idea, but I hadn't been in Philly that long and wasn't ready to commit to him or his religion.

And then I met Elijah, who seemed to be the ideal man for me. We had similar careers and family values and cherished being in each other's company. His strong and reassuring presence made me feel secure, and it felt natural for us to get married. However, our relationship started to fall apart when I unexpectedly discovered that he was involved in weapons trafficking and that he was close friends with Sémile, almost like brothers.

Don't all men lead to another?

At a party on his yacht in Tampa, Lady Zoë introduced me to White Magic as a potential client, who, on her advice, hired me to complete a forensic analysis of his accounts. She seized that opportunity to lure me into an intense threesome that began with us sharing the unicorn known as Lady Zoë. I'd be lying if I said I didn't enjoy being with them, but sometimes, I'm unsure who satisfies me more, Lady Zoë or White Magic.

Although Ranger Johnson was a good mistake, spending a night with a man who didn't require a commitment had been a relief. Once we got past his hunger and his corniness, I needed his sweet and tender care of my body to soothe me, as if we'd agreed to be in love for one night. We never made it to his bedroom but stayed wrapped around each other under heavy blankets in front of his fireplace. I've chosen not to reply to his text messages to savor those memories.

Having dozed off full of memories and a yearning for sex, I'm startled at the touch of someone's hand caressing my back.

"Get up. It's time to get ready."

His attire overlays Bryce's good looks as he's dressed in an almond-colored sports coat, slightly darker pants, and a crisp white shirt for the evening. From where he sits, his eyes follow me as I prance around the room wearing hi-cut panties and fresh-out-the-box 4-inch Louboutin sandals. While standing in front of the mirror, I realize it's been a while since I've dressed up. I've been wearing my bohemian look for the past six months, maybe even a year. Applying eyeliner and mascara, I feel him taking in every curve of my body. I pull my hair up, expose my neck, and apply my Fenty Fuchsia Flex across the bottom, then top lip, and when I see him shifting in his seat, bending slightly, my legs gapped, I add a light spray of Queen Silk to my ankles, behind my knees, wrists, and ears, a gift from Lady Zoë.

I further indulge in the satisfaction of his straining glance when I slip into a short, white Khaite dress, and for once, not having had children is a plus as my full breasts stand up without support inside its mock neck front, yet exposing a deep V-back to which I add a ball-chain lariat necklace that glitters with diamond accents stopping at the crevice of my ass. Briefly, I smile when my thoughts return to Agent Solano and her sultry attire while I was standing around in shorts and a halter top; if only she could see me now.

"That's what you're wearing?"

When I purposely ignore him, Bryce takes three long strides across the room and forcefully grabs a handful of my low messy bun, and says, "You're gonna learn to stop fucking with me."

Instead of taking his car to the party, he's hired a driver who gets stuck in a line of luxury vehicles backed up for screening, giving paparazzi time to snap pictures, frustrating Bryce. When security finally approaches our car and scans the barcode on Bryce's phone instead of mine, our driver is directed to drop us off near a lot filled with golf carts. It's Bryce, then, who must drive the cart around a bend that leads onto the property, where the undeniable voice and music of DJ Diamond Kuts fill the air.

Strolling behind other guests, approaching us and walking hand in hand is White Magic and Hailey. With some trepidation, I embrace Hailey, whose long white dress perfectly complements her glowing tanned skin. When White Magic hugs me, he whispers, "Damn you smell fine."

I feel Bryce's body stiffen behind me, making it the first time I've ever seen him intimidated.

White Magic offers his hand to Bryce who shakes it, simply greeting him with, "Magic."

"Bryce Goodman, how you making out?"

"I'm here."

"Bryce, meet my wife, Hailey. Babe he's the man who knows

how to flip bad money into good money and has access to all the right places."

I'm positive Bryce doesn't like that reference.

Hailey offers her hand to Bryce, "Mr. Goodman, nice to meet you, and Isabella, I'm so sorry to hear about what happened to you, to the both of you," she says her eyes on Bryce instead of me.

"Thanks, we're trying to put that behind us."

"Have they arrested the person responsible?"

"Babe, chill. They didn't come here to be interrogated; it's a party."

"I'm sorry, he was so worried," she says, snuggling up against White Magic, "We would hate for anything to happen to you."

What exactly does Hailey know about her husband's sexual preferences, and why haven't I ever bothered to ask him?

I can see this conversation is making her husband uncomfortable, so he cuts in by offering Bryce a gel-cooled leather packet of his custom-made and illegal cigars.

"Here man, c'mon, see the house."

The four of us cross a white 6-foot-long garden bridge into the party's heart, where a camera crew awaits to take pictures of arriving guests. Hailey hesitates in her steps to walk beside Bryce while White Magic disappears into the crowd in search of whatever pleases him.

"Bryce, when you have a moment, and Izzy, when you can spare him, I'd like to introduce you to a coterie of friends who would welcome fresh and unfiltered investment advice. You have a stellar reputation among some very important people."

Of course, she has those friends. Her father was one of the few Wall Street brokers who profited from the 911 tragedy, adding millions to the money he'd made from the oil refineries he owned in the U.S. and abroad. Talk about generational wealth, as an only child, even her great-great-great grandchildren will be billionaires.

"I'd welcome the opportunity," he says, his eyes traveling across her tanned and glittery body.

Whatever game Hailey is playing, the joke is on her. Trailing her inside the glass house, she brings me back into the conversation, saying, "Isabella, let me know when you can spare him for a few moments."

In reply to her shameless flirting, I reply, "He's all yours."

While Bryce orders drinks, I make a quick trip to the bathroom and upon my return, I find him on the second-floor balcony.

"I thought you went off with that fucken Magic, if so, maybe I'll take a shot at his wife," he teases, handing me a salted Margarita while he sips Blanton's on a big rock.

The enchanting view from the balcony is mesmerizing. Watching the swaying sea of white below as the sun begins to set while the stars emerge in the sky is truly a magical experience. Bryce draws my attention to the intermittent circling spotlight from a lighthouse in the distance, guiding boats into the yacht-filled harbor. With his arm wrapped tightly around my waist, this setting becomes perfect for us.

Rather than looking down at the growing crowd, he states, "I'm not sharing you anymore, you understand."

"You won't have to," I lie, knowing that his inability to keep an erection will indeed send me to another man. Luckily, that conversation is cut short when Diamond Kuts hypes up the audience, announcing to the hard beat of *Good Kisser* the evening's first performer, Usher.

Swinging me around to face him, Bryce states, "Let me see you move."

"Right here?"

With a slow gyration, I begin moving to the rhythm then hike my dress up to tease what he can't have. To add to my provocative dance, I turn around, my ass up against his crotch, and twerk for him. I'm unsure if it's his repeating Usher's lyrics in my ear, "...*You do it so good...you pull it out, then you open wide...*" Because if this were the past, he'd take me right here on the balcony, and I'd do exactly as the lyrics suggest, "...*get lipstick on his leg...*"

His response is to wrap his hands around my throat, pulling my head back, biting my lips, and kissing me until I choke on his force. Before I can shake myself loose, he removes the big cube from his glass, reaches under my dress, and places it between my thighs, where, combined with my moistness, it drips down my legs.

"Don't tease me."

"Shut up and keep dancing."

The sexual tension abruptly ends when he leans forward, asking, "Isn't that your Aunt Sasha down there?"

My eyes look to where he's pointing, and sure enough, Sasha is standing near one of the bars with a man whose hand is positioned on her lower back.

"She is *not* my aunt! What the hell is she doing here, and who's that man she's with?"

Judging by his smirk, Bryce seems to find this funny.

"I don't know, he looks white. I guess she's done mourning."

Not that I care, but I am curious as to why she's ignored my text messages and emails, yet she's out here hundreds of miles from Sugar Hill at a party in the Hamptons.

"I'll be right back; I need to clean myself up."

"You want me to go with you."

"Don't worry, I won't stop to fuck anyone."

He yanks me around my waist, drawing me close enough that I can smell the Blanton on his breath, "I'm gonna teach you to watch this nasty mouth," he says, popping two fingers across my lips.

After sticking my tongue out at him, I head downstairs, briefly speaking to Kevin and Eniko who are engaged in a comedic conversation with Lebron and Savannah. I pass by the outdoor cigar room, where the Wall Street moneyed crowd mingles with Silicon Valley's newest billionaire, Maddy Bowen. There are others along the way whom I've met at Lady Zoë's private parties, we only make eye contact and smile in acknowledgment.

Near the center of the crowd, a few people I pass by offer condolences on the loss of my husband, which they probably never knew I had. I can't be certain if these people care, but it feels comforting for them to acknowledge my loss and my pain. When I'm close enough to put my hand on Sasha, the calling of a familiar voice fills me with loathing and desire.

"*My Love*, it is you!"

Bypassing Sasha, I keep moving through the pockets of dancing guests, appropriately singing along to *My Confessions*.

"*My Love*, where are you going?"

Shaking off her touch on my naked back, her beauty momentarily strikes me in an all-white dress with cutouts that show more of her skin than not, yet she hides her ruthlessness as she does her anatomy, making me regret every private moment we've spent together.

"What do you want? I'm here with Bryce."

"Can we go somewhere private?"

I know what that means and I imagine White Magic will be close behind.

"That's over. I'm not letting you take advantage of me anymore."

After a graceful toss of her hair, she says, "Why, *My Love*, do you always play the victim? You were the one who invited me to Sugar Hill." She steps in closer. "You relished every bit of the lovemaking with White Magic, especially me. Do you even remember the things you said, how you loved me?"

I do remember but that was in a moment of forbidden

passion. What woman wouldn't love being sexed by an able-bodied athlete and a Futanari?

"Why are you saying these things here?" I ask looking around to see who might be listening.

Taking both my hands in hers, she begs, "Let me please you tonight. Why do you keep denying how you feel?"

"I have to go!" I yell a little too loudly.

Winding my way around the various seating areas and bars, I keep going until I'm outside the perimeter of the party. The grass is not as manicured, making it hard to walk in my heels. I take them off and head toward the lights at the end of the property, disregarding a sign that reads, DO NOT CROSS.

Lady Zoë doesn't wait for me to stop. Aggressively she grabs my arm, spinning me around and then kissing me with so much force that I feel myself go soft until I'm returning her passion, my hands on her face, considering maybe I can do this one more time to fill the aching desire that Bryce can't.

She steps in close, her hands removing what's left of my messy bun, and in a tone, I've only heard her use in private, she whispers, "I love you, Isabella."

Those words bring me back to my senses. "Love? Are you crazy? I don't love you."

"I don't expect you to love me. No one has ever loved me, I only want to take you away from all this, satisfy you, and give you what you deserve."

"You used me. That's what you did, preying on me, pulling me into your web, controlling me with what you can offer between your legs. All for what? Money? No, you need the attention, you feed off it. I'm done with you, with both of you. I'm with Bryce now."

"Isabella, there are truths you haven't been privy to."

"What truth? I know everything there is to know about you and about every fucken penny you're hiding."

"If you fuck with my money, you'll end up like your husband."

"You bitch!"

"That rat got what he deserved although I wouldn't waste my money. Heed my warning, Bryce Goodman is wrong for you, but you can't take his dick out your mouth long enough to see him for who he really is."

What she doesn't know is that his dick hasn't been in my mouth or anywhere else.

Pushing her out of my way, I walk further into the dark. "Go to hell!"

"Wait, you can't believe he loves you?"

I can't listen to her; I have to get back to Bryce.

Stepping back too fast and too far, I lose my footing on the slippery grass, and she saves me from falling, making me realize she could hurt me out here and nobody would ever know.

"You're a commodity to Bryce, and when he's done with you, well, you figure it out, but we both know you'll never be satisfied with the weakness of men. You'll always want me and crave the Futanari even more."

The lighthouse is sounding off, and my head starts spinning. Is she right? Do I love her or love how she makes me feel? No one could imagine being with a woman as soft and feminine as Lady Zoë and, while embroiled in sweet lovemaking, the feeling of her growing between my legs and, what's more, in my mouth. I will not allow my sex drive to control me anymore. I snatch myself away from her embrace.

Disregarding my resistance, she pulls me to her until I can taste her words as her tongue circles my lips, and I know she's ready. We kiss wildly, and I return that passion until I believe her when she tells me, "Isabella, don't be a fool. Let me love you. Let me show you."

Her hands grope my breasts, pinching my swelling nipples, then traveling down my stomach until she's on her knees, and that's when I realize how heavy I'm breathing. To stop her and myself from falling into her trap, I put one hand around her neck; moaning, I plead with her, "Please shut up, please."

I can barely make out her face in the dark, but I know she's winning, with her hand having made its way down the back of my dress, her fingers pressing and searching deep inside me for the spot she knows is there.

"O-o-o-oh, you're so wet, cum for me, *My Love*, cum for me so I can give you the unicorn; you know it's ready. Feel it."

I give in.

Removing my hand from her neck, it's me who reaches between the split of her dress, and she's right; her manhood has grown, and it's swollen to capacity. I want this woman and what she's offering so bad.

"Take it *My Love*, put it inside you. Only I can satisfy you. Forget about Bryce Goodman."

Her words bring me back to reality. I snatch my hand away, and to shut her up, I grasp her neck with both hands until she gasps for air. Even then, I squeeze harder until I'm sure she can't speak.

"I could kill you," I say, tightening my grip around her neck.

"And…I could…fuck…you… if…"

Lady Zoë can't finish her words. My grip is too tight, causing her fingers to fall from inside me. She reaches to remove my hands, and my adrenaline is moving too fast to let her win. All I know is that the harder I squeeze, the less I can hear of her voice.

The crashing waves get louder, the lighthouse sounds off, and faintly I hear someone calling me.

"ISABELLA! ISABELLA! STOP! WHAT ARE YOU DOING?"

Not realizing that Lady Zoë's feet are off the ground when Sasha reaches out to grab me, I release my grip, and like a delicate bird, Lady Zoë drifts through the air and flies over the cliff.

Mercy, Mercy, Me

Sasha

Is that Isabella with Lady Zoë? I hope this isn't turning into one of their parties. If that's why Azmar brought me here, I can find my way home. I excuse myself from Azmar to use the ladies' room, and when I turn down his offer to escort me, he kisses me on both cheeks and mouths, "Hurry back."

I don't know why I'm being bothered. I call out to Isabella and step up my pace to keep her from embarrassing herself. She can't hear me above the sound of *Megan Thee Stallion* and what looks like a million asses twerking.

As I see them reaching the edge of the property, where the dim lights from the party give way to the bright stars in the sky, I think about returning to get White Magic to help with this situation. But then a horrific scene unfolds before me.

Isabella lets out an eerie scream; I slap my hand over her mouth.

"Shut up! Shut the fuck up right now!"
"I killed her! Oh my—"
A harsh slap cuts her words short.

Afraid to take another step without getting too close to the edge, I peer over the side of the cliff; there's nothing to see except boat lights in the distance.

"What did you do?"

"She fell! I swear I didn't mean to kill her. Call somebody, help me, Sasha," she begs, getting too close to the edge herself.

I yank her back by the fabric of her dress for fear she might take me with her.

"You have to walk away, NOW!"

"I can't. We need help."

"You can't fucken help her."

"Please, Sasha!"

"You cannot be involved in another scandal! First, your husband is murdered in your home, and now your employer, client, lover, whatever she is, ends up dead with you standing over her. Think Isabella, we gotta go now!"

"I didn't mean to; it was an accident, you saw it! Oh my God, please help me!"

"No one is gonna believe you!"

"But it's true."

"I don't know what she had on you, but if you walk into that crowd, you're going to jail."

If I walk away from this, I'll be as guilty as she is.

Forced to practically drag her away from what is now a crime scene, I warn her, "Bitch, shut up and listen to me! You won't say shit to anyone, you understand. Now, let's get away from here."

Almost running back towards the party, Isabella loses her balance, and that's when I realize she's not wearing shoes. Shit, where are they? Did she leave them at the scene? I can't afford to panic, but God, I could use an Ambien right now.

Suspicious as we might look, I shove her into one of the luxury porta pots and ask the attendant to excuse us. A long bench is where I sit her down, crying uncontrollably. I'm not even sure what to do next. First I need her to shut up. But what about her shoes? I can't go searching for them in the dark. Who do I call? Shit, I don't have my phone.

In between her nerve-wracking sobbing, her frightened face looks up and asks, "Why are you helping me?"

"You see anybody else around?"

As I pace back and forth, peeking under the four stalls, I ensure we're alone in the low-lit bathroom suite, with gold vanities for each porcelain toilet and floor-to-ceiling mirrors. Suddenly, the door pushes open, startling both of us.

Isabella jumps up, screaming and crying, "Bryce, I killed her! You gotta help me!"

"What the fuck is going on?"

Dropping Isabella's shoes from his hands, he opens his arms for her. His eyes question me. "What's she talking about? Is she high?"

I give him the once-over, noticing that all her men are different. Each of them good-looking, but unlike Elijah, or whatever his name was, and the other one, the Muslim, this one is moneyed.

"It was an accident. She and that Lady Zoë were arguing, and she stepped back too far."

"Sasha! That's not what happened. Tell him the truth."

This time I'm taking an exhausted seat on the bench when I tell him, "It's too late for the truth."

Bryce reaches back and locks the door, then turns to us and asks, "Where is she?"

"She fell over the cliff near the edge of the property, where the lights end."

"What about cameras?"

Isabella shakes her head. "He doesn't allow cameras or phones at his parties; he has them all removed. What if she's still alive?"

He holds out his hand, showing us he still possesses his phone.

"Nobody could survive that fall," I offer.

"Here's what's gonna happen. We're walking outta here, and in an hour, we both should be gone from this damn party; I fucken told you I didn't want to come to this bullshit."

"This is not the time," I tell him, wanting to get away from them both.

"You're right. You okay with getting out of here?"

"What choice do I have?"

"Alright, your white boy can meet us by the bar at the pool's far end; we'll have a few drinks, then leave."

"Excuse me, Azmar is not a boy, nor is he white. And you will not order me the fuck around."

"My apologies, but if you don't want to be an accessory to murder, then you'll listen to me. Wait, you're with Azmar? You stay here with him. I'll take care of her."

Confused about his response and the reactions of everyone who sees him, this isn't the time to question Bryce. I will get my answers directly from Azmar.

With Bryce on one side of Isabella and me on the other, we exit the bathroom, giving the appearance that she's drunk. Once we reach the bar, Bryce swipes a D'ussé bottle from a cart being rolled out to guests. After sitting a shaken Isabella on a couch, he slips her shoes back on. I try to help by pouring cognac for the three of us.

Now that Bryce somewhat controls Isabella, I get lost in the crowd in search of Azmar. Instead, when an arm slips around my waist, he finds me.

"I didn't mean to startle you. Are you okay?"

"No! I mean, yes, it's my niece. She's had too much to drink."

"Where is she? Does she need help?" he asks, looking around to offer his assistance.

"No, her boyfriend's with her. He's taking her home."

"Does that mean you're ready to go?"

I want to say yes, take me away from here, but I don't want to appear rushed.

"I sense you need a drink."

"Something stronger than wine."

He kisses me on the cheek.

"Be right back."

"I'll come with you."

As Azmar guides me through the dense crowd, I can't help but notice the ostentatious display of wealth and glamour. Despite the lavish attire and sparkling jewelry, I am one of three people who is aware of the unsettling presence of a dead body a few feet away.

Standing at a high-top table, Azmar asks a passing waiter to remove a bottle from a locked cabinet. Not even taking the time to savor what I'm sure is an expensive drink, I finish it in one swallow.

"You're surprising me, Sasha."

"There's been a lot of those in my life lately, including you."

Before I can question his background, he is greeted by a couple who, if I'm not mistaken, are Harry and Meghan. I want to be interested and engaging but I'm not up to it. Luckily, we're joined by Serena, who, along with her husband, says goodnight to us, and the four of them make their exit. Meanwhile, Azmar has turned to have an entire conversation in French with the easily recognizable Bradley Cooper. I slip the waiter a $100, and after downing another drink, every muscle and fiber in my body heats up. I drink a little slower this time, and that's when I hear someone calling my name.

"Ms. Sasha, is that you?"

Under my breath, I mumble, "Who the fuck is it now."

Frustrated that another person has recognized me, I squint my eyes to see the unfamiliar face of a woman coming toward me.

"Yes, can I help you?" I ask, trying to place this woman who looks to be in her mid-40s with shoulder-length hair and what might be a manufactured body among this crowd.

"We've never met in person except at Trent's funeral."

"I don't remember much from the funeral. It was all a blur. I'm sorry."

"Allow me to introduce myself," she extends her hand, "I'm your travel agent, better known as *My Travel Agent*."

"Nice to meet you," I respond, wishing I sounded more enthusiastic to meet the woman who's handled every move I've made over the last 15 years, but I fall flat.

"I never expected to see you here."

"My niece dragged me," I lie, confident that in her eyes, I'm disrespecting Trent's memory. The lie dissipates when Azmar returns to my side, his hand lacing mine.

I'm about to introduce them when she glances down at our laced fingers and questions, "Mr. Azmar?"

He doesn't respond.

"Ms. Sasha, enjoy the party. We'll talk soon."

Azmar whispers in my ear, "Shall I take you home?"

"Please," I respond to his lowered head.

With him leading me by the hand, we make our way to one of the exits, where we are handed heavy white leather gift bags imprinted with our names, certainly filled with high-end products.

Sitting in the car, my head is filled with thoughts of running into Phoenix Carter, meeting *My Travel Agent*, and the admiration Azmar received from guests. All of this is mixed with the shock of seeing Isabella drop Lady Zoë off a cliff. Hoping I made the right decision, closing my eyes I try to push these thoughts away. Azmar, always attuned to my emotions, takes my hand, kisses my palm, and then turns my face to his. He asks, "Did something happen back there with you and your niece?"

"I never should've come here."

Instead of convincing me otherwise, he taps a button on the back console, and when, overtop the crooning of October London's *Take Me Back to Your Place*, Azmar sings along, bringing a smile to both of our faces.

"I thought you only—"

My words disappear in his mouth until he takes a moment to tap the console, signaling the driver, who pulls to a stop and exits the vehicle.

"What are you…where's he going?"

"He's safe, but you brown butter are not."

He opens the door and guides me to the front of the idling Mercedes with its headlights still on.

Taking a step back, Azmar unbuckles and loosens his belt before stepping out of his linen pants and briefs. Unbuttoning his linen shirt, he tosses it aside, exposing his sculpted body illuminated by the moonlight.

"You can't be serious. It's dark out here." I say, seeing the bugs fly past the headlights.

As if being out here is normal, he undoes the ties that hold the front of my dress together until it slips off my shoulders, falling onto the ground. Taking his time, he runs his hands over the soft fabric of my bodysuit, then lifts it over my head until I'm standing before him naked.

Breathless at what's about to happen, I beg him, "Who are you? Why'd you bring me here?"

He responds in a dialect I can't decipher, nor do I want to take the time to translate. I may not know who he is, but I am learning that he is a master at foreplay. With one hand, he pushes my head back and licks from my chin down to my hardened nipples until I find myself focusing on the stars above that shine a spotlight on us.

Bending down to his knees in the dirt, knowing what's next, I grab hold of that beautiful head of hair to give me balance.

"Allow me to taste this, please," he asks, yet before I can

answer, his warm tongue licks around one side of my clit and then the other.

The intensity causes me to back away from him until by bare ass is on the hood of the car.

"I need a second give me a..."

He silences me with a kiss, and before I can utter another word, he turns me around, stretching my arms in front of me, and with my face touching the hood of the car, I hear him say, "Brown Butter you're all mine," and with that, not a drop of my juices is spared.

Beast of Burden

Isabella

Lady Zoë didn't deserve to die, at least not by my hands, and for that reason, I can't stop crying. The more I keep trying to explain the circumstances to Bryce, the more he ignores me until finally, he shouts, "ISABELLA SHUT UP SO I CAN HANDLE THIS SHIT!"

"HANDLE IT HOW?"

Without an answer, my paranoia grows. What if the driver can hear my panic? Does he know what I've done? What if he phones the police? He has no allegiance to me or Bryce.

On my phone, I repeatedly enter the incorrect passcode, until I realize it would be easier to reach the police if I hit the emergency button. When Bryce sees what I'm doing, he rips the phone out of my hand, turns it off, and shoves it into his pocket.

Once we're in our room, I rush into the bathroom, fall onto my knees, and hold onto the sides of the toilet, hoping to vomit until realizing I never ate. Why didn't they let me call the police, and why didn't Bryce take me home? How do I even begin to process the act I've committed? Who is this person I've become? Did I want to kill her?

Instead of removing my clothes, I turn on the shower and stand under the water until Bryce bangs on the door. When I step back into the bedroom, he hangs up the phone and hands me a glass of Tequila he's poured until he sees my clothes are soaked. Removing them, he towels me off and gets me into a robe until I can finally collapse on the bed. Rather than allow me to lay there, he pulls me up and, positioning himself on his knees between my legs, he cups my face with his hands.

"I need you to listen and hear what I'm saying. We're going to stay here for a few days, and besides me, the only person you can trust right now is your Aunt Sasha."

"She's not—"

Covering my mouth with his hand, he replies, "Not important."

"No calls, emails, or texting, you understand. I don't want you calling the police. You're not built for what comes after that."

"I'm guilty."

"Guilty of what? You didn't intentionally kill her. It wasn't premeditated."

"Then why can't we tell that to the police."

"They won't believe you. They'll dig up her life and yours, and we both know what they'll find."

"What about everything she's left behind?"

"I'll handle it. She's out of your life, our lives. Isn't that what you wanted?"

He doesn't understand or know that I've set things in motion that can't be reversed.

"Isabella, listen to me, please. I may never be able to repeat what I'm about to say."

With my head spinning, I nod in acknowledgment but not in

agreement and accept his second drink, hoping it will knock me out.

"Before you came along, I didn't care about Lady Zoë's business practices because I took a percentage for every dollar she made. Then she got close to you, which wasn't the perfect situation but you mattered. I watched and studied you, and that's when I knew you weren't like her. She bought out another side of you that would never have been possible, and I'm guilty of taking advantage of that."

"I don't understand what you're saying. How much do you know about us?"

"Lady Zoë never cared about you handling her finances, she planned to seduce you, but it backfired when she fell in love with you. I told you that shit. You gotta trust me Izzy."

"I've been with her so many times and—"

"I don't care who the fuck you've been with, including that fucken White Magic, it's me and you now, you got that!"

"Yes."

Caressing my face, he continues, "I'm not a man of regrets, but in this business of moving money, you do some shit because you believe it's the right thing, so you deal with the consequences. I made a hard choice a few years back. I couldn't risk going to jail nor could I lose you, so I chose to save you at the cost of losing someone else. You came at a high price. Do you understand?"

There's only one reason why he's making this half-ass confession. With my fists banging on his chest, I lose it.

"YOU KILLED ELIJAH, YOU KILLED MY HUSBAND, DIDN'T YOU?"

Taking hold of my wrists, he yells, "Stop fucking saying that and listen to what I'm telling you. Don't make me have to tie you down!"

"You think I don't understand what you're going through.

Killing someone or having someone killed tortures your soul. I'm tortured."

I glance up into his regretful eyes, seeing pain there, probably from a time before I knew him. Unfortunately, there are no words of comfort I can offer him.

"C'mon, you need to rest, and I need to clean up."

Hearing the water running, I climb out of bed to find my phone, searching through his suitcase, my suitcase, under the mattress, and in his pants pockets, but it's nowhere to be found. He must've taken it in the bathroom with him. I finish off the glass of tequila and climb back into bed.

With his awkward confession and the events of the evening, I convince myself that regardless of what Sasha and Bryce say, in the morning, I'm turning myself in. They don't understand, I can't live always wondering if my crime will be exposed. What if someone saw us? Sasha could even change her mind and turn me in. Everyone has a conscience regardless of the choices we've had to make. Before falling asleep, my last thought is of Lady Zoë's body dangling and then dropping. I should've held on.

A cold chill wakes me. When I reach for the covers, through blurred vision, I see Bryce standing naked at the foot of the bed, stroking himself. I reach for the lamp on the nightstand.

"Bryce?"

Instead of responding, he stares at me with eyes so hard, almost making me fear him.

"I won't be gentle."

"How?"

"The talented Dr. Cynthia Lampley got me right. You feel it too, don't you?"

He's right. The sight of his hard-on stirs a dormant excitement.

"You want it or not?"

"Are you sure you're gonna be okay?"

Uninterested in answering my question or foreplay, with one

hand on each ankle, he drags me to the edge of the bed, demanding, "Open your mouth. You're about to pay for that shit you been saying."

"What? What do you mean?"

And while I'm attempting to play coy, with one hand on my head and the other on my shoulder, he glides himself in and out until I'm gagging. When I manage to squirm away from him, he pushes me back onto the bed, pinning me down with his forearm, and with the other, he lifts both my legs up and, after taking a long slow lick of my wetness, he wipes his mouth with the back of his hand then penetrates me with a thrust I'd forgotten he was capable of.

There is no love language for this moment. It is raw with emotions; for him the ability to reaffirm his manhood and for me, the realization that I've taken someone's life.

Gripping my hips, he pulls me onto the oriental rug that covers only a portion of the hardwood floor. Once he has me on all fours, with his knee, he kicks my legs apart and drills down until my entire body erupts into multiple orgasms. I've become so wet that he must hold onto my hips to stay inside me, and that's when my walls tighten around him. His body begins to jerk, and it's him who screams out, shooting his reclaimed manhood inside me.

For the next two days, we order room service, and he makes up for all the sex we didn't have, giving me little time to dwell on the crime I've committed.

After confirming with his sources that nothing has been discovered, on Tuesday, we pack up to go home. When he returns my cell phone, I notice several text messages and missed calls, but Corey's voicemail and text messages alarm me. When I call him, he's excited to share that after 27 hours of labor,

Synearra has given birth to Zion, a 9-pound baby boy. His ask of us is to manage Barren Hill in their absence, and Bryce agrees to help.

For almost two weeks, guests come and go, mostly in three-day stints. With the help of the chef and housekeeper, we greet and respond to their needs. Bryce handles the minor list of repairs that Synearra has left for us and some of the household items that need replenishment. During this time, Bryce rarely leaves my side, preventing me from turning myself in or, better yet, going crazy carrying this burden of guilt. He constantly reassures me everything is fine, and that Lady Zoë's body may never be found; even so, when the constant calls from her accountant, Lemuel, suddenly stop, I know Bryce has handled him.

Being in Elijah's house with Bryce is a strange feeling, but like an animal, he stakes his territory, determined to make love in every room of the home that isn't occupied.

While Bryce is outside entertaining a group of female guests, I can't shake off the unsettling thought of what he meant by being a voyeur. Could he have been watching me before we met? Or our female guests? The unease of not knowing his true intentions gnaws at me. Since he's occupied elsewhere, I return a call to Betty, who has received information from Vesper. They've obtained Lady Zoë's redacted birth records, which didn't list any parents or siblings, as if she appeared out of nowhere. The idea of her not being missed by anyone fills me with unexpected grief.

Adding to the intrigue, Lady Zoë's net worth is almost $500 million. The question of where she may have been hiding all that money lingers in my mind. I was only privy to a small part of her business, but Vesper has discovered that she owns stock in some of the most high-profile and profitable companies, adding another layer of mystery. Even after paying her debt and taxes, whoever inherits her estate will undoubtedly become wealthy. Who stands to benefit from her wealth remains shrouded in secrecy, fueling my suspicion.

Homecoming

Sasha

Two weeks after the party, Lady Zoë's body washes ashore five miles from where she went over. The news outlets begin reporting, *"Global socialite Lady Zoë falls to her death at the annual white party of Tampa Bay's quarterback White Magic. Her body was discovered when a yacht owner was leaving the island."*

The first call that comes in is from Isabella, and I can tell from her guarded conversation that Bryce has coached her not to speak about the incident over the phone.

"We need to discuss your financial portfolio."

"Where are you?"

"Philly. My little sister had her baby."

"I thought you were an only child."

"I am. Are you still on the East Coast? I can meet you?"

Not wanting her to know I'm still on the island, I say, "I can come to you."

The only reason I'm still in Ditch Plains is because Azmar made it so damn comfortable. My extended stay wasn't planned, but he offered his cottage as a quiet place to continue processing

Trent's death. What he doesn't know is that it's more than my husband's death I'm processing.

After the party, Azmar had to leave for two days. When he returned, we spent most nights wrapped in intimate moments and afternoons strolling along the beach. He has a remarkable ability to sense when I need space or his comforting presence. Our early mornings at the kitchen table, enjoying freshly brewed coffee with the sun drenching the room became cherished. As he reads the papers in Arabic and French, I manage my team at the lodge via Zoom. Our comfort with each other has grown inexplicably, and he never questions my daily medication regimen. However, the disappointment in my visit is not getting the opportunity to see him surf, which he says will be whenever I decide to travel with him.

I appreciate his discretion in taking business calls in his room, especially since most of them occur while I am sleeping due to the time difference. I've made a conscious decision not to pry too deeply into his life, as doing so might lead to uncomfortable questions I cannot answer about my own. One of the most powerful moments is when I wake before sunrise and hear him engaging in Salat while dressed in a thobe. During these contemplative moments, I find myself considering moving forward from the emotional aftermath caused by Trent's actions.

When Azmar hears me on the phone with *My Travel Agent* arranging for a car rental and a room at the Rittenhouse, he offers and practically insists that he has the perfect vehicle for me to drive myself to Philly. The next morning, his Carbon Black Range Rover SVAutobiography is waiting for me at the helipad in Manhattan. I've been in my share of luxury vehicles, but this one with its meticulously handcrafted details, is exceptional. I never even knew there was a car packed with so much luxury; he assures me it's no big deal and that he'll send someone to pick the SUV up when I'm done with my business in Philadelphia.

Cruising down the turnpike and switching between SiriusXM

Watercolors and Azmar's Marvin Gaye playlist, when I get close enough to my hometown, I tune the radio to WDAS and the familiar voice of Patty Jackson playing Whitney Houston. Nothing could be better than crossing over the Ben Franklin Bridge and having the skyline of Center City welcome me until my serenity is interrupted by Patty's 411.

"The recent discovery of socialite Lady Zoë has led to photos appearing on TMZ and Page Six, and trending across social media. These photos feature celebrities from sports, music, and Hollywood who attended. For more information, you can visit our website's 411 section."

Unfortunately, the story isn't about Lady Zoë's death but about the celebrities who attended White Magic's party. I'm praying that I wasn't captured in any of those photos, but when my phone rings with a call from Arshell, screaming at me for being caught on camera hugging Phoenix Carter, I know I've been exposed.

It's fruitless trying to explain that I was Azmar's guest because my phone continuously beeps with a flurry of calls and text messages from people I haven't spoken to in years. Everyone is curious about my relationship with White Magic and Phoenix Carter and if I'm back at Platinum Images.

When I disconnect from Arshell, Parker calls to inquire about my relationship with Lady Zoë, as the locals claim she spent time at Sugar Hill. A FaceTime call from Owen, Briana, and even TJ cuts in on Parker's call. I offer them a brief rundown of the party and the celebrities who were present. Despite finding a moment to breathe and selfishly giggle at their curiosity and assumptions, I can't shake the anxiety about what they don't know. Thankfully, there is no mention or images of Azmar.

My plan for the remainder of the day is to check into my room, walk across the street to Parc, and sit down in one of the Rittenhouse Square-facing windows for lunch. I may do a little shopping on Walnut Street. Luckily, maybe tomorrow, before dealing with the real reason I'm in Philly, I'll get a massage.

Coming down Market Street, I see the familiar landmark of Wannamaker's, now Macy's. I wonder if they still have the Christmas light show I frequented as a little girl. Rounding JFK Boulevard, with the Comcast building looming, I stop at a light and admire the renovated LOVE Park and the family-friendly Dilworth Plaza.

When I turn onto 19th Street and into the carport for The Rittenhouse Hotel, my phone rings with a call from an unknown number.

"Sasha, it's Bryce Goodman."

Praying he isn't calling to tell me our cover-up has been exposed, I wave off the valet who's arrived at my door.

"I need your help. I'm in New York to claim Lady Zoë's body."

"Haven't I done enough? Wait, does this woman not have family?"

"She was an orphan and I'm the executor of her estate and, as of late, her business partner."

"Then how'd you allow her to get a stranglehold on Isabella?"

"That's not a phone conversation."

"What do you want from me?"

"You need to navigate the media before this thing gains traction."

"Are you kidding? I don't do that anymore. What you need is a crisis management team. I assume you have a lawyer."

"Woodridge & Wiggins will be handling things. I can't answer questions from the press. It's too complicated. Once an autopsy is completed, you'll understand."

"She's a unicorn," I casually joke, "Whatever that means."

"Yes, that's what she called herself, she was born with male and female genitalia."

"A hermaphrodite?"

"Futanari."

"What the hell is that?"

"She is typically average, but during arousal, her genitalia enlarge, sometimes beyond the typical size of a man's penis."

"You're serious?"

"Human anatomy is a strange thing."

"And you've seen this?"

"Seen it, never indulged."

"And Isabella?"

He's silent. Of course, they were lovers. Does that mean White Magic is bisexual?

"Now you see why I need you to calm the waters and stop the speculation. Every man and woman who's ever been in her company or attended one of her private parties will be panicked about being exposed, and these are powerful people."

"I can't get involved in this shit. I need to get back to Sugar Hill."

"I would think you'd have your own interests to protect."

He's right; I must protect myself. Even so, can I do this? "Are you sure your lawyer can't handle it?"

"They don't have your experience. I recall you cleaning up Philly's first lady's image when her extramarital affair was exposed."

"Yes, but this is mur—" I stop short of saying the word and offer, "I'll give you one week. Wait, does Isabella know what you're asking me?"

"No, I didn't have time. I was hoping you could explain it to her, so she understands. She listens to you."

I chuckle at his lie.

"Let me offer this, once you claim the body, forego the autopsy and instruct the morgue to have her cremated immediately. I'll compose a holding statement this afternoon to fend off the media. Your problem is going to be Lady Zoë's client base. They'll be nervous this could be another Ashley Madison leak, which please tell me it won't be."

"I can't say for certain until we locate her phone, but Sasha, whatever your fee is, I'll be very generous."

I don't have a fee, but after I research Bryce and Lady Zoë, his bill will contain lots of zeroes.

"Bryce, I can spin this, but you won't like it. Also, there's something I need from you."

"Tell me."

"Who is Azmar?" I ask, realizing he may have given me the watered-down version of his background.

"Your billionaire Saudi Prince belongs to a family that owns an international conglomerate of businesses involved in financial services, automotive, land, and real estate in over a dozen countries. Their influence is so widespread that it's nearly impossible to buy a car without their fingerprints on it. His family business has been operating since the 1800s, and their fortune is so vast that it's immeasurable.

"Fuck," I mumble under my breath for allowing myself to get close to a man I didn't know at all.

Instead of checking into my hotel, I pull out of the parking space, circle Rittenhouse Square, whip around to Walnut Street, and onto 76. The first person I can think of to assist me is Michael, the current CEO of Platinum Images.

"Sasha, my friend, how are you? I didn't expect to hear from you so soon. Is everything okay? Of course not, but it feels good to hear your voice."

"I'm in Philly and was hoping to work out of your office for a few hours."

"Sure, the movers don't arrive until tomorrow. You still have your key?"

It's slipped my mind that the offices are relocating from Manayunk, where I began the firm, to the newly renovated historic Bellevue Hotel on Broad Street. When I opened the shop, I never imagined Platinum Images growing to the extent it has, with over 70 employees covering PR across the globe.

"Michael, I don't want to get in the way, I can use my hotel room."

"Absolutely not! Tell me what you need."

"Since you asked, can you also do a little digging for me on a woman named Lady Zoë? She recently washed ashore in the Hamptons."

"We're following the story, a few of our clients were there. As for Lady Zoë, I've heard the rumors about her exclusive parties for the uber-wealthy. Anyway, count on me to get a complete dossier. Anybody else?"

"Local guy, Bryce Goodman, Goodman and Associates. Can you see what you can find on him?"

"I know Bryce. He has a concierge business we access for our clients, and we've been negotiating with his lawyers about purchasing that business. His real cash cow is his investments for the rich and the unsavory. He's not a man I'd mess with in the dark or the light. But I'll have everything ready for you."

"Thank you, Michael."

When I arrive onto busy Main Street, I'm lucky to find a parking spot a few doors from Expect Lace. According to their website, the owner of this high-end boutique is listed as Shaw Lewis, an African American woman. However, she's not the person I'm here to see. Exiting the luxury vehicle, people on the street and inside the boutique are craning their necks to see who's getting out.

Stepping inside the sweetly scented establishment and onto its gleaming hardwood floors, I'm greeted by an animated young woman. When I ask if Victoria is available, she descends the stairs, and the knot in my stomach wraps itself so tight that I'm forced to lean on the display table.

"I was hoping you'd visit. Welcome to Expect Lace."

How could she be expecting me?

"You're Victoria?" I ask the woman in her 30s whose breasts are spilling over her bustier, with a necklace charm that's lost somewhere within its cleavage. I can certainly understand if she was my husband's mistress.

"I'm Sasha Borianni, and my husband was Trent—"

Victoria doesn't allow me to finish when she says, "Let's get you into a dressing room."

Behind the oversized dressing room curtain, Victoria sizes me up, saying, "38D. I'll pull a few things."

Does she expect me to undress in front of her, knowing she may have had an affair with my husband? "I didn't come here for lingerie. I came to see you about my husband!"

"Trent was one of my VIP clients. I'm sorry to hear of his untimely death. Arms up, please."

She measures me, "Perfect, just like he said you were!"

Seconds later, she reenters with an arm full of beautiful lingerie, and without being instructed, I remove my shirt, and she begins adjusting my breasts into a skin tone bra with nipple cutouts that feel like a second skin. This is crazy. Why am I playing this game?

"Trent ordered these for you, and ma'am, I'll answer your questions, but please keep your voice down."

Half-dressed in front of this woman, I remove the panties from my purse, demanding to know, "Do these belong to you? Your card was inside."

"Ah yes! Japanese Akoya pearls to match a necklace and earrings he'd given to you. It took our vendor three months to switch out the rhinestones."

"What exactly was your relationship with my husband, and

how did he know about this place? Were you selling drugs for him?"

She appears alarmed. "Please lower your voice. If you're referring to *Get Right*, yes. Isn't that why you're here? I'm all out, and I figured you'd be carrying on his business."

Deflated, I take a seat on the dressing room chair, "You weren't having an affair with him?"

"Oh God, no! I would never sleep with a man that's occupied. Trent and I were business partners. He always talked about you."

"I don't understand why...."

"Listen, I have a VIP client arriving. Here's my number. If you have any questions, especially if you get your hands on *Get Right*, please call me; clients love that stuff."

When I reach Platinum Images, a shaken Isabella awaits me in the parking lot. I'm not ready for her, as I'm still reeling from my visit with Victoria. We go inside and upstairs to the conference room, where Michael has set up a tray of beverages, the television remote, and Zoom instructions. He's also left a portfolio, which I assume is the info I requested on Lady Zoë and Bryce. After setting my bag of gifts from Expect Lace on a chair with my purse, I open and down a bottle of water while wishing for something with high alcohol content.

"Sasha, I'm scared! What's going to happen? What if they find out? You must be scared, too."

"Bryce told me about her alternative lifestyle—a Futanari, you call it?"

Embarrassed, she slides into one of the leather chairs and hangs her head.

"Izzy, there's no need to be embarrassed, but you also can't be running around all jittery. Bryce's attorneys will handle the legalities, and I'll fend off the media. Meanwhile, don't you talk to anyone!"

"Wait, you talked to Bryce? What legalities?"

"He's retained me as his publicist. Were you aware that he was the executor of her estate?"

"Why didn't he tell me! Where the hell is he?"

"He's staying at the Kimberly in New York, so we haven't had an opportunity to get into the details. Have you spoken to White Magic?"

"Yeah, and I've never heard him this shaken. He's at training camp but if word gets out that he was personally involved with her, he'll be the joke of the NFL and his fans; they'd never forgive him. And Hailey, she's frantic that someone died at the party. The police have met with them both and Tampa Bay's PR department is prepping them for the media."

"What's the deal with the two of them? Does she know about his little threesome with you and the deceased?"

"Open marriage. She'd rather know than have him whoring across the globe."

"And does that stop him?"

"I think you can answer that. But Sasha, I can't make it through an interview."

"We won't let that happen."

"I may have done something that will backfire."

"Please don't tell me you've gone to the police," I ask while searching the cabinets for snacks and alcoholic beverages.

"I'm ashamed to say I've been secretly threatening to expose Lady Zoë's private life and those of her clients to the public. I've also leaked a few of her financial documents to the Feds. If you're saying Bryce is her legal business partner, do you think he'll find out what I've done? He has enough to hide."

"Why the fuck would you do that and who's been helping you?"

"Betty, my partner at The Source Foundation, a non-profit I

run, is working with a company called Vesper, hacked into her files."

"Vesper," I whisper, confused how my son has become involved in this mess. His business is supposed to prevent companies from being hacked, and now that I know he's taking money to do the opposite, I'm not even sure I can have that discussion.

"Why is everybody hiding something?"

"Aren't you?"

I shrug my shoulders, satisfied to have located a half-empty bottle of Captain Morgan's rum, which I fill two red plastic cups with.

"I feel so bad after what happened in Esterillos and now this. I don't understand why all this is happening to me. It's like I've become a sponge for everything dreadful."

With no energy to filter my words, to get her full attention, instead of slapping her, I bang on the table, "Stop playing the goddamn victim over decisions you made! It's time for you to grow all the way the fuck up!"

"Excuse me, you've never been through what I'm going through."

"You have no idea what I've been through."

"Okay, Sasha, you're the publicist, how do you suggest I deal with it?"

"With a combination of grit and grace. And keeping your mouth shut until I tell you what to say. Now, you've been leaving me messages about my finances. Tell me what you found."

She empties the bottle of rum between our two cups.

"The travel agency you use, *My Travel Agent*, were you aware your husband is its majority owner?"

Rearing back in my chair to distance myself from her claims, I say, "Help me understand."

"They have somehow turned it into mostly a cash business.

In addition to client payments, money flows in from another unidentified source. There are money trails with payments from Sugar Hill, specifically Signature Services, to *My Travel Agent*, which, for tax purposes, is based out of Delaware. Plus, there are inflated costs for repairs and upgrades to various properties. They may look legitimate to the average accountant and even the IRS, but I examine things beyond the books. And one more thing, were you aware that your husband had a separate business checking account?"

I'm not sure what pains me more, the pounding in my head or the knot in my stomach. "How'd you discover all this?"

"This information is buried in the records, and Aunt Millie may have unknowingly assisted them. On top of that, he was using funds from this separate account to construct a professional-grade pickleball court at Sugar Hill."

"I never agreed to that. I told him it would detract from the aesthetics."

"The court was costing him nearly a hundred grand, so I think the figure is inflated. All in, he's moved around about 2.1 million over the last six years."

"This can't be happening, Trent would never---"

"Let me stop you right there. What is it you haven't told me?"

Isabella is right. It's glaringly apparent that Ginger, in addition to supplying our guests with weed, they were also offering *Get Right* at $1,250 a vial, which the couple at the Wooden Floor and Victoria were also purchasing. If I'm not mistaken, I vividly remember Judge Rasso mentioning *Get Right*. What's even more concerning is that Trent would playfully suggest to me during the day, "We're going to get right tonight, woman." Initially, I took it as a term of endearment; now, it holds no affection. For all those reasons, I now confide in Isabella how I've uncovered Trent's illicit drug activities.

"So, what's next?"

"I don't know."

After a restless night during which I ate half of my steak dinner yet managed to drink a bottle of wine and ignore Azmar's calls, I texted *My Travel Agent*, demanding she meet me at 8:30 the following morning. She knew this call was coming, as she readily agreed.

Hesitant but curious, I also did a Google search for Futanari, which led me to Hentai and Adult Anime. After spending way too much time in that dark and sexually explicit space, I found myself longing for Azmar. At the same time, it's hard to comprehend the challenges Lady Zoë faced, explicitly growing up as a child with dual anatomy. According to Bryce, her family shunned her and sent her to an orphanage. Unsurprisingly, she sought love under the façade of power - it seems she had no other choice. This, of course, leaves me too emotionally drained to google Azmar.

At 8:15 a.m., I head down to LaCroix, where *My Travel Agent* is already waiting at the hostess desk. We're shown to a table by the window overlooking Rittenhouse Square.

Bryce is calling, and I decline. I then turn my phone on silent to ignore an incoming call from Azmar.

"Good morning, Sasha."

"Tell me about your business with my husband. Were you laundering money through his travel agency that I now own?

"Let me start by telling you we all went to college together, me, him, and Lee. Even then, your husband was a bit of a loan shark. Maybe that's why he was so good at being a union boss."

Dr. Lee never mentioned *My Travel Agent* and I certainly don't recall any stories of Trent being a loan shark in college.

"First, what is your name?"

"Vaughn Righter-Brown."

"Were you fucking my husband?"

"Trent and I had a brief affair."

I am gut-punched at her honesty.

"When and how goddamn brief was it?"

"It started about a year after you were married. During a challenging time, he offered me support that turned into, well, you know, something else. After a while, we both realized that our relationship wasn't beneficial for either of us. He struggled with the burden of guilt, and of course, I wanted more than he could give. Since we couldn't pursue a relationship, I found myself solely responsible for the kids and needing a steady income. That's when Trent proposed the idea of starting a travel agency. With my background as a former travel agent and his financial resources, it was a perfect match."

I can barely get the question out before she answers, "No, they're not his children. I'm divorced."

"How long were you fucking my husband?"

"Sasha, you don't have to be so crude."

Leaning across the table so she gets the wrath of what I'm feeling, I say, "Don't tell me how to react to my husband having an affair with someone who knows every detail of my life. Now how fucken long?"

"Almost two years," she whispers while coffee splatters onto the table from her shaking hands.

Every nerve in my body urges me to reach across the table and grab hold of her skinny neck, but I refuse to embarrass myself. Nor will I allow a single tear to drop from my eyes. How was this possible? Why did he need her? When did he have the time? I'm reminded that men always find the time, especially when Trent was balancing his time between my house in Philly and his condo in New Jersey. I shift my focus.

"The money, how were you able to move that money around undetected?"

"Cash payments for travel coupled with the sale of *Get Right* which was always paid in cash."

"Who sold it at Sugar Hill?"

"Ginger moved the product, and your CFO helped Aunt Millie cover the cash with her messy bookkeeping, is what Trent told me."

My head is spinning at her honesty and that even Aunt Millie kept Trent's secrets.

"This business, this *Get Right*, ends now, and you can tell Dr. Lee and whoever else is involved that if it doesn't stop, I'm turning you all in regardless of the consequences."

"You can't make that call; you see, Dr. Lee has finally received his approval from the FDA, so within 18 months, Eluvient-GR will be on the market; you'll need a prescription and a shit ton of money to purchase it, but it's coming."

Her statement stuns me, and now I've lost control of this conversation because all I can imagine is her making love to my husband. My trembling hands won't allow me to lift the glass of water I need for my dry mouth.

"Did you love my husband?"

"Did you? Because Trent wasn't sure."

How dare she question my love for Trent. Intending to leave, I push back my chair but stop short, and in an act of intimidation, I move to stand over her. Knowing I can't shove her through the glass window, I slap the shit out of her.

After my reluctant arrival in New York hours later, I am astounded to find the Kimberly Hotel swarmed by paparazzi and police. The

SVAutobiography draws their attention. Thankfully the officers push them back behind barricades. After presenting my ID, I'm granted access to the hotel and promptly escorted to Bryce's suite.

In the vintage-style suite overlooking 50th Street, I am warmly greeted by a young woman who seems to know me without introduction. Bryce welcomes me and suggests I indulge in the well-stocked bar and the delicious spread of food and beverages. Opting for a bottle of water, I settle in to absorb the unfolding drama.

The attorneys representing Bryce bring to my attention that Lady Zoë's identity has been leaked to the press and on social media. What worries Bryce even more is that her cell phone is still missing. Despite not knowing him for long, I can tell that Bryce is distressed. With all eyes on me at this moment, my PR skills begin to percolate, and I sit down to understand the real threat, how to navigate this complex situation, and how to craft a release to the media.

In the morning, we release the following statement:

"Mr. Goodman is deeply shocked by the unexpected and accidental passing of his business partner, Lady Zoë. Consequently, he will not be available to address any inquiries from the media. We kindly request that you respect his privacy as well as the privacy of those who were acquainted with Lady Zoë. Any questions should be directed to the police."

I stayed at the hotel for three nights, aiding Bryce and outwaiting the media frenzy until a new news cycle began. Every night, I found myself alone upstairs at the Kimberly.

On this night, sitting on the 30th floor of the rooftop garden under floating lights and a tasty dinner of black truffle pizza and a bottle of wine, I decide it's time to return to Sugar Hill. I follow that decision with a call to Marquise, who shares some concerning news. He informs me that the local media has been investigating my connections with White Magic, Lady Zoë, and Bryce Goodman. During our conversation, for that reason and so many others, I offer him the role of Chief Operating Officer. After readily accepting, he reveals that Aunt Millie is retiring at the end of the year. Though not surprising, this news saddens me, especially as I suspect *My Travel Agent* informed her of my discovery.

After my second glass of wine, when I can no longer ignore Azmar's text messages and phone calls, I call him, getting right to the point.

"Why didn't you tell me who you were? Please don't say it's because you wanted me to like you for you. This isn't *Coming to America*."

"I don't understand your reference, but during our brief time together, I wanted to focus on your needs."

"How can you travel the country without any protection, bodyguards, or security? What if something happens to you? Where's your family? You should be married with an heir."

"I am protected with counter-surveillance around the clock. You should know that every star you see in the sky isn't a star."

"Azmar!"

"Yes, Brown Butter?"

"You're no ordinary man, you're a fucken Saudi Prince. It would help if you had told me. I'm driving this car, and now you're telling me people have been watching us! I can't do this."

"Am I not the man you met on the beach in Costa Rica? The same man in Ditch Plains?"

"Are you though?"

"Sasha, I understand you may not need me or my money, but I need a woman of your caliber, grace, and beauty. I hope that's enough for you to consider me and where this could lead."

Isabella

I've been alone most days at Bryce's condo while he handles Lady Zoë's business. So far, he hasn't spoken of the threatened leak. This afternoon, though, a FedEx package from Marley arrives for me, along with a text instructing me to call him before opening it.

"Marley, it's Izzy, what's in the box?"

"What Marley must tell you is, wait, hold on, I got another call."

"MARLEY! STOP! Focus on one thing, please! What is this?"

"I'm sorry, you have Marley's attention now. Your husband had a lover."

"Is that a problem?"

I crack open the seal on the box, while asking, "Where'd you find this stuff?

"Work locker at the Home Depot."

"The store just gave you the key?"

"Marley has his ways; now open, please."

Inside the 12x12 box are a Phila Eagles hoodie, matching

sweatpants, Roka sneakers, and a framed picture of his hiking group. There's an iPhone and an 8x12 manilla envelope containing a stack of folded letters wrapped in a rubber band, a few of which I notice have the heading Moore and Less Foundation. I set that aside on the couch. Scrambling further through all the papers, I see about $1,500 cash and a ring box holding Elijah's wedding ring.

"Have you listened to the cell phone?"

"You'll need to charge it, there are many messages between them. Some are hot hot! Marley thinks you shouldn't listen, but they will be evidence."

"What's with these letters?"

"Read one, you will see."

Before reading it, I glance at the signature at the bottom of the pale pink paper, *"Lovingly, LS."*

"LS?"

"Solano, Luciana Solano, she was your husband's lover!"

"The agent?" I can barely get the words out when laughter overcomes me. "Are you fucken kidding me? Do you think Castro knew, or was he covering for her?"

"Oh no, they are lovers, got engaged while on that vacation. This woman is the type that requires several lovers to be satisfied. Some women are like that, you know."

I want to tell him, yes, I know, I am one of those women.

"You're not reading."

> *Malcolm,*
>
> *I can't imagine living life without you. What we've shared has escaped me many times, that's how I know this is real.*
>
> *When I first met you and saw the pain in your face, I knew true love was all you needed to heal. I*

don't understand why you'd want to let that go. I love you.

I toss that one and pick up another that has pictures enclosed. Solano and Elijah having a snowball fight, another where they're enjoying themselves at a cigar lounge, with her sitting on his lap dressed provocatively. Pictures of them washing their cars and him hosing her down while she wears a dress with nothing underneath.

Malcolm,
I can be what you want. That woman will never be what I am to you. I beg you not to go back to her.

And another one.

Malcolm,
How can you continue to love such a heartless bitch? I won't let you leave me, Malcolm, Elijah; I'll call you whatever you want, but don't do it. I beg you, don't return to her.

"She knew he was coming back to me."
"Motive."
"She's a federal agent!"
"Women kill for love all the time."
"What am I supposed to do?"
"Call your friend Eddie. He'll know what to do. This is a big case for him and Isabella a box of those cigars from the Brown

Pipe is in there, too. According to one of his co-workers, they were living together."

"You really think she had someone come to my home and kill Elijah?"

"Marley thinks she did it herself; she was probably tracking him and took advantage of the opportunity to blame it on those Russians. I checked on that man. He's been stripped of everything. I doubt he'd have the money to pay for a hit."

"How could she be willing to risk her career, ruin her life, and potentially face jail time all for the sake of love? I can't understand it."

"Love always love."

I am paralyzed with disbelief. It turns out that Luciana Solano was the one responsible all along, despite my accusations towards Bryce, Lady Zoë, and the Russian. How do I tell Bryce? Once he knows the truth, he'll be obsessed with seeking revenge instead of allowing the authorities to handle it.

I call the Twins to get Eddie's number, and after relaying Marley's findings, he can barely formulate a response until he begins peppering me with questions I can't answer. Most importantly, he wants me to FedEx the box.

In the morning, with Bryce gone to his office, I decide to make my way to Barren Hill to visit Synearra and Zion. Halfway there, I receive a call from Christian Wiggins.

"Ms. Washington?"

"What's wrong? Where's Bryce?"

"The Department of Justice is interviewing Mr. Goodman for possible financial crimes related to the estate of Lady Zoë. We ask that you not speak to the press or anyone. We're reaching out to Ms. Borianni."

"Why aren't you there with him?"

"My partner has it covered."

I turn the car around and head back to the Ritz. I cannot let this touch my family. My first call is to Sasha.

"Sasha, where are you? They're questioning Bryce. His lawyer called! It's all my fault, everything backfired!"

"Don't say another word on this phone."

"Hold on, let me see who keeps texting and calling me from an unknown number."

"Don't answer. It could be someone trying to get information."

"It might be Bryce."

"Isabella, do you have a lawyer?"

"No, I mean yes, Alaina Kimmel, why? Okay, right."

"Call her, or better yet, go to her office and let her know what's happening, everything, and do what she tells you. I'll get back to you."

My phone rings again. It's Lemuel. When I don't answer, he sends a text, begging me to call him. Not heeding Sasha's warning, I return his call.

"Isabella, I'm certain we shouldn't be speaking, especially over the phone, but with Mr. Goodman in trouble, I'm worried about what'll happen to me. Nobody is answering my questions."

I almost feel sorry for him. Having been Lady Zoë's closest confidant, I'm sure he knows he will be questioned.

"I don't know anything."

"You were seen with her at the party."

"What do you mean? I went with Bryce."

"How could she have fallen like that and where is her cell phone? She never lets it out of her hand, especially not recently. I'm sure she told you, we've been getting threatening text messages."

"Like I said, I was with Bryce, and I'm sure she was trotting about making her own plans. Do you really think they'll find her phone in the ocean?"

"You may be right, but I'll tell you, and you can tell Bryce I will not be around to take the fall for anyone, nor will I have any of her clients coming after me. I'm certain someone has been following me, and I will not be the one paying for this."

Forty-eight hours later, when Bryce comes home, in response to my questions, he assures me that he has everything handled.

"Listen, I'm gonna jump in the shower; order some dinner from Vetri because I've been holding onto your Valentine's Day gift."

"Bryce now isn't the time for gifts. Do they know I killed Lady Zoë? Are they going to arrest you?"

His jaws tighten, and he squeezes me by my arms until it hurts. "Don't you ever fucken repeat those words out your mouth. Never! Forget you ever knew her. You understand me; never say those words."

"But you were being questioned."

"This is unrelated to that. We both know she hosted cash parties and now the authorities know it. The information they received predates my involvement. I only recently signed the partnership agreement. And if you're searching for it, I disposed of the phone I found in your bag when we were in the Hamptons."

I'm sure the shock is evident on my face. How could I have forgotten to dispose of it? When I attempt to explain lies yet to be formulated, he silences me by pulling one hand from his pocket. A diamond ring dangles on his middle finger—no box to open, no romantic gesture.

"I want you to focus on my next words."

Aware of what he's about he's about to ask, I still myself for the right response.

"Marry me, Isabella."

Quickly, I find myself recalling the final days I spent with Elijah. I married him a few months before our planned wedding so that we could enter witness protection together. Now, history seems to be repeating itself. Should I tell him about the call I received from Lemuel? Should I tell him about Solano?

"Bryce, are you sure?"

"Not unless four carats isn't enough," he jokes. "Listen, Isabella, whatever you want, I can give you. If it's a baby, I'll cum in you every night, and if we have to, we'll get a surrogate, in vitro, even adopt, as long as you're the mother of my child. First, I want to make this right, I need to be your husband."

As hard as I try, I can't stop the tears from falling. This man knows secrets I could never tell anyone; he even knows those I haven't told him. Despite that, it's his secrets that scare me, but if he's willing to give me what I want, then what choice do I have?

"Yes, I'll marry you."

Epilogue

Six months down the road

Sasha

One thing is certain, Trent has left me a wealthy woman, and I am grateful for that.

It feels good to be back at Sugar Hill and even better to be in my home, where the boxes have been removed and the only memories remaining are the ones I want to cherish. There was a bit of closure from a voicemail I received from Dr. DiBello that my husband did die from a heart attack caused by a small blockage.

I've been trying to work on forgiving him. Although I don't believe his intention was harmful when he drugged me with *Get Right*, it was still dishonest. I was worried about the potential of lingering side effects of his actions so much that I only felt better once I was cleared after a series of bloodwork showed no traces of anything foreign.

The disappointment from the affair with *My Travel Agent* is outweighed by the fact that I grew up surrounded by unfaithful men. It's disheartening to realize that despite the affair's brevity, I could not meet his needs at some level.

Isabella has graciously accepted the role of interim CFO, albeit working remotely. Her vision is to revamp our accounting department until we secure a comptroller. She aims to assemble a proficient team encompassing bookkeepers, accounts receivable and payable clerks, improved software, and the engagement of a new financial services firm, with Adam being the sole member retained from Trent's previous team. No one individual will oversee my financial matters.

The information Isabella shared and what the media has been reporting was shocking. It turns out Special Agent Solano was responsible for Elijah's tragic death and the attempted murder of Bryce. To avoid extradition, Solano has chosen to seek refuge in Venezuela, and for his association with her, Captain Castro has been stripped of his duties. This decision has understandably made Isabella anxious, but I'm relieved that Bryce is committed to ensuring her safety.

For me, I'm decided to take a month's vacation beginning with Arshell and spending the first seven days in Italy. This includes visiting Lake Trasimeno to see where the final piece of Trent's puzzle leads. After that, I'm flying to Nice, France, to stay at the Four Seasons in Cannes and meet Parker for a week of shopping, dining, and champagne tasting. The final leg of my trip excites me the most, as Azmar has arranged a Pied-à-Terre for me in Paris. I am undoubtedly looking forward to spending time with this man regardless of who he is. Can I blame him for not revealing the truth? I, too, have secrets I'm not willing to reveal. Depending on how things go, I'll tell my grown children about this new man in my life.

Before heading to the airport, while enjoying lunch at The Grille, I receive a text from an 800 number. Usually, these calls are about PR work, which I'm not interested in. This time, someone has included me in a group text with Isabella and Bryce. Either way, without reading it, I delete the message.

Bryce

Things are solid in my life, finances, business, and, more importantly, my life with Isabella. The one unresolved issue I will handle following our wedding in Houston is making the first stop of our honeymoon in Venezuela. Once that's resolved, I'll focus on starting a family and stop slipping her *Get Right*, but it's been challenging considering how much she craves satisfaction and the things she's willing to do. But it's also brought out my voyeuristic side, leading me to places and indulgences I thought I had left behind.

Today, without her knowledge, I'm meeting with a realtor as I consider moving to the suburbs to raise our child or maybe even children. I've even purchased a second cell phone for privacy and safety reasons, so I don't have to answer calls or text messages from unknown numbers. I'll tell her these things once she becomes my wife, but until then, I'll keep my secrets and hers.

Isabella

My peaceful slumber is disturbed by my cell phone, and as I reach across the bed for Bryce, I realize he's already up. He mentioned a 7:30 a.m. meeting with his lawyers about the complexities of unwinding an estate, which could take quite some time. However, what he's really focused on is my OB-GYN appointment this afternoon and the battery of tests to figure out why we haven't been able to conceive. It's certainly not for lack of effort, as our bond has only grown stronger lately.

I'd never tell him and try not to tell myself that there are times when I miss Lady Zoë, and the only person I speak about her to is White Magic. Somehow, he manages to come out of all this with his reputation unscathed by following Sasha's suggestion to create a charity in his friend Lady Zoë's memory supporting the LGBTQ+ community to which he's donated $5M.

While I'm getting dressed, the phone rings with a call that luckily isn't from an unknown number.

"Hey, Sémile."

"I need you to meet me."

"Are you in Philly?"

"Yeah, I'm at the Loews but you gotta come now, cause I'm checking out in a few hours."

Not sure of the urgency, when I get to his hotel room, he answers the door in a suit and tie; momentarily, the rise in my libido almost makes me forget why I'm here. When I open my arms to receive his familiar hug, he pulls me inside and closes the door.

"What's wrong with you?"

"I need to tell you something I've been figuring out for a while now."

"Okay, what is it?"

"Bryce was responsible for his sister's murder."

"What are you talking about? What sister?" I ask, hoping he's not confusing it with the murder of Lady Zoë because for that, I am responsible.

"Sit down. I'm going to pour us both a drink," he says, until while handing me a glass of what I'm sure is Hennessy, he sees the glistening diamond ring on my finger.

"I'm not drinking."

"Wait, you married that mothafucka? Please don't tell me you having his baby!"

"What's wrong with you? I didn't question your choices, so don't question mine. Now tell me what you're talking about, and how do you know anything about Bryce's family?"

"Bryce got in trouble when he was barely a teenager. He was accused of stabbing a kid over some dumb shit, so they sent him away. Kitty Kat was his older sister."

"He's told me about his family and never mentioned having a sister. Wait, you mean that friend of you and Elijah's, well, more than a friend; I remember she was killed in a robbery or something a few years ago? What does that have to do with me? And why are you saying she was Bryce's sister?"

"Hear me out. It was more than that. When Bryce found out the Russians and that freak you were hanging with were going to sacrifice you for Elijah being a snitch, they gave him a choice, either you or his sister. Someone had to pay."

"I don't believe you. This is stupid. It doesn't even make sense. Are you making this shit up?" I ask him, knowing Sémile wouldn't come to me if he weren't sure.

"That nigga got you fooled."

"Yeah, but a sister, c'mon Sémile, what are you trying to do here," I ask aloud, yet recall the night after Lady Zoë's death when he told me about a tortured decision he'd made. This can't possibly be what he was referring to.

Sitting on the coffee table across from me, his legs spread open, he leans forward and says, "Listen, you already know there's another side to him; I mean, what kinda man would sacrifice his sister for a piece of ass."

"ARE YOU SAYING HE DOESN'T LOVE ME? THAT I'M NOT WORTH IT?"

"Izzy, calm down. You're not listening? This man allowed his sister to be killed in cold blood, and now he's controlling you. He's probably behind that freak Lady Zoë winding up in the ocean."

Realizing that Sémile has gone too far in trying to blame

Bryce for everything that has gone wrong, I stand up and push him out of my way.

"Sémile, I'm walking out of this room, so please don't call me with this shit again. Bryce and I are trying to make a family. Goodbye."

Walking back to the Ritz, I carefully consider whether to share this information with Bryce. Even if it's true, which I doubt, what impact would it have? Bryce already had suspicions about Sémile, and I don't want to place Sémile in danger or risk upsetting Bryce with such a horrible accusation.

Lost in my thoughts while strolling across Broad Street, the jarring horn of a SEPTA bus brings me back to reality. At that moment, an incoming text notifies me of my inclusion in a group chat with Sasha and Bryce.

> Unknown number: Zoë was not an orphan; she was my twin. I know what you did and I'm coming for all of you.

The End -- Maybe

Phillywriter, LLC
www.brendalthomas.com
brendalthomas@comcast.net

Also by Brenda L. Thomas

FICTION
Heartless, when love isn't enough.
Woman On Top
Every Woman's Got a Secret
The Velvet Rope
Fourplay, The Dance of Sensuality
Threesome, Where Seduction, Power and Basketball Collide

NON-FICTION
Sayin' A Taste
Laying Down My Burdens

SHORT STORIES
Bewitched
Secret Service
Every New Year

ANTHOLOGIES
Four Degrees of Heat
Maxed Out
Kiss The Year Goodbye
Every New Year
Bedroom Chronicles

The Experiment

Indulge

The Watcher

www.ingramcontent.com/pod-product-compliance
Lightning Source LLC
Chambersburg PA
CBHW071859290426
44110CB00013B/1207